W9-BYU-557

WITHDRAWN

The Cambridge Introduction to
The Novel

Beginning its life as the sensational entertainment of the eighteenth century, the novel has become the major literary form of modern times. Drawing on a wide range of examples of famous novels from all over the world, Marina MacKay explores the essential aspects of the novel and its history: where novels came from and why we read them; how we think about their styles and techniques, their people, plots, places, and politics. Between the main chapters are longer readings of individual works, from *Don Quixote* to *Midnight's Children*. A glossary of key terms and a guide to further reading are included, making this an ideal accompaniment to introductory courses on the novel.

MARINA MACKAY is Associate Professor of English at Washington University in St. Louis. Her publications include *Modernism and World War II* (Cambridge, 2007) and, as editor, *The Cambridge Companion to the Literature of World War II* (2009).

The Cambridge Introduction to

The Novel

MARINA MACKAY

CAMBRIDGE
UNIVERSITY PRESS

CAMBRIDGE UNIVERSITY PRESS
Cambridge, New York, Melbourne, Madrid, Cape Town, Singapore,
São Paulo, Delhi, Dubai, Tokyo, Mexico City

Cambridge University Press
The Edinburgh Building, Cambridge CB2 8RU, UK

Published in the United States of America by Cambridge University Press, New York

www.cambridge.org
Information on this title: www.cambridge.org/9780521713344

First published 2011

Printed in the United Kingdom at the University Press, Cambridge

A catalogue record for this publication is available from the British Library

Library of Congress Cataloguing in Publication data
MacKay, Marina, 1975–
    The Cambridge introduction to the novel / Marina MacKay.
    p.   cm. – (Cambridge introductions to literature)
    Includes bibliographical references and index.
    ISBN 978-0-521-88575-1 – ISBN 978-0-521-71334-4 (pbk.)
    1. Fiction–History and criticism.   I. Title.
    PN3353.M245   2010
    809.3–dc22
    2010034946

ISBN 978-0-521-88575-1 Hardback
ISBN 978-0-521-71334-4 Paperback

Contents

Acknowledgments

Writing this book would never have crossed my mind had it not first crossed the mind of Ray Ryan at Cambridge University Press. It's a real pleasure to express my gratitude to Ray for his truly extraordinary support over a number of years and projects. I would like also to thank his colleagues for their exemplary responsiveness, and to thank the Press's readers for reviewing the proposal with such insight and generosity. A number of collaborations and conversations in recent years helped me to figure out what I wanted to say, and my thanks to Miriam Bailin, Robert Caserio, Michael Gardiner, Andrzej Gasiorek, Allan Hepburn, Peter Kalliney, Pericles Lewis, Leo Mellor, Petra Rau, Neil Reeve, Wolfram Schmidgen, Lyndsey Stonebridge, and Steve Zwicker. Much older debts, unthinkingly incurred but gratefully remembered, are owed to Mr. Tony Ashe, Professor Jon Cook, Professor Robert Crawford, Dr. Michael Herbert, Dr. Ian Johnson, Dr. Paul Magrs, Mr. Phillip Mallett, the late Professor Lorna Sage, and Professor Victor Sage. Sincere thanks, too, to my senior colleagues David Lawton, Joe Loewenstein, and Vince Sherry for moral support and more, and to my wonderful undergraduates at Washington University in St. Louis for their braininess and sheer good will. My affectionate thanks, finally, to Lara Bovilsky and Donald MacKay for timely comic distraction, and to my best friend Dan Grausam for everything else.

St. Louis, May 2009

About this book

Many of the eighteenth-century critics who observed the appearance of this new literary species would have been astounded to learn that the frivolous, fashionable "novel" so beloved of silly females would eventually be considered deserving of a scholarly introduction (with the Cambridge University Press imprimatur, no less!). And not even the novelists themselves could have imagined that they were contributing to what would ultimately become the major literary form of modern times, both inside and outside the university. This book begins by telling the story of that extraordinary rise, before going on to describe in more detail the particular formal characteristics and qualities we associate with the novel. Later chapters are concerned with *types* of novel: the genre novel, the experimental novel, the novel of nation and community.

Each chapter addresses a formal or historical aspect of the novel, drawing examples and illustrations from a range of novels often from very different times and places. Between these main chapters are more sustained readings of individual works, intended to suggest how the generalizations of the summary chapters might be put to specific uses. Arranged mostly in the order of their publication, these interchapters collectively offer, well, certainly not *the* story but *one* story of the novel running from Cervantes to Rushdie. But these should be considered optional reading, and, if the main chapters work as they were intended, student readers will be able to think of favorite novels with which to replace mine. Although the book's broad drift is historical, moving closer to the present day as it proceeds, the main chapters are fairly self-contained, and can be read selectively and/or out of order.

When what may be an unfamiliar term appears in **bold** on its first use you will find it defined in the glossary at the end of the book – there is very little jargon in what follows, but sometimes the precise terminology can be genuinely clarifying because it allows you to see things you might not notice if you didn't have the language to describe them. Also at the end of the book is a short list of supplementary reading arranged by chapter headings: this names the scholarly works to which individual chapters are most indebted.

The novels and novelists discussed here were chosen primarily for the familiarity attendant on their cultural stature, in some cases positively monumental; my hope was to find the common ground that comes of a shared body of reading. Listing what has been left out would be more than a life's work, but there are novels I eventually decided not to write about because I thought them too hobbyhorsical (as Tristram Shandy would say), many more I would have written about if I had space to include them, and, above all, countless novels I might have included had I ever encountered them in the first place. Needless to say, the limitations of *The Cambridge Introduction to the Novel* reflect the limitations of its author's knowledge.

Chapter 1

Why the novel matters

In the famous schoolroom scene that opens Charles Dickens's *Hard Times* (1854), the pedantic Mr. Gradgrind asks the novel's heroine to define a horse. Although she has spent her life around circus ponies, Sissy Jupe is struck dumb. Her horrible classmate Bitzer supplies the answer:

> "Quadruped. Gramnivorous. Forty teeth, namely twenty-four grinders, four eye-teeth, and twelve incisive. Sheds coat in the spring; in marshy countries, sheds hoofs, too. Hoofs hard, but requiring to be shod with iron. Age known by marks in mouth." Thus (and much more) Bitzer.[1]

Dickens wants us to feel that this definition is as wrong as it is right, that for all its factual precision it doesn't really bring us much closer to apprehending the object of study. After all, Sissy the circus girl knows horses far better than Bitzer does, but she couldn't care less about grinders, incisors, and the shedding of hooves in marshy countries.

This is the risk you run when you try to define the novel. In response to the Gradgrind imperative to begin by saying what a novel is, we might propose something along these lines: "A novel is a self-contained piece of fictional prose longer than 40,000 words." There are famous exceptions to this definition – Pushkin's *Eugene Onegin* (1833) is a novel in verse, for example, while the modern "**non-fiction novel**" pioneered by Truman Capote tells you that a novel needn't even be fictional. As a general rule, though, it does the job of identifying what makes the novel different from other forms of **narrative**, even if it stops far short of explaining why we feel the way we do about it. If I say that those of us who read *fiction* know better than to share Gradgrind's conviction that "facts" are "the one thing needful," of course I don't mean to suggest that

1

facts about fiction always miss the mark, but only that stripped of their human relevance they don't take you far enough.[2] Reducing a novel or a horse to its constituent parts, whether you're talking about four legs, forty teeth, or forty thousand words, leaves out the huge social, historical, cultural, and emotional significance of the thing you meant to describe.

Novels are like horses to the extent that you generally know one when you see one, and the definition of the novel offered in this book is mostly a matter of slowing down to consider what we take for granted in that first unconscious instant of recognition when we see a novel and know that's what it is. This is why most of the following chapters are about characteristics and qualities that novels share, features such as **narration** (Chapter 3), **character** (Chapter 4), **plot** (Chapter 5), **setting** (Chapter 6), time (Chapter 7), and finitude (Chapter 11) that seem as easily taken for granted as the four legs of a horse. Those chapters aim to explain how and why critics and theorists have brought particular aspects of the novel into the foreground. But there are other questions to be asked: When did novels first appear and where did they come from? (See Chapter 2.) How do we categorize different kinds of novel? (See Chapter 8.) What do we do with novels that resist or overturn our expectations of the genre? (See Chapter 9.) What role does the novel play in the making of communities and nations? (See Chapter 10.) So, in short, this book is about what novels are and what they do. I'll return in the next chapter to the problem of defining the novel when we address the question of its origins, but I want to begin by considering the claims that have been made for its unique importance – or why we think the novel is worth studying in the first place.

Passions awakened: the dangers of fiction

You might call it a backhanded tribute to the novel that it aroused such suspicion and hostility in its early, eighteenth-century years. If the novel mattered in those first decades when it really *was* "novel," it was because this wildly popular new genre seemed too dangerous to ignore. A typical indictment of the novel in its first century in English is put into the mouth of an imaginary critic in the novelist Clara Reeve's *The Progress of Romance* (1785), one of the first book-length studies of the novel, and an attempt to rescue good fiction from the prevailing critical prejudice. Reeve's character argues that, first, novels leave the habitual reader "disgusted with every thing serious or solid"; second, "seeds of vice and folly are sown in the heart, – the passions are awakened, – false expectations are raised"; and, last, novels make "young people fancy themselves capable of judging of men and manners."[3] In other words, novels instill intellectual frivolity, give girls unrealistic ideas of what to expect from their future (for "future" read "suitor"), and mislead the young into believing they know how the world works. These common eighteenth-century claims help to explain what was so unusual about the novel when it first appeared in English: *its seductive proximity to the real world.*

So those books we call novels were felt to be different from the fanciful **romances** of earlier centuries, even if, somewhat confusingly, you often find the terms "romance" and "novel" used interchangeably in the eighteenth century (as in the title of Reeve's own book, *The Progress of Romance*). On this view, novels were distinctively dangerous because distinctively **realistic**: while no one would be foolish enough to model his or her behavior on the wildly implausible fictions of earlier times (so the argument goes), this new type of narrative fiction, with its complex characters, its recognizable settings, and its broadly credible sequence of events, might dupe the sequestered and susceptible into believing it a reliable guide to the world. It would be hard to overstate the importance of this feeling that the novel matters because of its closeness to the real world; over the last three centuries, many claims for the novel's significance have rested on exactly this sense that, among all the literary forms, the novel – for better or worse – has an especially intimate relationship to ordinary life. As the novelist Milan Kundera has recently put it: "'Prose': the word signifies not only a nonversified language; it also signifies the concrete, everyday, corporeal nature of life. So to say that the novel is the art of prose is not to state the obvious; the word defines the deep sense of that art."[4] Although Kundera approves of it, this emphasis on the "everyday" was once felt to be the novel's most troubling characteristic.

The novel, according to Samuel Johnson in 1750, focused on "life in its true state, diversified only by accidents that daily happen in the world, and influenced by passions and qualities which are really to be found in conversing with mankind."[5] The trouble with persuasive "realism," however, is that it may not be as realistic as it seems:

> These books are written chiefly to the young, the ignorant, and the idle, to whom they serve as lectures of conduct, and introductions into life. They are the entertainment of minds unfurnished with ideas, and therefore easily susceptible of impressions; not fixed by principles, and therefore easily following the current of fancy; not informed by experience, and consequently open to every false suggestion and partial account.[6]

By appealing to the wrong people for the wrong reasons, novels could influence their readers in all the wrong ways. "Example is always more efficacious than precept," a character points out in Johnson's one fictional narrative,

Rasselas (1759), a philosophical fable about the life well lived.[7] Indeed, Johnson's decision to convey philosophy through fiction underlines his alertness to the novel's exemplary force; a characteristically mid-eighteenth-century awareness of the "trite but true Observation, that Examples work more forcibly on the Mind than Precepts," as Henry Fielding put it in his novel *Joseph Andrews* (1742).[8]

Of course, the idea that novels teach by examples realistic enough to elicit the reader's identification was necessarily a double-edged affair: if fiction can make you a worse person, it can surely also make you a better one? This question is especially important to the eighteenth-century novel, the product of a culture profoundly interested in the links between imagination and empathy. In his immensely popular **novel of sensibility**, *The Man of Feeling* (1771), Henry Mackenzie would reprise a familiar attack on the novel when he attributed the downfall of the prostitute Emily Atkins to a habit of novel-reading that left her easily seduced by the scoundrel Winbrooke, and yet as we read the novel we feel that Mackenzie is *also* encouraging the reader to learn from the sympathetic capacities of the novel's weepy hero, Harley, the "man of feeling" in the book's title.

The eighteenth-century attentiveness to the novel's capacity to effect change through example helps to explain why even quite risqué early novels should reach us buttressed by authorial preambles announcing virtuous designs – however scandalous the ensuing material. From the title page alone of Daniel Defoe's *Moll Flanders* (1722) we learn that Moll was a thief, a "whore," and a bigamist who married her own brother, but the preface tells us that Moll's outrageous career has to be seen in the properly edifying light of her subsequent repentance. And if the reader finds Moll's repentance less interesting than the crimes she commits at such voluptuous length throughout the novel, this is because of "the Gust and Palate of the Reader": your problem not Defoe's, because "it is to be hop'd that … Readers will be much more pleas'd with the Moral, than the Fable; with the Application, than with the Relation."[9] Not *very* likely, and Defoe surely knew it. Prefatory claims separating the novelistic substance from its ostensibly edifying "moral" were commonplace in the eighteenth century, and thankfully never convincing enough to make you want to put the book down.

Women and the novel

It's unlikely that such prefatory declarations of virtue made the novel seem any more respectable – or any less appealing. Looking ahead to the other end of the eighteenth century from Defoe, Frances ("Fanny") Burney first published her **epistolary novel** *Evelina* (1778) anonymously, for reasons that become clear in her preface where she writes of the novelist's situation that "among the whole class of writers, perhaps not one can be named, of whom the votaries are more numerous, but less respectable."[10] She goes on to mount an attack on the novel *generally* at the same time as she defends the one we are about to read: if novels in their entirety could be wiped out "our young ladies in general ... might profit from their annihilation," but since the "distemper" or "contagion" has taken such inexorable hold, "surely all attempts to contribute to the number of those which may be read, if not with advantage, at least without injury, ought rather to be encouraged than contemned."[11]

Although certainly indebted to Burney (whose novels are socially sharp accounts of young women on the marriage market), Jane Austen had little time for this opportunistic sort of maneuvering. Her passionate reading helps Marianne Dashwood to put the "sensibility" into *Sense and Sensibility* (1811) but her vice is poetry rather than the novel. Initially, however, the heroine of Austen's *Northanger Abbey* (1817) seems to fare worse. While a guest at the ancient abbey, the avid novel reader Catherine Morland becomes convinced that her host, like a villain from one of her favorite **gothic novels**, has murdered his wife; General Tilney, however, proves to be simply a greedy bully of the everyday kind. And so far, so familiar, you might think: reading novels is bad for impressionable young women. This is not the whole story, though, because in a very famous defense of the novel Austen's **narrator** intervenes on behalf of novelists, "an injured body" whose works (whatever the snobbish male reviewers say) "have only genius, wit, and taste to recommend them":

> "I am no novel reader – I seldom look into novels – Do not imagine that *I* often read novels – It is really very well for a novel." Such is the common cant. – "And what are you reading, Miss – ?" "Oh! it is only a novel!" replies the young lady; while she lays down her book with affected indifference, or momentary shame. – "It is only *Cecilia*, or *Camilla*, or *Belinda*"; or, in short, only some work in which the greatest powers of the mind are displayed, in which the most thorough knowledge of human nature, the happiest delineation of its varieties, the liveliest effusions of wit and humour are conveyed to the world in the best chosen language.[12]

Rather provocatively, Austen defends the degraded novel by invoking the highly traditional, neoclassical criteria for judging art: *utile dulci*; the novel pleases and instructs. Although the feminist element in Austen's defense of the novel ("And what are you reading, Miss – ?") sounds much more modern than her use of neoclassical precept, such attention to the woman reader is no less embedded in Austen's own time, when women were coming to be a powerful force in literary culture.

That women were believed to be the major consumers of fiction during the eighteenth century is evidenced by the alarmist rhetoric about the corruption of impressionable minds, and by an explosion of comic caricatures of the charming but silly novel-reading girl (Austen's Catherine Morland is only one of many). Lydia Languish in Richard Brinsley Sheridan's play *The Rivals* (1775) refuses to be wooed by the impeccable Captain Absolute because what could be less romantic than marrying someone of whom everyone approves? This is "the natural consequence of teaching girls to read," Captain Absolute's absurd father expostulates: "I'd as soon have them taught the black art as their alphabet!"[13]

And women had already come into their own as novelists, too, because this kind of writing did not require the classical education to which men enjoyed privileged access. As Fielding explains in his romping but erudite *Tom Jones* (1749), "all the arts and sciences (even criticism itself) require some little degree of learning and knowledge … whereas, to the composition of novels and romances, nothing is necessary but paper, pens, and ink, with the manual capacity of using them."[14] Critics often point out that women writers like Aphra Behn, Delarivier Manley, and Eliza Haywood began to produce their sexy and much-read novels many decades before the **canonical** triumvirate of early novelists Defoe, Fielding, and Samuel Richardson. Indeed, it was long believed that most eighteenth-century novels were authored by women – and, rather strikingly, a male character in Tobias Smollett's novel *Humphry Clinker* (1771) goes so far as to speculate that women write not only *more* novels but *better* novels: a paid-by-the-volume hack novelist, his career is over because "that branch of business is now engrossed by female authors, who publish merely for the propagation of virtue, with so much ease and spirit, and delicacy, and knowledge of the human heart, and all in the serene tranquility of high life, that the reader is not only inchanted by their genius, but reformed by their morality."[15]

In view of the new importance of women as novelists and novel readers, it's no wonder that the experiences of women should have provided so much of the novel's traditional subject matter: "the whole domain over which our culture grants women authority," Nancy Armstrong summarizes: "the use of leisure time, the ordinary care of the body, courtship practices, the operations of desire, the forms of pleasure, gender differences, and family relationships."[16] Although Armstrong goes much further than this, proposing that the novel wasn't *describing* a female field of knowledge so much as *inventing* one, at least it can be said with certainty that such "feminine" concerns as those she lists were central to the gentrification of the novel during its first century in

English, novels written by men as well as by those genteel lady novelists who put Smollett's hack writer out of business in *Humphry Clinker*. With this gentrification in mind, the most important of the major male novelists of the eighteenth century is the one with, to put it crudely, the most stereotypically "feminine" sensibility, Samuel Richardson.

Richardson's psychologically absorbing *Pamela* (1740) and *Clarissa* (1747–8) purport to be collections of the heroine's letters, and so aim to represent the operations of her mind as intimately and immediately as possible. "Writing to the moment" was Richardson's term for this practice, and he has a character in *Clarissa* contrast "lively and affecting" letters written "in the midst of *present* distresses" with "the dry, narrative, unanimated style of persons relating difficulties and dangers surmounted."[17] Richardson's epistolary form was not new; the libertine Behn had imported the style from France sixty years earlier with her *Love-Letters Between a Nobleman and His Sister* (1684–7). The technical common ground, the epistolary form, shared by Behn and Richardson is not coincidental, since Richardson's accomplishment with the **sentimental novel** would be to refocus those interests that had made the novel such a dubious and (of course) pleasurable affair in the first place. In the story of how the novel came to be taken seriously, Richardson is vitally important because he helped to redirect the erotic energies of fiction like Behn's toward the socially respectable ends of the courtship novel.

Ever alert to fiction's exemplary potential, Johnson admired Richardson because he "taught the passions to move at the command of virtue."[18] "Virtue" is the key term here because the full title of Richardson's sensationally popular first novel is *Pamela, or Virtue Rewarded*. The servant girl Pamela is kidnapped and locked up by her rich employer Mr. B because she refuses to have sex with him, and, after a timely, rape-averting swoon (Clarissa will be less fortunate), Pamela's moral superiority compels the chastened Mr. B to "reward" her virtue with marriage (to him!). So the "virtue rewarded" in the subtitle comes down in the end to a sort of spiritualization of bodily intactness, and Richardson's single-mindedly tenacious attention to Pamela's virginity tells us that the early novel's sexual preoccupations may be serving new purposes but they haven't really gone away. Probably envious of Richardson's splashy success, many of his contemporaries produced sometimes very funny send-ups of *Pamela*, drawing out the pornographic prurience and vulgar opportunism underlying its ostentatious moral rectitude. In *Shamela* (1741), the wittiest and best-known of these, Fielding appropriated Richardson's epistolary form in order to expose the heroine as a sexual adventuress cannily exploiting the brainless Squire Booby: "I thought once of making a little Fortune by my Person," Fielding's sham heroine tells a correspondent, "I now intend to make a great one by my Vartue."[19]

To a correspondent who queried his potentially compromising use of the novel as a vehicle of moral education, Richardson explained that "Instruction, Madam, is the Pill; Amusement is the Gilding."[20] You might recall that Defoe had attempted a similar splitting of form and content when he divided "Moral" from "Fable," "Application" from "Relation," in the preface to *Moll Flanders*. Going further back still, the Puritan proto-novelist John Bunyan had prefaced his **allegorical** *The Pilgrim's Progress* (1678) with a warning to the reader along the same lines: "Take heed also, that thou be not extream, / In playing with the out-side of my dream."[21] The "pill" Bunyan asks us to swallow in that book is a pretty uncompromising fundamentalism; its "gilding" consists of novel-like qualities that Bunyan certainly never intended to be taken as such – unexpectedly vivid characterization, for instance – but which helped to make *The Pilgrim's Progress* one of the most popular fictions of all time. Because most readers of fiction are pretty adept at, so to speak, spitting out the moral pill, what Richardson was trying to do when he followed Protestant forefathers like Bunyan and Defoe in distinguishing between alluring forms and rigorous moral content is much too neat because good novels have a habit of jeopardizing their declared aims. Just as *The Pilgrim's Progress* can be admired for what Bunyan would have thought of as exactly the wrong reasons, and just as – I have to assume – no one has ever read *Moll Flanders* for the purposes of moral edification, Richardson's intensely vivid scenes of sadistic compulsion stay with you long after the virtuous pronouncements have been forgotten.

This was the propensity for unraveling-from-within that the English novelist D. H. Lawrence diagnosed as endemic to the form when he wrote in a 1925 essay that the novel "won't *let* you tell didactic lies, and put them over."[22] "If you try to nail anything down," he wrote in another essay on morality and the novel, "either it kills the novel, or the novel gets up and walks away with the nail."[23] Directly in opposition to attempts to redeem the novel by harnessing it to socially and morally respectable ends, this resistance to the single didactic purpose would be another reason "why the novel matters." I took the title of this chapter from Lawrence's essay of the same name.

The novel becomes an "art"

In the almost two hundred years that separate Richardson and Lawrence the novel shed its air of moral hazard but still had much further to go than simply passing as harmless entertainment. After all, to say that the novel is not *actively harmful* seems a weak case for its importance. Through the nineteenth century the novel's popularity and perceived suitability as "family" reading only accelerated, and the novelists Sir Walter Scott (or "the author of *Waverley*" as he was initially known) and Charles Dickens were international superstars in their lifetimes. Even so – or perhaps thus – the novel still had none of the prestige of poetry, and none of the credibility it would need in order to be studied in universities as it is now.

The late nineteenth and early twentieth centuries saw a number of books on the novel authored by academic literary critics (as distinct from gentleman amateurs). Broadly, those early efforts come in two forms: the synoptic history and the structural analysis of the novel. Exemplary of the historical approach are Walter Raleigh's *The English Novel* (1895), which begins with the ancient romance and ends with Scott, and George Saintsbury's still very readable *The English Novel* (1913), which goes all the way up to the 1890s. Exemplary of the structural approach is Selden L. Whitcomb's grim manual *The Study of a Novel* (1905), of historical interest because it lets you see what critics considered worth saying about narrative technique in the years before the novel was fully institutionalized ("The paragraph has undergone great development in the course of its history").[24]

However, much of the credit for making the novel what it is in our time, institutionally speaking, should be attributed not to scholars but to novelists at the turn of the last century. Particularly influential was the American-born Henry James, who argued most forcefully in "The Art of Fiction" (1884) that the English novel needed to start taking itself seriously as a highly crafted form, that there was something deeply philistine about the inclination to think that "a novel is a novel, as a pudding is a pudding, and that our only business with it could be to swallow it."[25] It was high time, James argued, to jettison moralistic assumptions that would sound downright nonsensical in the discussion of other art forms: "You wish to paint a moral picture or carve a moral statue…? We are discussing the Art of Fiction; questions of art are questions (in the widest sense) of execution; questions of morality are quite another affair."[26] One of his contemporaries, the Polish-born Joseph Conrad, also tried to elevate the novel by likening it to more prestigious forms, to the *fine* arts:

> [The novel] must strenuously aspire to the plasticity of sculpture, to the colour of painting, and to the magic suggestiveness of music – which is the art of arts. And it is only through complete, unswerving devotion to the perfect blending of form and substance; it is only through an unremitting never-discouraged care for the shape and ring of sentences that an approach can be made to plasticity, to colour, and that the light of magic suggestiveness may be brought to play for an evanescent instant over the commonplace surface of words: of the old, old words, worn thin, defaced by ages of careless usage.[27]

Here Conrad evoked sculpture, painting, and music as models, as if to suggest that we might attribute their higher prestige to their being less hampered by crude expectations of real-world **representation**; after all, no one could confuse their artistic medium with the ordinary means of communication, whereas novels have to be assembled from "the old, old words" of everyday life. Although the novels of James and Conrad were so profoundly interested in moral questions that it would be a mistake to represent their position as "art for art's sake," they were clearly trying to make a case for the novel as something to be judged on its formal execution rather than on its subject matter alone. Many writers of the next generation would share their sense of artistic mission, and thus create the **modernist** novel – or the "art-novel," as Mark McGurl instructively terms it in his study of James's legacy.[28] "I have had my vision," ends Virginia Woolf's *To the Lighthouse* (1927) as the authorial surrogate, the artist Lily Briscoe, puts down her paintbrush.[29]

To recover the force of this claim that a novel could be as legitimately artistic as a painting it is important to remember that no one had ever felt the same need to reclaim *poetry* for the realm of high art. Even the novel-advocate Saintsbury had taken an apologetic turn at the end of his 1913 history of the novel when he began to acknowledge the "inferiority" of fiction to poetry ("a higher thing by far").[30] So the extravagant claims made on the novel's behalf by early twentieth-century writers – "The novel is a great discovery," Lawrence wrote: "The novel is the highest form of human expression so far attained"[31] – would have sounded even more inflated to those reading Lawrence in an era when the novel was thought of primarily as popular entertainment. Showing why the novel was more than this was the aim of such critical landmarks as Percy Lubbock's *The Craft of Fiction* (1921), Q. D. Leavis's *Fiction and the Reading Public* (1932), and F. R. Leavis's *The Great Tradition* (1948).

By the 1940s, the novel was well on its way to becoming an essential object of literary study. For this, much is owed to the Leavises, two married Cambridge scholars who thought of themselves as outsiders but who would have massive influence around the middle of the century. Lawrence's claim that "being a novelist, I consider myself superior to the saint, the scientist, the philosopher, and the poet … The novel is the one bright book of life" sounds exorbitant, but the Leavises would have agreed with him.[32] Q. D. Leavis argued in her groundbreaking *Fiction and the Reading Public* that the purpose of novels "is not to offer a refuge from actual life but to help the reader to deal less inadequately with it; the novel can deepen, extend, and refine experience by allowing the reader to live at the expense of an unusually intelligent and sensitive mind."[33] The ultimate target of her book was a culture in which people read mediocre commercial fiction as an escapist way of killing time when they should instead be turning to novels to "obtain assistance in the business of living" and "enrich the quality of living by extending, deepening, refining, coordinating experience."[34]

The novel, then, is experience in its own right, and experience that improves our real, non-fictional lives. In asserting this, the Leavises took their cue from the great nineteenth-century realists they admired. Leo Tolstoy, for instance, had used their respective capacities for human engagement to mark the difference between the magnificent Anna Karenina and her unsympathetic husband: while Anna cannot read a novel without identifying with its hero or heroine, her husband's moral downfall lies in his belief that any attempt to "put himself in thought and feeling into another being was ... harmful and dangerous romancing."[35] "The greatest benefit we owe to the artist, whether painter, poet, or novelist, is the extension of our sympathies," George Eliot had famously declared in an 1856 essay.[36] For novelists like Tolstoy, Eliot, and then Henry James (Q. D. Leavis's line about a novelist's "unusually intelligent and sensitive mind" is pure James), fiction helps you to live in a more engaged way. The Leavises theorized this passionately humanizing aspect of the novel as the ultimate justification of literary criticism.

You can probably see the tension between moral and artistic claims in these early efforts to elevate the novel. For instance, even though the Leavises and Lubbock both turned to Henry James as an exemplary novelist they took very different things from him. Lubbock had followed James in arguing that because the novel is *art* and not simply a transcript of life it needs to be evaluated on the quality of its execution, whereas the Leavises had no interest in technical achievement for its own sake, and so James joins Austen, Eliot, and Conrad in the elite group that F. R. Leavis designated "the great tradition" because his interest in artistic technique "is the servant of a profoundly serious interest in life."[37] The enduring legacy of Lubbock's attention to fiction as craft is implicit every time we speak of narrative form or technique (the subject of my Chapter 3), but it is easy to see why the Leavises' uncompromisingly moral view of the novel should have had a substantial impact in its own time, rethinking as it did both the novel and novel criticism as transformative spiritual forces.

"The peculiar property of a good novel," Q. D. Leavis wrote, "is the series of shocks it gives to the reader's preconceptions."[38] The notorious trouble with Leavisite criticism was that it tended to find literary shocks less interesting than moral ones. So, to name some of the rasher judgments of *The Great Tradition*, Lawrence is more important than James Joyce, the tract-like *Hard Times* is Dickens's best novel, and Laurence Sterne's experimental *Tristram Shandy* is "irresponsible (and nasty) trifling."[39] You can see from these judgments that the Leavises were not trying simply to show that the novel mattered but were demarcating what *kind* of novel mattered. If Austen, Eliot, James, and Lawrence are in the great tradition, and Sterne, Dickens, and Joyce are not, realist fiction must be the only fiction that counts. Linguistic exuberance and a love of the grotesque, bizarre, and fantastical – the features that Sterne, Dickens, and Joyce share across the centuries dividing them – evidently don't make for literary greatness. It had taken the channeling of sexual passion into narratives of "virtue rewarded" to make the novel socially respectable; intellectual respectability on the Leavisite model would require additional disciplining of this unruly form.

Novelistic realisms and realities

The privileging of realism in claims made for the novel at mid-century was by no means unique to English criticism, and in the work of continental critics made a far stronger case for why the novel matters in political and social (as distinct from moral and artistic) terms. Although Erich Auerbach's monumental *Mimesis: The Representation of Reality in Western Literature* (1946), which begins with Homer and ends with Woolf, was not overtly (or even intentionally) a book about the novel, the story it tells is of the triumph of the realist novel, unmistakably the standard by which Auerbach measures everything that precedes it. Three main features constitute realism here: the mixing of styles, from the high literary style to ordinary demotic language; the serious treatment of the everyday lives of the ordinary, un-aristocratic masses; the embedding of those ordinary lives in their very specific social and historical contexts.

The last of these – let's call it "realist embedding" – was the focus of many politically minded critics. Writing around the same time as Auerbach, Georg Lukács championed the realist novel because he believed that this was the only literary form capable of addressing the fractured conditions of modernity. So, whereas the ancient **epic**, one of the long narrative forms predating the novel, was the product of an epoch of stability and wholeness, the novel was the outcome of a less stable, no longer inherently meaningful world order, and "an expression of this transcendental homelessness."[40] What Lukács understood by realism was the type of novel that shows the subjective, private life in its relations with the public, exterior world of social, economic, and historical forces, and which presents the two – the private self, the social self – as inextricably bound together. Importantly, Lukács was not especially interested in the political views of particular novelists (many of those he admired held conservative attitudes radically at odds with his own Marxism) but rather with the realist novel as a form: historically and politically vital, he thought, because it explains who we are, where we are, and how we got there.

A near-contemporary of Lukács and Auerbach, and perhaps every bit as influential for novel theory in the long run, the Russian Mikhail Bakhtin began in the same place by contrasting the novel with the epic, celebrating the diverse, decentered new world of which he (like Lukács) took the novel to be the characteristic literary expression. According to Bakhtin, the fact that contemporary reality is its subject gives the novel two essential features: *laughter* and *polyphony*. Laughter is the province of the novel because the novel engages a familiar, incomplete, and fluid present rather than the sealed-off, semi-mythic, monolithic national past of epic poetry; and whereas epic necessarily "has something of an official air," the novel has its roots in folklore and popular culture, and so "is associated with the eternally living element of unofficial thought (holiday forms, familiar speech, profanation)."[41] Underscoring that sense of the novel as subversive, demotic, and "unofficial" was Bakhtin's definition of the novel as a **dialogic** form. Whereas the epic takes place in a world which knows its own unified literary language, and thus its own view of reality, as the only true one, the novel emerges in a modern world in which numerous languages meet and collide, and in which every living language is *itself* internally multiple ("**heteroglossia**" was his term for this multiplicity). For Bakhtin, then, the many-voiced novel is the truest, most *realistic* reflection of the uncertain modern condition.

Bakhtin's influential arguments presented an immensely attractive political case for the novel: in describing the novel as *inherently* dialogic he makes it a relativistic and democratic literary form – to understand the political implications of the "dialogic" think of the difference between **dialogue** and monologue. No wonder Western critics were so excited to encounter Bakhtin's mid-century writings for the first time decades later: here was an account of the novel that explained not only its emergence (the collapse of epic), and its characteristic styles (multiple languages) and interests (everyday reality), but also made the case for its political relevance (an inbuilt pluralism and relativism).

The late twentieth century, though, produced less cheering political interpretations of the novel's characteristic realism, understanding it not as "lifelikeness" but as the narrative techniques most associated with the realist novel: its all-encompassing social range, its all-knowing narrator. Deploying arguments about the link between surveillance and power postulated by the French historian of ideas Michel Foucault, critics noticed that the controlling consciousness of realist narration – the **omniscient narrator** who, invisible, can see everything and everyone – might be seen to model the organizing principles of the state, a state that no longer relies on force but on centralized knowledge. (Foucault had argued that a distinctive aspect of modern state power was that it had rejected violence against the body – torture, branding, mutilations, and so on – in favor of instilling the kind of self-policing attendant on learning to see yourself as the object of perpetual surveillance.) As a form, then, the novel is not the subversive, "unofficial" affair that Bakhtin imagined, but the model of the modern state. That the novelist Henry Fielding was one of the founders of the first professional police force in England is suggestive given that it was also Fielding who pioneered the characteristic omniscient narration of realist fiction, a narrative mode based on a controlling authorial consciousness. You can see what was innovative about this now-traditional form if you recall that Defoe presented himself as only the ghostwriter of Moll Flanders's autobiography, and that Richardson pretended to be simply the compiler of characters' letters.

Realism, then, has been the key term in most accounts of why the novel matters, and it has come to mean many things. But one point unites all these claims: that realism means more than just representing what "really" is. That is to say, the novel may act upon us as all cultural texts do, and thus potentially change the world in the act of describing it. A story often told about Harriet Beecher Stowe's blockbusting abolitionist novel *Uncle Tom's Cabin* (1852) recounts that when they met for the first time during the American Civil War Abraham Lincoln addressed Stowe as "the little lady who made this big war."[42] Is it possible that a novel could start a war? Can a novel change the world simply by making people look at it differently? Stowe for one certainly thought so when she proclaimed in her rousing final chapter that there is "one thing that every individual can do" to combat slavery: "they can see to it that *they feel right* … See then to your sympathies in this matter!"[43] "Sympathies" is literally the operative word; novels are *doing* something by teaching you how to feel, and, in theory, when we "feel right," we act rightly.

If this is true, we have to take novels seriously as potential agents in the world rather than imagining them as the innocently reflective surfaces that the term "realism" implies. Are they agents for good? Yes – and no. What makes *Uncle Tom's Cabin* such a useful example is that its considerable narrative power has notoriously proved a curse as well as a blessing. Which is to say that even though the novel professes a documentary aspiration in its rendering of African American slavery – its subtitle is "life among the lowly" – this book has looked less than realistic to many modern eyes; indeed it has seemed impossibly, even dangerously, sentimental. Thus the saintly Uncle Tom, who dies praying for his master/murderer, would become a byword for any perceived African American collusion with white racism. Stowe's powerful novel is an extreme example of the novel managing our minds as it moves our emotions, controlling our consciousnesses and acting upon our behavior, seeming merely to describe a world but in reality altering that world in ways that could never wholly have been desired or even imagined at the outset.

Back in 1750, Samuel Johnson, you'll remember, worried about how a novel can affect real-life behavior because it seems to represent it so convincingly. We have lived with novels for so long that it is hard to recapture the extent of his unease when he wrote about the force of fiction in the middle of the eighteenth century. Nonetheless, in the centuries that separate us from Johnson, many critics have, albeit in very different ways, conceded his central point: that it is precisely because the novel is so intimately connected to real-world representation that it can do so much to shape the world it purports only to be describing,

Miguel de Cervantes, *Don Quixote* (1605, 1615)

As God slowly departed from the seat whence he had directed the universe and its order of values, distinguished good from evil, and endowed each thing with meaning, Don Quixote set forth from his house into a world he could no longer recognize. In the absence of the Supreme Judge, the world suddenly appeared in its fearsome ambiguity; the single divine Truth decomposed into myriad relative truths parceled out by men. Thus was born the world of the Modern Era, and with it the novel, the image and model of that world.

Milan Kundera, "The Depreciated Legacy of Cervantes"[1]

I wrote above that no one would be foolish enough to model their behavior on the unrealistic old **romance**, but a famous exception comes in the most important early novel of all: Cervantes's *Don Quixote*, published in two parts in 1605 and 1615, a novel in which a middle-aged Spanish farmer saddles up his scrawny workhorse and sets off to put the world to rights in the heroic style of his beloved chivalric romances. Turned into something close to **parody** by their incongruence with the hero's own prosaic world, the extravagant conventions of chivalric romance seem to give way to the representation of reality in all its ordinariness. Did *Don Quixote* represent the triumph of modernity and reason? Did Cervantes liberate fiction from fantasy and falsity? Perhaps – but the novel speaks more ambivalently than this about the value of disenchantment.

Since it is often said that the novel arose out of the romance, as *Don Quixote* emerged out of the works it parodied, the distinctions posited by the Restoration playwright William Congreve in the famous preface to his 1692 novel *Incognita* usefully summarize the difference between the book Cervantes writes and those his hero reads:

> Romances are generally composed of the Constant Loves and invincible Courages of Hero's, Heroins, Kings and Queens, Mortals of the first Rank, and so forth; where lofty Language, miraculous Contingencies and impossible Performances, elevate and surprize the Reader into a giddy Delight … Novels are of a more familiar nature; Come near us, and represent to us Intrigues in practice, delight us with Accidents and odd Events, but not such as are wholly unusual or unpresidented, such which not being so distant from our Belief bring also the pleasure nearer us.[2]

His reading of romances has prepared Quixote for "wonders": impossible love and peerless courage, giants, monsters, and damsels in distress, castles, dungeons, and enchantments. But from the very opening of the novel, it is clear that we are in a world of "a more familiar nature," in Congreve's phrase, and that Quixote himself is its product.

In that opening, we see the mixture of social particularity and typicality that will ultimately come to seem distinctive of the novel as a genre. "In a village of La Mancha, the name of which I purposely omit, there lived not long ago, one of those gentlemen, who usually keep a lance upon a rack, an old target, a lean horse, and a greyhound for coursing," Cervantes writes, before going on to supply a long list of the **protagonist**'s dietary, sumptuary, and household habits, all in keeping with his social class.³ In what would eventually become recognizable as a definitively novelistic manner the book opens by deploying very precise cultural detail to place the hero for us in a recognizable social world – realist embedding, I called it earlier. The protagonist is thoroughly ordinary, just "one of those gentlemen," but what makes him hero-worthy, what turns him from a social type into what we think of as an individual, is his faith in the historical truth of fictional romance. And so he sallies off with his prosaic squire Sancho Panza and his skinny Rosinante in search of maidens, widows, and orphans to succor.

Some of Don Quixote's knightly misadventures have the currency almost of proverbs: he bravely attacks a cluster of windmills, believing them wicked giants; he routs two converging flocks of sheep, thinking himself on the field of battle between warring armies; he slashes a wine bag to shreds, taking it for the head of a monstrous villain, usurper of a princess's kingdom. He is astonished when he surveys the fruit of his victories – a clump of windmills, some dead sheep, a room awash with spilled wine – and "realizes" that a malevolent enchanter has sought to rob him of his triumphs by transforming giants into windmills, armies into sheep, a severed head into a wine bag. In a truly glorious twist of perceptual logic, Don Quixote cannot see that he has magicked the banal into the fantastical, but believes that a grudging nemesis has done exactly the opposite. "Depend upon it, Sancho," he says in one of Cervantes's many **metafictional** jokes, "that the author of this our history must be some sage enchanter" (483). To the extent that Quixote believes in giants, giants are what he really, truly sees, and even the doggedly materialistic Sancho Panza, who sees windmills, sheep, and wine bags as they are, is willing to be taken in. As of course is the reader, willing to suspend disbelief (after all, the novel is scarcely *plausible*) for the sake of the story's fun.

Indeed, all Quixote's loyal friends are drawn into a madness they profess to reject. The local priest and barber masquerade as a distressed damsel and her squire in order to lure the hero back to his native village with the promise of a new adventure, and, in an absurd transformation every bit as silly as the hero's conviction that the tin basin on a barber's head is the legendary helmet of Mambrino, one of Quixote's friends disguises himself with a beard made from the – surely unconvincing – material of an ox's red and white spotted tail. Even as they think they are tricking Don Quixote, they have been seduced into sharing his characteristic habit of remaking the drab materials of the real world into something richer and stranger. "You are mad," an un-seduced bystander tells Don Quixote, and "you have the property of converting into fools and madmen all that converse, or have any communication with you" (873).

This happens again in the novel's magnificent second volume – perhaps the best novel sequel ever written – when Don Quixote and Sancho Panza encounter characters who have read not only the first volume of Cervantes's novel but also a counterfeit second volume (which really existed, written in these pre-copyright times by an Alonso Fernández de Avellaneda). Among those new characters are an elegant duke and duchess who tease Quixote and Sancho by pretending to take them deadly seriously, all the while sending them on extravagant "adventures" inspired by their own readings of the fictions that drove Quixote mad. In one, the heroes are made to believe that they have traveled the world on an enchanted wooden horse; in another, Quixote is promised that his beloved lady Dulcinea El Toboso has been turned into a plain country wench (i.e. the plain country wench she "really" is) and can be restored only by 3,300 strokes of the lash to Sancho's brawny behind. It is as though "the mockers were as mad as the mocked; and that the duke and duchess were within two fingers' breadth of appearing to be mad themselves, since they took so much pains to make a jest of two fools" (919).

"But every day produces new things," a character says, "jests turn into earnest, and jokers are joked upon" (781). And so our laughter rebounds on us, because however much we hope to keep our mocking distance from the hero's exploits Cervantes draws us in by exploiting the same pleasures that seduced Quixote. In fact, by a very early stage of the novel, in the eighth chapter of seventy-four, the reader is becoming as susceptible as the hero himself. Here, Quixote meets a Biscainer on his travels: they argue, then they challenge each other, then they draw their swords, then the bystanders gasp and pray, then the combatants attack each other … and then the story breaks off! The narrator can hardly believe it, but his source has left the story unfinished! A new chapter begins:

> In the first part of this history we left the valiant Biscainer and the renowned Don Quixote with their swords lifted up and naked, ready to discharge two such furious and cleaving strokes, as must, if they had

lighted full, at least have divided the combatants from head to heel, and split them asunder like a pomegranate: but in that critical instant this relishing history stopped short, and was left imperfect, without the author's giving any notice where what remained of it might be found. This grieved me extremely. (66)

The joke is on us, and it is a good joke too. Don Quixote and the Biscainer, swords aloft, have been caught and frozen in a ridiculous position – and so has the reader. The jolting interruption of the narrative serves to highlight just how absorbed we have become in the outcome of this daft fight. We've become engrossed by the most absurd of exploits, have lost altogether that detachment on which the novel has tricked us into priding ourselves – the readerly detachment that distinguishes us from the novel's insane hero – and Cervantes has caught us out.

But there is, finally, a more profound sense in which the joke is on us for finding Don Quixote a figure of fun. More is the pity if it is absurd to believe that the world can be changed. Aware of his fallen world, a world in which "sloth, idleness, gluttony, and luxury triumph" (581), the hero's aim is only "to succour the wretched, and destroy the oppressor" (806), "to do good to all, and hurt to none" (674). For all his absurdity, the novel's hero tells us that a world more generous and equitable than this one is only possible if it is first imaginable. The demand that we be "realistic," that we act as if the way the world *is now* is the only way the world *could ever be*, forecloses the possibility of transformation. *Realism* becomes the tyrant, the giant monster Don Quixote was trying to kill.

I imagine this is why so many novelists across the centuries have found this an inspiring novel, and why we are disappointed when Don Quixote renounces fiction and dies repentant. When Dostoevsky designated this the saddest book ever written, he was surely thinking of the final chapter, which recounts *"How Don Quixote fell sick, made his will, and died."*

> "I am now no longer Don Quixote de la Mancha ... [N]ow all the histories of knight-errantry are to me odious and profane: I am now sensible of my folly, and of the danger I was led into by reading them; and now, through the mercy of God, and my own dear-bought experience, I detest and abhor them." (940)

As a seventeenth-century Catholic he could do nothing else. In the passage I quoted earlier, Milan Kundera proposed that the new secular relativism at the heart of *Don Quixote* would come to define both modernity and "its image and model," the novel. For Kundera, the novel matters because it shows that reality is plural, that truth is relative. But when the hero throws out his "odious and profane" books and embraces "reality" in that final capitulation, we realize, perhaps more wistfully than Kundera allows himself to say here, that the force of social orthodoxy is such that it can masquerade as absolute reality itself. "May Don Quixote never be recovered!" one character says, speaking on behalf of the reader who rebels against the imminent ending (895). But Don Quixote is cured of his madness, and the cure kills.

Chapter 2

Origins of the novel

The story of the novel's emergence can be told differently depending on what you think a novel actually is. And depending on how you define the novel, you could attribute its emergence to the Mediterranean and Middle Eastern empire of the ancient Greeks or to England over a millennium and a half later. So the divergence is enormous, both geographically and temporally: on the one hand, the novel is the product of a culturally hybrid classical antiquity, and, on the other, the outcome of Britain's transition into a capitalist modernity. This chapter surveys some very different accounts of the origins of the novel, and it turns in closing to a follow-up question: why do we want to be able to pinpoint when, where, and how the novel emerged?

Dates and definitions

"This book is the revelation of a very well-kept secret," Margaret Anne Doody writes in the opening line of *The True Story of the Novel* (1996): "that the Novel as a form of literature in the West has a continuous history of about two thousand years."[1] Doody goes on to offer a history of prose narrative which suggests that the novel is as old as Western civilization itself, beginning with ancient Greek fictions written around the time of Christ, among them those works that Bakhtin had considered when he sought to distinguish the irreverent novel from the stately classical epic. But are these all really *novels*? According to Doody's capacious definition they are, because a novel is a novel "if it is fictional, if it is in prose, and if it is of a certain length."[2] For many critics, though, this definition is too open-ended and inclusive, so generous that it tells us little about the novel as a form. But since definition is a project of exclusion and containment, Doody's point is that when it comes to defining the novel our exclusions have often been arbitrary and our acts of containment driven by the critical desire to present the eighteenth-century English novel, very much a latecomer in the history of long prose fiction, as the first "real" novel.

So with its inclusive definitions and its massive historical scope, Doody's account of the novel's origins deviates dramatically from the received critical wisdom on the subject, a received wisdom that leaves out not much less than two millennia of long prose fiction. J. Paul Hunter offers a very useful but much more conventional definition of the novel in his study of the eighteenth-century context from which the English novel emerged. For Hunter the distinctive features of the novel are these: *contemporaneity* (novels tend not to be set in remote times and places); *credibility* (plots and characters operate in believable ways); *familiarity* (the world of the novel is a recognizably everyday one); *rejection of traditional plots* (unlike, say, Chaucer or Shakespeare, novelists tend not to reuse existing stories); *tradition-free language* (the novel eschews elevated "literary" diction in favor of everyday speech); *individualism* (novels care less about types than about individual subjectivities and their different ways of viewing the world); *empathy and vicariousness* (novels invite us to inhabit sympathetically the interior lives of characters); *coherence* (a narrative strand unites the whole); *inclusiveness, digressiveness, and fragmentation* (even if novels close by tying up their loose ends they also roam in unpredictable ways); and *self-conscious innovation* (in the eighteenth century, novelists had a strong sense that they were doing something new).[3]

Hunter's definitions are worth cataloguing at such length because, above all, they are so plausible and intuitive. What they also help to show, though, is how we habitually generalize about the novel on the basis of the most canonical eighteenth-century examples. You can probably think of many novels as counterexamples to Hunter's definitions (some gothic novels, for example, undermine the assertions about *contemporaneity* and *credibility*) but this criticism can be answered with the claim that these are not "mainstream" novels. The obvious problem, though, is that what constitutes the "mainstream" is an institutional judgment, its legitimacy conferred by its antiquity and by consensus, rather than an innocently descriptive fact. I said at the start of this chapter that your understanding of the origins of the novel depends on what you think a novel *is*; the biggest problem, however, is that what you think the novel *is* will depend on which historical moment in the long history of prose fiction you have decided to foreground. I have presented the choices as classical antiquity and eighteenth-century Britain, but it's more complicated even than that: after all, countries as different as England, France, China, and Spain had produced long prose fictions – "novels"? – in the sixteenth century, and by then Lady Murasaki's Japanese classic *The Tale of Genji* was already half a millennium old.[4] So are you going to generalize about the novel on the basis of Apuleius or Murasaki, Rabelais or Richardson, Cervantes or Defoe? The definition of "novel" used to confirm that the novel emerged in the eighteenth century has, in reality, *already* presupposed that eighteenth-century emergence by virtue of having been reached on the basis of eighteenth-century examples (rather than, for example, ancient or Renaissance prose fiction). More succinctly put, your dating of the novel depends on your definition of the novel, but your definition depends on your dating.

The (eighteenth-century) rise of the novel

The book that did most to establish the conventional story of the novel's emergence in eighteenth-century Britain is Ian Watt's *The Rise of the Novel* (1957), a book of such rare critical importance that it continues to elicit elaborations and corrections over half a century after its publication. Focusing his study on Defoe, Richardson, and Fielding (and again you can see how much gets left out when critics address the emergence of the novel), Watt argues that "the lowest common denominator of the novel genre" is its "formal realism":

> Formal realism, in fact, is the narrative embodiment of a premise that Defoe and Richardson accepted very literally, but which is implicit in the novel form in general: the premise, or primary convention, that the novel is a full and authentic report of human experience, and is therefore under an obligation to satisfy its reader with such details of the story as the individuality of the actors concerned, the particulars of the times and places of their actions, details which are presented through a more largely referential use of language than is common in other literary forms.[5]

What characterizes the novel, then, is, first, a focus on the plausible particulars of individualized characters and their contexts (that **verisimilitude** discussed in my Chapter 1), and, second, the use of language in a primarily denotative or "referential" way, language treated as a transparent medium rather than used for its own rhetorical sake (this is what Hunter implies by "tradition-free language"). Very influentially, Watt argued that although there are moments of particularizing detail in the otherwise intricately stylized long prose fictions of classical antiquity and early modern Europe, these are anomalous, and it was not until the novels of Defoe, Richardson, and Fielding that "formal realism" became the norm.

Watt and the many critics who have followed him have argued that Britain's early transition into capitalism made the novel possible. A print culture was emerging there for the first time: new technologies allowed for a wider circulation of written materials, and for the transmission of this reproducible, portable, and even purchasable commodity. Furthermore, although the eighteenth century was by no means an era of universal literacy, the novel differed from earlier literary forms because it was produced outside elite systems of aristocratic patronage, subscription, and private circulation. In his famous opening to *Tom Jones*, Fielding likened the novelist to a pub landlord: the novel is a democratic form, then, even if it's only the democracy of the pub, where your cash secures your welcome. The "patrons" of this new genre would be a much less select group: the booksellers, the new circulating libraries, and the novel's borrowers, buyers, and readers. Most critics agree that the new possibilities for publication and distribution must have played a massive part in the eventual ascendancy of an emergent literary form.

The wider culture of which these new publishing conditions were part would also be massively significant in shaping the concerns of the novel, Watt argued, because not only did the birth of capitalism make the novel *materially* possible as a print commodity, but it also created the powerful, literate, self-confident middle class from which the novel's writers and readers would come. From these social transformations emerges the characteristic worldview of the eighteenth-century novel: capitalistic, individualistic, and entrepreneurial. Watt takes as exemplary of this worldview the solitary and self-interested protagonists of Defoe's fiction: his restless pursuit of wealth is what lands Robinson Crusoe on his desert island, while the pickpocket Moll Flanders and the courtesan Roxana approach conventional morality with the dog-eat-dog attitude of the emergent entrepreneur. Traditional ideas of birth and status, notions of a person's supposedly "natural" station in life, are breaking down, and there is everything to play for.

Michael McKeon argues in his substantial extension of Watt that the novel worked to negotiate "questions of virtue" and "questions of truth" that appeared as the traditional belief in a divinely sanctioned order of things started to crumble in the transition from feudalism into capitalism, and from the medieval into the modern era.[6] If your birth is no longer the measure of your worth, and if it is now possible to imagine honor as a matter of character rather than caste, then ideas of selfhood become newly interiorized and newly contingent. McKeon offers an evolutionary narrative with an important twist: that the erosion of aristocratic values fueling progressive **ideology** carried within it the means of critiquing progressive values themselves, because once status is no longer "natural" but a factor of economic accomplishment, the inevitable question arises of why anyone should consider the new aristocracy of cash somehow better than the aristocracy of birth it replaced. McKeon's "questions of truth" work in a similar way because once you challenge "universal" truths with the relative truths of empirical knowledge (or what is learned by human experience and not known as, say, divine law), you create the conditions under which your supposedly "truer" truth is in turn subject to debate.

The novel emerged in England, scholars often propose, because this was a rapidly secularizing Protestant culture, and, anticipating the obvious challenge from readers of the Spanish Catholic Cervantes, McKeon suggests that *Don Quixote* was a false start because the arrival of the Catholic revival known as the Counter-Reformation terminated the skeptical lines of inquiry which Cervantes and others were advancing. Just as progressive ideas of individual self-making made possible their own undoing at the very moment in which they undid ideas of birth-as-worth, and just as empiricism unleashed the forces that enabled its own dismantling, Protestantism started by eroding the authority of the Church but ultimately eroded the basis of its own claims to religiously sanctioned truth. Because the middle class of eighteenth-century England was a Protestant one, the novel it produced would, in keeping with the Puritan tradition of individual self-scrutiny, be introspective rather than civic in its emphases, but what follows from that "Protestant" internalization of authority is a valorization of private judgment that ultimately renders religious authority superfluous because it inadvertently exposes the subjectivity and relativity of *all* knowledge.

In a historically relocated counterpart to Lukács's and Bakhtin's arguments that the novel, emerging out of epic, speaks of a world in which ideas of universal truth have been dissolved, critics like Watt and McKeon present the novel as the product of a Protestant-inspired but ultimately secularizing rejection of the traditional and timeless in favor of the contingent, circumstantial, and empirically and individually knowable. So the novel emerged within the intellectual climate that was also producing the empiricism of scientists and philosophers like Francis Bacon and John Locke – "the early modern epistemological revolution," is how McKeon characterizes this historical moment.[7] Indeed, Watt argues that Defoe's focus on what the protagonist knows through *personal* experience, knows from the evidence of his or her senses, is "as defiant an assertion of the primacy of individual experience in the novel as Decartes's *cogito ergo sum* [I think therefore I am] was in philosophy."[8]

That novels emerged with modern individualism makes sense in relation to how we actually read them. Whereas the reception of earlier literary forms reinforced communality – plays are watched with others, and poetry often read aloud – the novel is consumed in privacy and solitude. And the novel is very much concerned with the interior lives of individuals, interior lives at odds with their social circumstances. You see this very clearly in the striking inwardness of the modernist novels of the early twentieth century, but perhaps theirs is only the continuation of a novelistic concern with interiority that has been distinctive of the novel since its earliest days; you might say that Robinson Crusoe's twenty-eight years on a desert island has an almost allegorical appropriateness, but the many hundreds of private letters that make up Richardson's *Clarissa* also tell us how interested eighteenth-century readers were in life as it is experienced from the inside. Or, looking back still further, there is Madame de Lafayette's wonderful *The Princess of Clèves* (1678), a psychological study of a woman trapped between marital obligation and adulterous desire. Married under duress to the Prince of Clèves, the Princess falls in love with the Duke of Nemours. The novel begins like a romance – the men are paragons of valor, the women of beauty – but ends up as something psychologically much knottier: duty clashes with desire, but the Princess cares as much for her reputation as her moral duty, while her desire for the Duke of Nemours is tempered by a suspicion that he is more interested in the chase than in her. This is a **historical novel** set in the French court of a century earlier, but the main "events" of *The Princess of Clèves* are more psychological than social.

However, although it is easy to catalogue examples like these to show that the novel is essentially an individualistic form, concerned primarily with questions of subjectivity, psychology, and interiority, any argument along those lines needs to register the fact that defining the novel in a particular way reflects reading habits and experiences consolidated long after those novels were written. If you have decided after, say, James and Woolf that the novel is about the subjective life then the subjective life is probably what you are going to see when you look back at Lafayette, Defoe, Richardson, and the other early novelists. The risk of anachronistic reading is always with us. You read Behn differently after reading Richardson, Richardson differently after Proust, and while Eliot makes Austen read differently, and Woolf makes Eliot read differently, Dickens sheds light on Fielding, and Joyce on Dickens. Successors shape our reading of precursors.

But is it a *novel*?

Indeed, even the designation of "novel" is potentially anachronistic. In *From Fiction to the Novel*, Geoffrey Day goes so far as to suggest that what we unhesitatingly think of as eighteenth-century novels "were not perceived as such by the readers or indeed by the major writers of the period, and that, so far from being ready to accept the various works as 'novels', they do not appear to have arrived at a consensus that works such as *Robinson Crusoe, Pamela, Joseph Andrews, Clarissa, Tom Jones, Peregrine Pickle* and *Tristram Shandy* were even all of the same species."[9] A number of scholars have argued that it is only when you get to the very end of the eighteenth century and the beginning of the nineteenth, and to writers like Jane Austen and Sir Walter Scott, that the novel has really taken shape as a single form. This is why, these critics explain, the stories we tell about "the rise of the novel" need to attend to the after-the-fact status of their terminology.

In view of the long tradition of reading their works as *the* "eighteenth-century novels," it would be perverse to suggest that writers like Defoe, Richardson, and Fielding cannot be novelists on the grounds that our novelistic expectations did not exist when they were writing. However, one of the things their longstanding canonization *as* novelists tends to obscure is their books' indebtedness to a huge range of preexisting textual forms: *Pamela* is part conduct book and part fairy tale; *Robinson Crusoe* recalls the travelogue and the spiritual autobiography; *Clarissa* aims at tragedy; Fielding thought that he was adapting the lofty epic into prose comedy. If you look back a little further than the eighteenth-century novel to some of its plausible antecedents in Renaissance prose fiction, Thomas Nash's *The Unfortunate Traveller* (1594) and Thomas Deloney's *Jack of Newbury* (1597) are, among other things, pseudo-biographies and jest-books, with a touch of the cautionary (Nash) or exemplary (Deloney) fable, and, in Nash's case, confession, chivalric fantasy, and travelogue on top of all that. Unless you keep in mind those debts to other written forms, the interestingly mongrel quality of the novel in the eighteenth century and beyond threatens to disappear. "For the novel least of all forms of literature can boast a pure extraction," wrote the critic Walter Raleigh in 1895: "it is of mixed and often disreputable ancestry."[10]

Imposing total coherence on the novel would be disastrous if it meant flattening out either the rich diversity of its textual sources or the extraordinary capacity for transformation that it continues to demonstrate. Rather oddly, both Watt and McKeon conclude that the novel would spend the next few centuries just recapitulating what the major eighteenth-century novelists had already done. This is a strange conclusion because it obliterates the intellectual and formal variety of everyone from Jane Austen to James Joyce, making the novel sound a good deal less interesting than most of us find it, and because it ignores how subsequent writers have shaped our reading of their predecessors. The conventional story of the rise of the novel is least convincing when it presents the novel and its history as if they were sitting there waiting to be discovered rather than constructed (and reconstructed over and over again) by modern readers. The massive differences in critical narratives of the history of the novel are an important reminder that all literary histories are put together in accordance with the particular interests of the periods in which they are being written.

You can see this most clearly when you contrast the insularity of the classic "rise of the novel" story with the globalized consciousness of the critiques and revisions that it provoked at the end of the twentieth century. The Ian Watt tradition picks out three English novelists and nationalizes the novel, sidestepping the problem of its relative belatedness compared to what was happening on the continent through what William Warner shows to be a critical sleight of hand: "if one understands 'the' (first real modern) novel as the expression of middle-class (democratic, Protestant) culture, then the novel is an English invention."[11] England gets the credit for inventing the novel, and the English "invention" of the novel turns descriptive claims about the novel at a single stage in its history into prescriptive claims about the novel generally. Thus, Warner goes on, "empiricism, Protestant individualism, moral seriousness," and other distinctive aspects of English culture at a particular historical moment, "are promoted from secondary characteristics of novels which happen to have been written in England to primary features of the novel's generic identity."[12]

This nationalizing of the novel would have been meaningless to eighteenth-century readers who read promiscuously, linguistic competences and translations permitting, across national boundaries. As importantly, one of the most striking aspects of Doody's alternative history is in its reminder that prose fiction, "the novel," predates the nation-state by many centuries. Even the "Greek" and "Latin" tags attached to these early works refer only to the languages in which early prose fiction has survived, and not to any easily predictable site of geographical origin. Translate their places of origin into modern-day geography and Apuleius (*The Golden Ass*) was born in Algeria, Achilles Tatius (*Leucippe and Clitophon*) in Egypt, Chariton (*Callirhoe*) was Turkish, and Heliodorus (*Aethiopica*) Syrian. "The Novel was produced in antiquity by people from non-Greek and non-Roman areas, by writers who came from the Near East and from Africa," writes Doody:

> The Novel, that is, is a "foreign" import – or rather, it is the product
> of combination, of contact between Southern Europe, Western Asia,
> and Northern Africa. And behind these regions, the regions of Greece
> and Syria and Ethiopia and Egypt, there lie other areas, hinterlands
> not without influence. We can assume the possibility of story and style
> filtering in from the Balkans and the Celtic lands in the West, from

Persia and India in the East, from the Sudan and Kush and Katanga in the South. The homeland of the Western Novel is the Mediterranean, and it is a multiracial, multilingual, mixed Mediterranean.[13]

The world opens up as a more capacious view of the history of a familiar-seeming form enables a more capacious view of the world, or, as Doody puts it in another context, "Multiculturalism begins at home."[14] So much for national claims about the novel: as we look back at the novel, its family tree, like our own, traverses countries, continents, and then recedes out of historical view.

Origins in the novel

When she titled her book *The True Story of the Novel*, Doody pointed to the *narrative* desires that underpin inquiries into where the novel came from. Does the novel have a "story"? Does it have a "true story"? The desire for a good story helps to explain why we read novels, and is a desire that the novel as a form has continuously fed: literary history, Doody's title proposes, shares the novel's narrative compulsions. As if the novel were the protagonist of a long and complicated plot, we have sought origins as if they will explain everything that followed. I want to end this chapter by outlining the connection between how we think about the history of the novel ("but where did it *really* come from…?") and what novels have historically been about: questions of genealogy and origin.

Right from "the start" – what the canonical narrative designates as the start – the English novel has created mysteries around parental origins. The heroine of *Moll Flanders* is united with her long-lost mother when she unknowingly marries her own brother; at the end of the novel she inherits her mother's estate. Although this is only part of rather than the climax to Defoe's **episodic novel**, successors like Fielding with an interest in more tightly constructed plots will turn the story of origination and inheritance into their main story (a literally "stagey" plot, you might say, since drama had been using the discovery narrative for centuries). The full title of Fielding's novel is *The History of Tom Jones: A Foundling*, and the novel begins when Squire Allworthy discovers the infant Tom in his own bed and decides to bring him up himself. The locals speculate that Tom is no "foundling" at all, but the Squire's illegitimate child – incorrectly, as it happens, but who can resist a good story about true origins? Fielding's earlier *Joseph Andrews* likewise turns on the hero's discovered origins.

The statistically remarkable population of orphans and foundlings in English fiction indicates how important the origination plot has been. It was certainly enough of a cliché by Austen's time to be worth deflating in *Emma* (1816) when the heroine befriends a local orphan. To Emma, Harriet is "the natural daughter of somebody"; to the wiser Mr. Knightley, she is "the natural daughter of nobody knows whom."[15] Obscure origins mean creative opportunity because they allow Emma to speculate that Harriet must be of socially distinguished origins, and so she divides her from the man she loves because this local farmer must be too plebeian for her friend. As usual, Emma is wrong. Harriet turns out to be, in drab reality, the product of a tradesman's embarrassing indiscretion. Emma is mortified: "Such was the blood of gentility which Emma had formerly been ready to vouch for! The stain of illegitimacy, unbleached by nobility or wealth, would have been a stain indeed."[16] The genealogical mystique founders on the most prosaic of origins.

But the origins of the most famous nineteenth-century foundling remain forever obscure. "Do you know anything of his history?" a character asks about Heathcliff in Emily Brontë's *Wuthering Heights* (1847): "I know all about it," replies his informant Nelly Dean, "except where he was born, and who were his parents, and how he got his money."[17] There is nothing to contextualize Heathcliff prior to his arrival at Wuthering Heights as the grubby toddler that Mr. Earnshaw picked up on the streets of Liverpool, "a dirty, ragged, black-haired child; big enough both to walk and talk … yet, when it was set on its feet, it only stared round, and repeated over and over again some gibberish that nobody could understand."[18] Terry Eagleton proposes that Irish would be a likely origin for a dark, savage, "gibberish"-speaking Liverpool foundling, while there's a very longstanding critical suspicion that he is the illegitimate son of Mr. Earnshaw, and Cathy's half-brother.[19] Like Fielding's nosy villagers, critics cannot help filling in the missing origins.

However, Nelly tries to console the young Heathcliff by focusing, like Austen's Emma, on the rich possibilities of the foundling plot:

> "You're fit for a prince in disguise. Who knows, but your father was Emperor of China, and your mother an Indian queen, each of them able to buy up, with one week's income, Wuthering Heights and Thrushcross Grange together? And you were kidnapped by wicked sailors, and brought to England."[20]

And indeed he does eventually buy both houses up – *not* because he discovers an elevated birth but in revenge against those to whom the estates belong. In view of this novel's interest in the specifically environmental forces that make people what they are ("We'll see if one tree won't grow as crooked as another, with the same wind to twist it!"), it is absolutely essential that Heathcliff's birth remain unaccounted for.[21]

This shift from blood origins to environmental determinisms is immensely important for how we read the nineteenth-century novel, and especially one of its dominant forms, the **Bildungsroman**, or novel of formation. The differences between two Dickens novels about boy orphans, *Oliver Twist* (1837–9) and the much later *Great Expectations* (1859) are instructive because, although both novels are concerned with the question of origins and inheritance, they outline two very different views of what a person "really" is: a move away from nature towards nurture, and away from the recuperation of preexisting status toward a more evolutionary understanding of the relationships between self and society, where you become not what you "always" secretly were but what your situation makes you.

Born in a workhouse, abused throughout childhood, and captured by evil Fagin's gang of thieves, the trusting, mannerly Oliver Twist is scarcely a product of these environments, the only ones he has ever known. So where does he really belong, and to whom? In the course of the novel, Oliver finds two pseudo-parents: the scholarly Mr. Brownlow and the kindly Mrs. Maylie, already an adoptive parent to the beautiful girl who turns out to be Oliver's Aunt Rose (her equally shady origins also have to be vindicated in the course of the novel). These are the proper homes for Oliver, who has spent his entire life among criminals, prostitutes, and the abjectly poor, and yet has a thoroughly socialized sense of right and wrong. We know that Oliver will turn out to be the product of genteel parents, and predict an inheritance for him; as in Fielding (whose influence is felt through this novel), you can be illegitimate in the narrow sense and yet otherwise vindicated as a worthy heir. All the same, the real mystery of the novel, the unsolved puzzle that all critics remark, is the extraordinary resilience of Oliver's practically *genetic* middleclassness: Oliver remains throughout what Oliver was born to be and not what circumstances ought to have made him.

Similar ingredients of an abused child, substitute parents, and how people are (or are not) made and remade by social circumstances are combined more darkly in *Great Expectations*. Like the character in *Oliver Twist* of whom Dickens jokes that he can "trace his genealogy all the way back to his parents,"[22] the working-class orphan Pip knows where he has come from; indeed, it is in the cemetery where his parents lie buried that he meets the escaped convict who will transform his life with the "expectations" of the novel's title. Pip's beloved Estella, another adoptee, has taught him to despise his humble birth, but Pip comes to learn that his newfound gentlemanliness is more tarnished yet by the source of its enabling wealth. Both Estella and Pip have been "made" by fake parents using them to get their revenge: Miss Havisham has brought Estella up to break men's hearts in revenge against the man who broke hers, and Magwitch has made Pip a gentleman to get his revenge on the gentry: "If I ain't a gentleman, I'm the owner of such. All on you owns stock and land; which on you owns a brought-up London gentleman?"[23] And these nightmarish manipulations of Estella and Pip are only the most dramatic instances of their status as hostages to fortune; both will change again as their treatment by others changes ("I have been bent and broken, but – I hope – into a better shape," a humbled Estella chillingly tells Pip at the end of the novel).[24] Origins cannot predict outcomes, and there is no sense in which the destinies of Pip and Estella are already there in their beginnings.

If the novel has trained us to think genealogically – where did it come from? – it should also have trained us to think contingently. "Men can do nothing without the make-believe of a beginning," George Eliot wrote in the opening line of *Daniel Deronda* (1876), another novel structured around discovered origins, but "no retrospect will take us to the true beginning."[25] For sure, Fielding and Richardson both had a sense of doing something new – Fielding called himself "the founder of a new province of writing" and Richardson felt he was founding "a new species of writing"[26] – but we do not conventionally think of theirs as the first novels. A whole range of novels from *The Tale of Genji* to *Don Quixote* to *Robinson Crusoe* have been proclaimed the true parent of the novel, and in a nicely ironic twist the designation *novel* used so disparagingly in the eighteenth century has now become a term of advertisement and approbation. Witness the case of William Baldwin's 1553 *Beware the Cat*. You could be forgiven for never having heard of this tale about a man who makes a potion that allows him to understand what the cats on the London rooftops talk about. It doesn't strike me as much of a novel, but in recent times the book has been republished as *Beware the Cat: The First English Novel* because up until then, its editor writes, "we can find no original work of English fiction of more than short-story length in which we see consistent character portrayal and a sequence of events that form a coherent plot."[27] So is this the first English novel? It depends – as always – on whether or not you buy the editor's definition of a novel.

But the un-answerability of the question may be no bad thing. Even if we could identify with greater assurance the point at which prose fiction turned into the novel, we would be making a serious mistake in thinking that the future of the novel is immanent in its conception, à la Oliver Twist, a form of determinism to which "rise of the novel" stories are notoriously liable. Rather, the novel may be more like Heathcliff because its origins can be enjoyably guessed at but never definitively explained, and because its identity is a contingent affair, the product of circumstances. If we want to know where the novel really came from, it is in no small part because so many of them have seduced us with promises, sometimes deferred and sometimes broken, of an origin that would explain everything if we could only discover it. "What is clear," Homer Obed Brown writes, "is that the linear history of the novel as having an 'origin' and 'rise', the history we have been brought up on, with its genealogies, lines of descent and influence, family resemblances, is itself a fictional narrative – a kind of novel about the novel."[28] In literary history as in literature itself, explanatory beginnings and revelatory endings are as artificial as they are alluring.

Laurence Sterne, *The Life and Opinions of Tristram Shandy, Gentleman* (1759–67)

If you really want to hear about it, the first thing you'll probably want to know is where I was born, and what my lousy childhood was like, and how my parents were occupied and all before they had me, and all that David Copperfield kind of crap, but I don't feel like going into it, if you want to know the truth.

J. D. Salinger, *The Catcher in the Rye* (1951)[1]

Tristram Shandy is the most typical novel in world literature.

Viktor Shklovsky, *Theory of Prose* (1925)[2]

Tristram Shandy is a novel about what we expect novels to be. Through Tristram's unorthodox storytelling, plot dissolves into digressions ("take them out of this book … you might as well take the book along with them"); linear storytelling proves impossible; and the individuality of characters turns out to be a matter of bizarre private fixations, hobbyhorses.[3] *Tristram Shandy* is the story of Tristram Shandy as *Robinson Crusoe* is the story of Robinson Crusoe, but even the seemingly simple structuring of the novel as a fictional autobiography turns out to be vastly more complicated than it sounds when Tristram tells the reader in his fourteenth chapter that he has been writing for six weeks and hasn't managed to get himself born yet. On the face of it, *Tristram Shandy* is so eccentric a work that it may be reckless to try and make it stand for anything other than itself; still, thinking about *Tristram Shandy* in relation to the rise of the novel can be illuminating for the very reason that our expectations are so brazenly thwarted at every stage. Because there are no expectations without conventions, this refusal to conform helps to throw light on what Sterne's readers think a novel is supposed to do.

Exploiting the convention that narrators may address their imagined audience ("reader, I married him," and all that), Tristram rebukes the reader for not paying proper attention. One early chapter begins with a scolding for the sloppy reader: "How could you, Madam, be so inattentive in reading the last chapter? I told you in it, *That my mother was not a papist*"; her penance is a rereading: "I do insist upon it, that you immediately turn back, that is, as soon as you get to the next full stop, and read the whole chapter over again" (51–2). But supposing you identified enough with the address to reread the chapter – and of course Sterne knows that we understand the difference between our real-world selves and the conventionally implied reader – you would learn nothing whatsoever about Mrs. Shandy's religion. That's the point. *Only* if you already knew the comically recondite fact that the Catholic Church once debated the baptizing of the infant in the womb would you have been able to infer Mrs. Shandy's religion from her difficult labor. Sterne, knowing just how unlikely that is, mocks the usually easy, taken-for-granted relationship between narrators and implied readers by making Tristram an inept teller of his own story.

And Tristram is magnificently inept. Here we are in the fourth volume of the book, and Tristram is still discussing the night of his birth. He breaks off mid-sentence:

> I will not finish that sentence till I have made an observation upon the strange state of affairs between the reader and myself, just as things stand at present – an observation never applicable before to any one biographical writer since the creation of the world, but to myself …
>
> I am this month one whole year older than I was this time twelve-month; and having got, as you perceive, almost into the middle of my fourth volume – and no further than to my first day's life – 'tis demonstrative that I have three hundred and sixty-four days more life to write just now, than when I first set out; so that instead of advancing, as a common writer, in my work with what I have been doing at it – on the contrary, I am just thrown so many volumes back. (256–7)

The more of his life Tristram writes the more remains to be written. Reminding us of the conventional gap between narrative time and lived time that so-called realist fiction tends to gloss over (with, say, a new chapter beginning "It was on my eighteenth birthday that …") his story recedes further into the past the longer he goes on telling it. After all, Moll Flanders, Jane Eyre, and all the many other tellers of their own life stories know that it is okay to leave things out. Tristram, on the other hand, seems not to have realized that narrative is necessarily *selective*. Instead, he feels compelled to recount all the circumstances surrounding his birth because "I know there are readers in the world … who find themselves ill at ease, unless they are let into the whole secret from first to last, of everything which concerns you. It is in pure compliance with this humour of theirs, and from a backwardness in my nature to disappoint any one soul living, that I have been so very particular already" (8). Obliging as ever, he tells you that you may "skip over the remaining part of this Chapter" if you are not one of those readers: "_____Shut the door_____" (8) And, the door shut, Tristram goes on to explain "for the curious and inquisitive" how he came into the world (8).

Now travestying the expected relationship between the novel and the writing of a formatively damaged childhood – "all that David Copperfield kind of crap," as Salinger's Holden Caulfield dismisses it – Tristram explains how he has been cursed from the start: first, his father is interrupted at the moment of ejaculation, thwarting his flow of "animal spirits"; then Tristram's nose is flattened at birth by the midwife's forceps; and finally, worst of all, he is christened Tristram rather than the portentous Trismegistus on which his father had decided. A catalogue of minute contingencies, elaborately and non-sequentially narrated, brings about each disaster. Walter Shandy winds the clock and has sex with his wife on the first Sunday of the month, and her inadvertent association of the two spousal obligations explains how Mrs. Shandy comes to interrupt her husband at the critical instant by asking if he has wound up the clock. Then Tristram's nose is flattened at birth because Mrs. Shandy has forfeited her right to give birth in London (a long story) and so is at the mercy of a mediocre male midwife who has cut his finger (another long story) untying the knotted bag that contains his obstetric instruments (yet another long story). And as if all that were not bad enough, Tristram is misnamed because while Mr. Shandy struggles to get dressed the maid hurries to convey the implausible name, Trismegistus, to the curate, who assumes she means Tristram.

Dickens's *David Copperfield* (1849–50) begins with the simple "Chapter I: *I am Born*," but Tristram struggles to get himself even to that point. Not even his conception will do as a point of origin in view of all the circumstantial factors that will have a bearing on what he will be. Because whether you think of Tristram's conception (the disturbed ejaculation), or his birth (the flattened nose), or his christening (the misnaming) as the real beginning of "Tristram Shandy" – and the novel is telling us just how arbitrary all beginnings really are – the fully catastrophic quality of these inaugurations makes sense only when you know what his father is. And knowing Walter Shandy means knowing his hobbyhorses. Walter believes wholeheartedly in his own masculine power: he is a disciple of Robert Filmer, author of *Patriarcha* (1680), a defense of the absolute authority of kings, based on the divine and domestic authorities of God and the father. A political framework, even what Sterne would consider a preposterous one like this, is too grand to constitute a hobbyhorse, but it does explain his others. So, for this paterfamilias, Tristram's conception is a disaster because the sperm carries the child in miniature, the "homunculus" (women don't have much to do with things in Walter Shandy's world; later in the novel the men conclude that mothers are not related to their children); then Tristram's birth is a disaster because Walter Shandy believes a really big, long, substantial nose is the key to power (so unabashedly phallic a symbol that Tristram keeps asking us to remember that he really *means* the nose); and, last, the christening is a catastrophe because Walter believes that names are the key to the destiny of their bearers. He might have basked in the glory reflected from a Trismegistus Shandy, Walter believes, but you can't expect much from a Tristram.

All the way through Tristram's efforts to recount his beginnings the authority conventionally attributed to parental origins is rendered meaningless, Mr. Shandy robbed of any power to determine what Tristram will become. But what still continues to surprise new readers is just how bawdily the novel literalizes Sterne's denial of phallic power: you don't expect a clergyman to write a book full of penis jokes; and Tristram affects to be very shocked indeed to hear that early volumes have been censured for their indecency, warning young lady readers against the temptation to misread his **anecdote** about women being maddened by their desire to handle a stranger's abnormally large nose. This is what comes of "depending so much as I have done, all along, upon the cleanliness of my reader's imaginations" (196). Yet it's one thing to have Walter Shandy symbolically emasculated by contingencies that rob him of his paternal power, but another to threaten every male character with literal castration.

"'Twas nothing – " the chapter on Tristram's accident begins, "I did not lose two drops of blood by it – " (339). Since this has no apparent relation, or, rather, not an immediately apparent one, to the previous chapter's discussion of Walter Shandy's *Tristrapaedia*, the rigorously determined plan to which Tristram's life fails so conspicuously to conform, the reader wonders what this "nothing" is. With none-too-ambiguous ellipses, Tristram explains:

> The chamber-maid had left no ******* *** under the bed: – Cannot you contrive, master, quoth *Susannah*, lifting up the sash with one hand, as she spoke, and helping me up into the window seat with the other, – cannot you manage, my dear, for a single time to **** *** ** *** ******?
>
> I was five years old. – *Susannah* did not consider that nothing was well hung in our family, – so slap came the sash down like lightening upon us; – Nothing is left, – cried *Susannah*, – nothing is left – for me, but to run [flee] my country. (339)

Rumor travels countywide about the heir to Shandy Hall, and although Tristram assures us that all is well, Sterne's jokes invite us to speculate on the damage: "nothing was well hung in our family," Tristram muses, while Susannah cries out ambiguously that "nothing is left." The word "nothing" is used suspiciously often in the – truncated – chapter dealing with Tristram's accident.

We soon discover that the accident was caused by Uncle Toby's hobbyhorse. Uncle Toby is fixated with military fortifications and he and his man Corporal

Trim spend their time reenacting famous sieges: the window fell on Tristram's infant penis because the lead from the sash window went as raw materials for their bowling-green fort. Like uncle like nephew, since it was a projectile in the groin at the Siege of Namur that ended Uncle Toby's military career, hence *his* military hobbyhorse. A hobbyhorse is to be straddled, Tristram reminds us often, and you can truly know a man by his hobbyhorse because of the "friction" between the horse and "the heated parts of the rider" (67); "a man's HOBBY-HORSE is as tender a part as he has about him" (101). Only when Tristram offers his long-promised account of Uncle Toby's romance with the Widow Wadman in the final chapters do we finally find out what, other than his hobbyhorse, Uncle Toby keeps between his legs.

Metaphors of generation and origination are literalized in the crudest way in *Tristram Shandy*: the novel ends – although it's a bit of a stretch even to call it an ending – with the story of how the bull Walter Shandy bought to service the local cows has proved sterile, a cock and bull story in the most indecent sense. If the novel's dominant **theme** of generation might be read allegorically, the problem raised by the unpredictability of reproduction in *Tristram Shandy* is the nature of *origination* and *originality* in the novel: where do novels come from? And even though novels are not reproducible in any straightforward way – not like, say, sonnets – we know them as novels because we recognize certain distinguishing conventions. "Shall we for ever make new books, as apothecaries make new mixtures, by pouring only out of one vessel into another?" Tristram asks in defense of his own oddity, but the devastatingly entertaining novelty of *Tristram Shandy* in fact resides in its appropriation and disruption of narrative conventions recognizable from earlier novels (309). Not even the most mechanical of the novel's conventions escapes Tristram's mishandling. The fourth volume lacks its twenty-fourth chapter, for reasons Tristram explains in the twenty-fifth, and chapters eighteen and nineteen of the ninth volume consist only of headings, the chapters to be written later. Even the novel's prefatory material ceases to be prefatory in Tristram's hands, appearing only in chapter twenty of the third volume: "All my heroes are off my hands; – 'tis the first time I have had a moment to spare, – and I'll make use of it, and write my preface" (173). The novel has only just got off the ground when it produces its **anti-novel** in the shape of *Tristram Shandy*.

Chapter 3

Narrating the novel

> Nobody can work in material of which the properties are unfamiliar, and a reader who tries to get possession of a book with nothing but his appreciation of the life and the ideas and the story in it is like a man who builds a wall without knowing the capacities of wood and clay and stone. Many different substances, as distinct to the practiced eye as stone and wood, go to the making of a novel, and it is necessary to see them for what they are.
>
> > Percy Lubbock, *The Craft of Fiction* (1921)[1]

What makes the narration of *Tristram Shandy* so striking is that we are never allowed to forget that everything we learn reaches us mediated by the idiosyncratic voice of Tristram himself. You could put it more strongly than this and say that the *telling* of events constitutes the main event, as would later become the case in many twentieth-century novels: "There is the story of one's hero," Henry James wrote of his novel *The Ambassadors* (1903), "and then … the story of one's story itself."[2] That novels are never simply unfolding before our eyes but are narrated from somewhere is one of the most important factors to keep in mind as we read them. Although other predominantly narrative forms such as theater and film have strategies of their own to direct our perceptions and make particular meanings possible, they usually present events as if they are happening before our eyes rather than being "told" to us: unlike the events of a novel, dramatic and cinematic events are enacted rather than narrated.

So when we read novels we must always be acutely conscious of the nature of the telling because it shapes to an immeasurable extent how we respond to what is being recounted – I say "recounted" because novels are usually written in the past tense, as if describing events that have already occurred somewhere in the non-fictional world. Because, as I've suggested earlier, the novel has always been thought of as the literary form most closely identified with real-world representation, it is sometimes easy to forget the art that goes into their construction; and, seduced into not seeing that constructedness, we excavate the novel's content and take that to be its meaning. This chapter, then, sets out to survey some of the novel's most characteristic narrative tactics and techniques, and to show how narrative form doesn't so much convey meaning as create it.

Omniscient narration

"Vanity was the beginning and end of Sir Walter Elliot's character," Jane Austen writes of the heroine's father early in *Persuasion* (1817):

> He had been remarkably handsome in his youth; and, at fifty-four, was still a very fine man. Few women could think more of their personal appearance than he did; nor could the valet of any new made lord be more delighted with the place he held in society. He considered the blessing of beauty as inferior only to the blessing of a baronetcy; and the Sir Walter Elliot, who united these gifts, was the constant object of his warmest respect and devotion.[3]

This is an example of omniscient narration, "omniscient" coming from the Latin adjective *omnis* ("all") and the verb *scire* ("to know"). Austen's narrator knows all about Sir Walter Elliot: vanity is no less than *the beginning and end* of his character; and, handsome in his youth (which she knows all about, thirty years on), he may still be judged "very fine" to look at; she knows, too, that he has one "constant object of his respect and devotion" – himself. There is no room for doubt here about the essence of Sir Walter Elliot.

In one important respect, the idea of "omniscience" is misleading because it implies that the narrative world and its inhabitants have a reality beyond the narration itself, as if they are not simply made-up figments of Austen's imagination, and as if they are not coming into being for the very first time in the words through which we encounter them. Of course her narrator *knows* everything: she invented it all. But "omniscient" remains a useful designation precisely because it characterizes the kind of novel that asks to be read in just that way, as if it were not an invention but a representation of something existing prior to and outside the text in which it appears. When critics speak of "realist" fiction, they are typically not commenting on the lifelikeness or plausibility of fictional content; rather they are registering the *effect* of reality produced by narration like Austen's. "Realist" describes the kind of novel that asks us to believe in the prior actuality of what the narrative represents (indeed, this is exactly what the word *re*-presentation denotes).

The concept of narrative omniscience identifies the degree of trust that the reader is asked to place in the truth-value of the story's telling: in stark contrast with the many novels told by fully characterized first-person narrators with some personal involvement in the stories they tell, you get a strong sense when you read realist fiction that the narrator's judgments are to be accepted rather than questioned. If you look again at the Walter Elliot passage, you will see how Austen establishes the contract, the common ground, between **implied author** and **implied reader**. "Few women could think more of their personal appearance than he did," Austen writes, "nor could the valet of any new made lord be more delighted with the place he held in society." As if a crisp summary of the "beginning and end of Sir Walter Elliot's character" were not enough to instill total confidence that this narrator knows what she's talking about, the amplification works to imply a shared cultural world: Sir Walter is vainer than most women; he is more snobbish than the menservants of the *nouveau riche*. The worldly authority with which Austen circulates these received ideas – that women are conceited and that new money (as opposed to landed wealth) is vulgar – helps to build a bridge between the author and a reader who is expected to recognize conceited women and vulgar valets as real-world phenomena with which Sir Walter Elliot can be compared.

Here, it is as if writer and reader are exchanging knowing nods over the oblivious head of the character being described: we know that Walter Elliot could never describe himself as Austen has. But let's not be too smug about this comfortable conspiracy: though the reader doesn't know it yet, the novel is going to turn on their heads these misogynistic and snobbish assumptions about female vanity and *nouveau riche* vulgarity: only when the heroine Anne Elliot has lost her marriageable youthful beauty and Captain Wentworth has made his vulgar new fortune will they finally get together. Indeed, one of the things that make Austen so entertaining is that she has her cake and eats it too: establishing a bond with the reader through a common fund of received ideas that she then throws into question. When, in the famous opening of *Pride and Prejudice* (1813), Austen pronounces it "a truth universally acknowledged, that a single man in possession of a good fortune, must be in want of a wife," her comically inflated "universally acknowledged" reminds us of the thoroughly contingent status of the easy social "truths" on which her conspiracy with the reader relies.[4]

Omniscient narration is the dominant mode of the nineteenth-century novel, the marker of a novel often referred to as the "classic realist text." A particular hierarchy of voices is its primary characteristic: there is the narrator's authoritative voice and then there is the dialogue; and the omniscient narrative voice is to be taken as objective while everything in quotation marks is to be understood as subjective, and thus in need of the narrator's explanatory wisdom. Just as when we put words in "scare quotes" in order to indicate ironic distance, the quotation marks in a classic realist text tell you that, while the words enclosed within these quotation marks (the dialogue) are subject to debate and interpretation, the truth of the narrator's voice (never framed by quotation marks) is beyond doubt. This means that the narrative "voice from nowhere" can interpret what the quotation marks present as the "voice from somewhere," a biased or limited voice of a character and only one voice among many, but resists interpretation itself.[5]

Because George Eliot's novels are usually considered exemplary classic realist texts, here is a short passage from her *Felix Holt* (1866) that helps to make clearer the relationship between "subjective" dialogue and "objective" **third-person narration**, between voices that are to be interpreted and the single narrative voice that is to be taken as authoritative. After many years, the haughty Mrs. Transome is reunited with her son Harold, who, having returned to England with his imperial fortune, is about to stand for election to Parliament:

> "But I shall not be a Tory candidate."
> Mrs Transome felt something like an electric shock.
> "What then?" she asked, almost sharply. "You will not call yourself a Whig?"
> "God forbid! I'm a Radical."
> Mrs Transome's limbs tottered; she sank into a chair. Here was a distinct confirmation of the vague but strong feeling that her son was a stranger to her.[6]

This is straightforward enough so far: dialogue between mother and son interspersed with narrative commentary summarizing Mrs. Transome's horrified reactions, reactions which an omniscient narrator is in a position to describe (that "vague but strong feeling that her son was a stranger to her" could be apprehended only by Mrs. Transome and the narrator). But now look at the work of elaboration explaining how this disappointing meeting has come about:

> She was ignorant what sort of man Harold had become now, and of course he must be changed in many ways; but though she told herself this, still the image that she knew, the image fondness clung to, necessarily prevailed over the negatives insisted upon by her reason.

And so it was, that when she had moved to the door to meet him, she had been sure that she should clasp her son again, and feel that he was the same who had been her boy, her little one, the loved child of her passionate youth. An hour seemed to have changed everything for her. A woman's hopes are woven of sunbeams; a shadow annihilates them.[7]

Notice how the passage moves from what we take to be an entirely trustworthy explanation of Mrs. Transome's reaction to a general real-world claim about the fragility of "women's hopes." The rhetorical authoritativeness – no quotation marks around any of this – of the classic realist text makes for, some critics argue, a specifically political content because the novel presents a subjective, culturally contingent claim (here, about women's hopes) as unqualifiedly objective truth. Although I suspect that, as the example of Austen suggests, realist novelists often have a far more ironic relationship to "universally acknowledged" truths than such readings imply, the crucial point is that for many critics narrative form should not be understood simply as a vehicle for fictional "content," but as material that should be interpreted in order to bring its *own* ideological content to light.

I begin with omniscient narration because it raises one of the most useful questions to guide your reading of narrative techniques: What does the narrator *know*? Thinking in terms of the narrator as an implied subjectivity that may or may not know certain things is an indispensable personification so long as we keep in mind that often it is *only* a personification. There are two more questions to ask yourself as you read: "Who is *speaking*?" and "What is their *perspective* or **point of view**?" We're so familiar with those dead metaphors of speaking and seeing that we forget that they *are* metaphors, intended to evoke aural experiences (as if we were listening to someone rather than reading in solitude) and visual privileges or limitations (as if the scene were being surveyed from a particular physical location). The differences among the categories of narration discussed in this chapter become clearer if you keep in mind these three metaphors of knowing, speaking, and seeing: the narrator knows or does not know certain things; communicates and withholds information from a particular narrative situation; and views the object from one vantage point or many.

Focalization and free indirect discourse

You should immediately recognize the passage below as an example of broadly realist narrative from a later historical moment – it bears emphasizing that literary realism is not solely a nineteenth-century phenomenon. In Angus Wilson's *Anglo-Saxon Attitudes* (1956) the medieval historian Rose Lorimer is on her way to a café to meet the novelist Clarissa Crane for the first time. Importantly, this is also the first time that the reader encounters these characters:

> Rose Lorimer, struggling with weighed-down shopping baskets, made her immense way among the marble and mosaic of the Corner House, caught a passing view of herself in a mirror and was pleased. She had always affirmed that women scholars were primarily women and should not disregard the demands of feminine fashion. To advertise learning by disregard of dress was to be odd, and Dr Lorimer disliked oddity more than anything. The vast intellectual excitement of her researches since the war had not left her a lot of time for thinking about clothes, but her mother had always said that with a good fur coat, however old, one could not go wrong; and for her own part, she had added a bold dash of colour to cheer our drab English winter – woman's contribution to banish gloom. Twenty years ago, of course, she reflected, straw hats with flowers would have been out of place in December, but the dictates of fashion were so much less strict nowadays, it seemed. And then Dr Lorimer had always loved artificial flowers, especially roses.
>
> ...
>
> Clarissa Crane, searching the vast marble tea-room with a certain distaste, suddenly recognized her learned hostess and felt deeply embarrassed. In all this drab collection of matinée-goers and pantomime parties, that only could be her. She had expected somebody dowdy, indeed had worn her old green tweed suit in deference to the academic occasion, but she had not been prepared for someone quite so outrageously odd, so completely a "fright." Dr Lorimer was mountainous, not only up and down, but round and round as well, and then her clothes were so strange – that old, old fur coat, making almost no pretence of the large safety-pins that held it together, and, above the huge, aimlessly smiling grey face, a small toque composed entirely of artificial pink roses and set askew on a bundle of tumbling black coils and escaping hairpins. Clarissa, with a sensitive novelist's eye, dreaded to think into what strange realm the poor creature's mind had strayed.[8]

What makes this passage so crafty is how it uses their first meeting to dramatize the meeting between a novel's reader and its characters, and to expose how the reader makes judgments according to where he or she is looking from. We see events through the eyes of two characters consecutively, having our view transformed when we see the first character through the eyes of the second.

We're initially taken in by Rose Lorimer's self-image: pleased to catch a glimpse of herself in the mirror, she sounds so dress-conscious and conventionally socialized that it doesn't immediately occur to you to question her self-perception. As if to underscore the reader's susceptibility to taking characters at their own evaluation, details from the first passage are reused in the second when Rose is seen anew through the eyes of the fashionable novelist Clarissa Crane: "Dr Lorimer disliked *oddity* more than anything," we're told in the first passage; the second tells us that Clarissa "had not been prepared for someone quite so *outrageously odd*" (my emphasis). That sensible and stylish fur coat, "however old," has now become the "old, old fur coat, making almost no pretence of the large safety-pins that held it together"; Rose's "bold dash of colour" is now "a small toque composed entirely of artificial pink roses" perched on a "huge, aimlessly smiling grey face." Clarissa correctly concludes that Rose has lost her mind.

This passage is indicative of the cunning with which even relatively traditional-seeming writers deploy point of view. The narrative technique that does the most work in this passage is **free indirect discourse** (sometimes termed **free indirect style**). If you ask yourself "who is thinking?" you'll notice that the passage begins with a distant summarizing voice: Rose Lorimer is introduced as she goes "on her massive way." Who could describe her thus? Well, certainly not Rose because she is too un-self-knowing to see herself as fat; and it cannot be Clarissa because, although Rose's "mountainous" bulk will be the first thing she notices, she hasn't spotted Rose yet. So we know that an omniscient narrator is describing Rose as she appears from the outside. But what about "her mother had always said that with a good fur coat, however old, one could not go wrong; and for her own part, she had added a bold dash of colour to cheer our drab English winter – woman's contribution to banish gloom"? Something has changed, narratively speaking. These must be Rose's thoughts rather than those of a reliably omniscient narrator: we know this because the sentiment recalls in a conversational idiom Rose's reported views on "feminine fashion" and because you can indeed "go wrong" with an old fur coat (as the encounter with Clarissa will instantly confirm). You recognize the technique as free indirect discourse, then, once you notice that, even when there is nothing explicitly identifying the owner of these thoughts, and even though the narrative remains in the conventional past tense and in the third person, the words and ideas belong to the character herself: this is free *indirect* discourse because there are no quotation marks and no "she thought" explicitly marking the thought process as Rose's.

Free indirect discourse is probably the most common of novelistic techniques, and this passage from *Anglo-Saxon Attitudes* is a characteristic use of a narrative strategy that lends itself brilliantly to ironic effects at the expense of a character – we end up knowing much more than he or she does. I used Austen to illustrate omniscient narration but the fact that she also pioneered free indirect discourse in the English novel tells us something essential about the inextricability of narrative form and thematic content: that is, the plots of her novels are driven by the need for the protagonist to recognize and overcome the limitations of her immature knowledge. So, for instance, early in *Emma* (1816), Austen's omniscient narrator describes the potential pitfalls awaiting the charmed and charming Emma Woodhouse as "the power of having rather too much of her own way, and a disposition to think a little too well of herself."[9] This is the same crisply synoptic method Austen uses to characterize Sir Walter Elliot at the beginning of *Persuasion*. But notice how Austen later uses free indirect discourse to dramatize the heroine's thought processes as Emma impertinently "improves" Harriet Smith away from good Robert Martin:

> The friends from whom she [Harriet] had just parted, though very good sort of people, must be doing her harm. They were a family of the name of Martin, whom Emma knew well by character, as renting a large farm of Mr. Knightley, and residing in the parish of Donwell – very creditably she believed – she knew Mr. Knightley thought highly of them – but they must be coarse and unpolished, and very unfit to be the intimates of a girl who wanted only a little more knowledge and elegance to be perfect. *She* would notice her; she would improve her; she would detach her from her bad acquaintance, and introduce her into good society; she would form her opinions and her manners.[10]

To recall the convenient distinction between "showing and telling" that Percy Lubbock supplied in *The Craft of Fiction*, whereas the omnisciently narrated passage *tells* you outright that Emma has an ominous streak of willfulness and self-importance, this passage of free indirect discourse *shows* you these things through Emma's highhanded musings on Harriet and the Martins. We can see Emma's limitations quite clearly here, and our adult knowledge is precisely what Emma must develop in the course of the novel.

The traditional prevalence of the coming-of-age narrative helps to explain the ubiquity of free indirect discourse through the nineteenth century and beyond. This is a narrative strategy that is all about ignorance surmounted and knowledge difficultly attained. Again, I used Eliot to speak of omniscience, but she too is an author who uses free indirect discourse extensively. As you read this introduction of Dorothea Brooke, the gracious, gifted heroine of *Middlemarch* (1872–3), you should now be able to recognize the movements between external summary and interior thought, between statement and demonstration, and between the pseudo-objectivity of omniscient narration and the subjectivity of free indirect discourse.

> She was open, ardent, and not in the least self-admiring; indeed, it was pretty to see how her imagination adorned her sister Celia with attractions altogether superior to her own, and if any gentleman appeared to come to the Grange from some other motive than that of seeing Mr Brooke, she concluded that he must be in love with Celia: Sir James Chettam, for example, whom she constantly considered from Celia's point of view, inwardly debating whether it would be good for Celia to accept him. That he should be regarded as a suitor to herself would have seemed to her a ridiculous irrelevance. Dorothea, with all her eagerness to know the truths of life, retained very childlike ideas about marriage. She felt sure that she should have accepted the judicious Hooker, if she had been born in time to save him from that wretched mistake he made in matrimony; or John Milton when his blindness had come on; or any of the other great men whose odd habits it would have been glorious piety to endure; but an amiable handsome baronet, who said "Exactly" to her remarks even when she expressed uncertainty, – how could he affect her as a lover? The really delightful marriage must be that where your husband was a sort of father, and could teach you even Hebrew, if you wished it.[11]

Having essentially told us that we are going to like Dorothea (who is "open, ardent," and so on), the omniscient narrator now announces that Dorothea has "very childlike ideas about marriage," and through the access to Dorothea's reasoning supplied by free indirect discourse, we get to see just how wrongheaded these notions are; the implicitly older, wiser reader knows that an "amiable handsome baronet" is a very desirable thing, that marriage to a notorious misogynist like Milton would be absolutely wretched, and that looking for a husband who is "a sort of father" is (as for Dorothea it will prove to be) a very bad idea. Indeed, the chapter in which Dorothea falls for the scholar Casaubon – she thinks him a genius; everyone else knows that he is a dried up old stick – is prefaced with an **epigraph** from *Don Quixote*, citing the episode in which Don Quixote mistakes a barber on a donkey for a nobly mounted cavalier.

Middlemarch is especially useful for thinking about narrative perspective because it is so preoccupied by the subjectivity of perception, with how much depends on where you are looking from. Eliot likens the individual's perspective to a candle held against a scratched mirror; the scratches are randomly distributed, but the light of the candle makes them resemble concentric circles radiating around the candle: the candle is human consciousness, which rearranges random events into a pattern, with the self right in the middle. But the difficult thing is recognizing that everyone else has "an equivalent center of self, whence the lights and shadows must always fall with a certain difference," and the extensive use of free indirect discourse mimics the possibilities of empathy that the novel advocates.[12] If only in fiction, we can transcend our natural egotism in seeing the world from other people's perspectives. In another very famous moment in the novel, Eliot's narrator draws attention to the relationship between narrative perspective and the manipulation of readerly sympathy: "But why always Dorothea?" the narrator interrupts herself just as she is about to describe the unhappiness of Dorothea's life with Casaubon: "Was her point of view the only possible one with regard to this marriage?"[13] We then learn how that failed marriage looks to Casaubon.

As an aside, it's worth remembering that the use of multiple points of view is by no means unique to the realist novel, with its blend of omniscient narration and free indirect discourse. At its most complex, the epistolary novel had also deployed different perspectives brilliantly. Think of Clarissa Harlowe recounting to Anna Howe events that we will learn of in a completely different way when her seducer Lovelace writes to his friend John Belford, and you'll see how much of *Clarissa's* sustained hold over the reader (and this is a very, very long novel!) comes from Richardson's multiperspectival technique. You can see what a difference this makes if you compare *Clarissa* with an epistolary novel like Goethe's *The Sorrows of Young Werther* (1774), a novel of unrequited adolescent love leading to suicide, told from the single point of view of the rejected lover's letters; that its publication provoked a rash of copycat suicides attests to the novel's emotional force, certainly, but there's a sort of narcissism built into the form that doesn't make for the moral complexity of a novel like *Clarissa*.

While the epistolary novel is an unmistakably eighteenth-century form, free indirect discourse has had a much longer life, one of the nineteenth-century forms that the **modernist** writers of the 1910s and 1920s embraced and extended. James Joyce's *A Portrait of the Artist as a Young Man* (1916) deploys third-person narration, but always filtered through the consciousness of the autobiographical central character Stephen Dedalus. Because *A Portrait of the Artist* is a **Künstlerroman**, a novel about an artist's growth from infancy to adulthood, the language "grows up" with Stephen. We begin with a fragment of story about a moocow – "His father told him that story; his father looked at him through a glass; he had a hairy face"[14] – and end with the forbidding jargon of the advanced aesthetics to which the self-important young artist is in thrall. Joyce's exact contemporary Virginia Woolf also shows how even a fairly traditional narrative device like free indirect discourse can look unfamiliar in the hands of modernist writers. The main reason why her novels can be so hard to follow when you encounter them for the first time is that the summary remarks and narrative signposts of the omniscient narrator have been so substantially eroded. Look at the beginning of *Mrs. Dalloway* (1925), for instance, when the heroine walks out of her London home:

> What a lark! What a plunge! For so it had always seemed to her, when, with a little squeak of the hinges, which she could hear now, she had burst open the French windows and plunged at Bourton into the open air. How fresh, how calm, stiller than this of course, the air was in the early morning; like the flap of a wave; the kiss of a wave; chill and sharp and yet (for a girl of eighteen as she then was) solemn, feeling as she did, standing there at the open window, that something awful was about to happen; looking at the flowers, at the trees with the smoke winding off them and the rooks rising, falling; standing and looking until Peter Walsh said, "Musing among the vegetables?" – was that it? – "I prefer men to cauliflowers" – was that it? He must have said it at breakfast one morning when she had gone out on to the terrace – Peter Walsh. He would be back from India one of these days, June or July, she forgot which, for his letters were awfully dull.[15]

This passage of free indirect discourse following Clarissa Dalloway's point of view makes it seem almost as though the guiding narrator has disappeared altogether; only belatedly do we realize that the passage has remained in the third person throughout ("so it had always seemed to *her*," "*she* forgot which," and so on). It makes for a demanding read because it imitates what Woolf felt the interior life was really like: associative rather than sequential, past and present commingling. Focalization can shift, of course, and although most of the novel is focalized through Mrs. Dalloway or her double, the shell-shocked war veteran Septimus Smith, we see the world from the viewpoint, too, of the minor characters they encounter in the course of their day. So there *is* an omniscient narrative consciousness here who moves among all the novel's characters, but only rarely does the narrator speak at a remove from the characters as Austen and Eliot's often do; the narrative voice tends to be immersed in the consciousness of whichever character is in the foreground at that moment.

One absolutely essential qualification, though, is that occasionally Woolf's narrator speaks "for" a character. Notice what happens to point of view in *To the Lighthouse* (1927) when the young James Ramsay is angry with his father for constantly demanding his mother's attention:

> Standing between her knees, very stiff, James felt all her strength flaring up to be drunk and quenched by the beak of brass, the arid scimitar of the male, which smote mercilessly, again and again, demanding sympathy.[16]

The prefatory "James felt" prepares us for James's thoughts, but there is no way that this very young boy could articulate his murderous Oedipal jealousy in the language Woolf supplies. Here, the narrator has stepped in with an obscure but powerful set of phallic metaphors – a "beak of brass," the "arid scimitar of the male" – to convey the passionate intensity of James's rage against his father. Both the content and the method here recall Woolf's contemporary, D. H. Lawrence, who at similar moments of emotional and erotic intensity focalizes a scene through a character but uses a linguistic register wholly unavailable to the character himself. Here in his **short story** "The Thorn in the Flesh" (1914), for instance, a young soldier has fled to his lover after disgracing himself during military exercises:

> He buried his face into her apron, into the terrible softness of her belly. And he was a flame of passion intense about her. He had forgotten. Shame and memory were gone in a whole, furious flame of passion.
>
> She was quite helpless. Her hands leapt, fluttered, and closed over his head, pressing it deeper into her belly, vibrating as she did so. And his arms tightened on her, his hands spread over her loins, warm as flame on her loveliness. It was intense anguish of bliss for her, and she lost consciousness.[17]

Roughly divided, the first paragraph comes from *his* point of view (the soldier feels the "terrible softness of her belly") and the second from *hers* (the young woman feels his warm hands "spread over her loins"). But neither character, speechlessly inarticulate all the way through the story, could describe his or her experiences as Lawrence has. With its focus on states of obliterated consciousness – "He had forgotten," "she lost consciousness" – the passage underscores the modernist interest in the subconscious life, and that interest helps to explain why a narrative voice distinct from the character must articulate feelings that the character cannot voice. Like young James Ramsay, Lawrence's characters do not know – and could never put into words – what they are experiencing.

Interior monologue and stream of consciousness

In contrast to this kind of authorial rephrasing of thought is the **interior monologue** that modernist writers made famous in their effort to convey the "stream" of human consciousness. The phrase "**stream of consciousness**" comes from the philosopher and psychologist William James (brother of the novelist Henry James), who was trying to explain why consciousness must be thought of not as a chain of ideas as some earlier philosophers believed, but as something whose components are seamlessly merged: "A 'river' or a 'stream' are the metaphors by which it is most naturally described. In talking of it here-after, let us call it the stream of thought, of consciousness."[18] The phrase entered literary criticism through a review of the modernist Dorothy Richardson, who used this form for her long **novel sequence** *Pilgrimage* (1915–67).

But perhaps the best-known example of interior monologue in all of modernist fiction comes in the closing pages of Joyce's *Ulysses*. This is how the novel's final episode begins:

> Yes, because he never did a thing like that before as ask to get his
> breakfast in bed with a couple of eggs since the *City Arms* hotel when
> he used to be pretending to be laid up with a sick voice doing his
> highness to make himself interesting to that old faggot Mrs Riordan that
> he thought he had a great leg of and she never left us a farthing all for
> masses for herself and her soul greatest miser ever was actually afraid to
> lay out 4d for her methylated spirit telling me all her ailments she had
> too much old chat in her about politics and earthquakes and the end
> of the world let us have a bit of fun first God help the world if all the
> women were her sort…[19]

And so on, for the final, unpunctuated (because we don't think in sentences) fifty pages of the novel, as Molly Bloom, wife of the novel's hero, lies in bed. Here, first-person narration mimics the not random but certainly rambling movements of the mind: Bloom has asked for breakfast in bed, which reminds Molly of the last time he did that, and of the circumstances in which he did it, and of the disappointment with which that episode ended, and so on, and so on, and on. Joyce seems almost to be speaking Molly Bloom rather than speaking for her.

The distinction between "speaking" and "speaking for" characters need not coincide with the distinction between **first-person narration** and third-person narration. One of the many striking narrative features of the modernist William Faulkner's *As I Lay Dying* (1930) is that even in interior monologue characters may speak in a language beyond their reach. *As I Lay Dying* is the story of the death and burial of Mrs. Addie Bundren, and is told in chapters narrated from the various perspectives of her husband, children, and neighbors – and, at one point, the dead Addie herself. Darl Bundren, especially, is given to flights of lyric intensity, as when he describes his brother Jewel with his horse: "rigid, motionless, terrific, the horse back-thrust on stiffened, quivering legs, with lowered head; Jewel with dug heels, shutting off the horse's wind with one hand, with the other patting the horse's neck in short strokes myriad and caressing, cursing the horse with obscene ferocity."[20] The stylized syntax ("short strokes myriad and caressing") and diction ("obscene ferocity") tell you that passages like these are not meant as imitations of how poor Southern white boys speak. If having the dead Addie Bundren narrate one chapter were not enough to make the point, Faulkner continually reminds us that it would be a mistake to think about point of view only in terms of verisimilitude.

Of course, it is certainly the case that writers of Faulkner's generation often tempt us to think of their interest in perspective only in terms of lifelikeness – Woolf, for example, defended her method as an effort to show what the interior life is really like – and as a way of giving the reader a deeper intimacy with the character whose perspective is being represented. However, lifelikeness wasn't the only thing Woolf herself was interested in when she experimented with narrative form. Throughout her most demanding novel *The Waves* (1931), characters verbalize the body's submarine erotic life in ways that one can never imagine doing. "Now I smell geraniums; I smell earth mould," announces one character, recounting her experiences of the morning; "I dance. I ripple. I am thrown over you like a net of light. I lie quivering flung over you."[21] (Try saying that to someone in real life.) While Woolf's most famous statements on fiction stress the failures of so-called realism to be *real* enough, it would be a mistake to emphasize easy ideas of lifelikeness at the expense of modernism's other interests in the literally unspeakable poetry of the subconscious life, which necessarily presents a challenge to our rationalizing, real-world expectations.

First-person narration and the problem of reliability

From interior monologue, then, to novels narrated in their entirety by a single character. Obviously we call this first-person narration for its use of the grammatical first person singular ("I") or, much less commonly, plural ("we"). (The grammatical third person is "he," "she," "it," or "they.") **Narratology** uses the adjective "**homodiegetic**" for a narrator who is also a character within the story, as opposed to "**heterodiegetic**" for a narrator that is not personalized, not a part of the story. I mentioned in relation to Austen that omniscient narration – which is always heterodiegetic – invites us to put our trust in the un-attributed voice that recounts the story, but first-person narration works differently because the speaker is explicitly identified as part of the story. Can we place our trust in the speaker? Is he or she a reliable interpreter of the events being described?

The idea of the **unreliable narrator**, first formulated in Wayne Booth's enduringly useful *The Rhetoric of Fiction* (1961), is especially useful for thinking about the many modern novels you may end up misunderstanding altogether if you don't recognize the narrator's intent to deceive: famous examples include

Agatha Christie's *The Murder of Roger Ackroyd* (1926), the narrator of which turns out to be the murderer himself; Vladimir Nabokov's *Lolita* (1955), the sumptuous but self-justifying fake memoir of the pedophile Humbert Humbert; and Albert Camus's *The Fall* (1956), about the aftermath of Nazi collaboration in Europe. Structured as a confession, Camus's novel, with its continual address to the reader, solicits our identification with the creepy speaker, as if to act out on the level of style the novel's thematic interest in what makes people collaborate with evil: "I have no more friends," the reader is ominously told: "I have nothing but accomplices."[22] Perhaps more usual than deliberate deception is the crucially limited status of modern fiction's many first-person narrators: the narrator of Ford Madox Ford's *The Good Soldier* (1915) is too repressed to understand the catastrophically destructive sexual obsessions with which his story is concerned; the opening of Faulkner's *The Sound and the Fury* (1929) is narrated by the mentally handicapped Benjy; while, at the other end of the twentieth century, the narrators of Kazuo Ishiguro's *An Artist of the Floating World* (1986) and *The Remains of the Day* (1989) are so deeply implicated in the destructive values of an imploded imperial past that they do not understand (although the reader must) how the world has changed around them.

It's important to remember, though, that there are modern first-person narratives that aren't intended to be unreliable: in his avowedly non-judgmental way the sensible Midwesterner Nick Carraway acts as a moral compass for the reader of *The Great Gatsby* (1925), quietly damning the American cult of wealth and celebrity even as he demonstrates its capacity to seduce; Nick Jenkins in Anthony Powell's twelve-volume novel sequence, *A Dance to the Music of Time* (1951–75), is almost certainly to be taken as largely an authorial surrogate, an astute observer of the period described in the novel, and (as his name suggests) the same is true of "Christopher Isherwood" in Christopher Isherwood's fragmentary novel about the rise of Nazism, *Goodbye to Berlin* (1939): "I am a camera with its shutter open," he famously begins, "quite passive, recording, not thinking."[23]

More important still is that the very long history of first-person narration creates real difficulties for the distinction between reliability and unreliability. Take the very early example of Aphra Behn's *Oroonoko* (1688), told from the point of view of the young Behn, daughter of the governor of an English colony in Surinam, where she has befriended Oroonoko, an African prince who has been tricked into slavery and is eventually killed when he rebels against his captors. "I do not pretend, in giving you the History of this *Royal Slave*, to entertain my Reader with the Adventures of a feign'd *Hero*," Behn begins: "I was my self an Eye-Witness to a great part of what you will find here set down."[24]

This is all true then – except it is not true at all because Behn's biographers know that she was not the daughter of a colonial governor. Of course, modern readers will simply distinguish between the real-world Behn and her first-person narrator and not mind the "deception." All the same, what about the reliability of the narrator herself? Why is she never around when her friend is being tortured? Why can't the governor's boastful daughter save Oroonoko? Whose side is she on? Even if we don't *really* believe that Behn intended her speaker to seem a false friend to the royal slave she professes to admire so warmly, homodiegetic narration raises questions that heterodiegetic narration would not.

Or notice how Defoe raises our suspicion in this very famous episode in *Robinson Crusoe*. Crusoe has waded out to the wreck of his ship to see what he can salvage to help him survive alone on his island. In one drawer he finds such useful commodities as razors, knives, and scissors, but in another he finds only cash, useless on his desert island:

> I smil'd to myself at the sight of this money, O drug! I said aloud, what art thou good for? Thou art not worth to me, no not the taking off of the ground, one of those knives is worth all this heap, I have no manner of use for thee, e'en remain where thou art, and go to the bottom as a creature whose life is not worth saving. However, upon second thoughts, I took it away, and wrapping all this in a piece of canvass, I began to think of making another raft … [25]

The bathetic disparity between Crusoe's lofty dismissal of the cash ("O drug … what art thou good for?") and his pragmatic "second thoughts" is amusing because it seems to cut Crusoe down to size so sharply, to make him a figure of fun. Defoe's novels, fictional autobiographies, are full of moments like this one when an enormous ironic gap suddenly opens up between how the narrator and the reader interpret what is happening. Historically minded critics have argued that Defoe didn't think he was being funny, that what resembles a comic undercutting of his narrators is a factor of Defoe's haste rather than his craft (in an era that despised the novel, Defoe wrote them for money not glory), and that even if we see a moral contradiction between acquisitiveness and piety the contradiction was built into Defoe's own culture and invisible to the author himself. On this reading, modern readers see irony here only because they are so accustomed to artful unreliability.

Aside from and at a very sharp angle to such challenges from historicist approaches, the other potential pitfall of the reliable/unreliable distinction is that it does not quite take into account the element of distance that *critical* reading often requires. Think of the first-person narrators of, say, *Jane Eyre* and *David Copperfield*. You'd have to think it pretty unlikely that Brontë and Dickens wanted us to read "through" their semi-autobiographical narrators, to collude with the implied author over Jane's and David's heads in the way that we must when we read unreliably narrated texts. Nonetheless, we find ourselves pausing over some of the values that Jane and David, and perhaps Brontë and Dickens, surely took for granted. Perhaps we notice that Jane quite viciously racializes the monstrosity of the West Indian Bertha Mason, the first Mrs. Rochester; that David has blundered from one reactionary idealization of womanhood into another when he replaces the infantile Dora with the martyred Agnes. Although we should always avoid congratulating ourselves on our superior political wisdom as modern readers of older texts (we can count on looking preposterous if not downright wicked to our descendants too), the distinction between unreliable and reliable first-person narrators doesn't take into account how we read novels with a critical eye on the historically specific **ideology** to which they give voice.

A number of other nineteenth-century novels keep the question of reliability and unreliability wholly unresolved, leaving us altogether uncertain of how to read the narrator, how to interpret the interpreter of the story relayed. The final chapter of Nathaniel Hawthorne's *The Blithedale Romance* (1852), the story of a socialist utopia blown apart by the devastating individual passions of its four founding members, includes an admission from the narrator Miles Coverdale: "I have made but a poor and dim figure in my own narrative, establishing no separate interest, and suffering my colorless life to take its hue from other lives."[26] But in the very last sentence we get a confession: Miles Coverdale was futilely in love with one of the three main characters all along – a belated revelation that asks us to review everything the "colorless" Miles has told us in the course of his narration, and yet leaves us wondering if Miles really *has* enough "color" for the real story to have been any different from what he actually told us.

Or, to take a still more complex example, think of the uncertainties raised by Emily Brontë in *Wuthering Heights*. Having rented a house in the Yorkshire moors, Mr. Lockwood catches a chill on his way back from the home of his new landlord, Heathcliff. His housekeeper Nelly Dean entertains him on his sickbed with the story of two houses, Thrushcross Grange, where Lockwood lies in bed, and Heathcliff's house, Wuthering Heights. It is Lockwood, then, who recounts the story to us, which makes him our narrator and Nelly Dean's narratee. Lockwood and Nelly Dean might *both* be unreliable narrators, but *differently* unreliable. Perhaps Lockwood is doing his honest best according to his own dim lights: "A capital fellow!" he calls the thug Heathcliff: "Mr Heathcliff and I are such a suitable pair to divide the desolation between us."[27]

His misunderstandings are one way for Brontë to underscore the very difficulty of any outsider understanding this terrifyingly introverted world. Nelly
Dean, though, has known it from the inside all along: brought up in Wuthering
Heights with Catherine and Heathcliff, she becomes Catherine's housekeeper
at Thrushcross Grange, and nurses her on her deathbed. Or maybe she doesn't.
In fact, Nelly is so deeply implicated in the story she tells that there is some
hint that she is even implicated in Catherine's premature death (Edgar Linton
thinks so). But we never know. So the hapless Lockwood tells the perhaps self-
justifying story of Nelly Dean telling the story of Wuthering Heights. Brontë is
using a doubled **frame narrative**, and critics sometimes refer to this structure
as "Chinese boxes," but "Russian dolls" would do just as well – the idea is that
there's a story within a story (and sometimes a story within a story within a
story), and it typically works to leave us even less certain about what has really
happened, because, with no omniscient narrator, everything we learn comes
mediated by speakers who have their own investments, their own limitations.

Stories within stories and other composite fictions

Right from the start, novels have incorporated other stories, often described
as embedded, interpolated, inset, or subordinate narratives (because they
are "embedded," "interpolated," or "inset" into the main narrative, and "subordinate" to it). This is true however early you start from: the main story of
Apuleius's comic *The Golden Ass*, a second-century Latin "novel," describes the
misfortunes of nosy Lucius, accidentally transformed into a donkey, passing
through the hands of robbers, pimps, and slave-drivers before he manages to
get himself turned back into human shape; but throughout the book are separate self-contained stories, some of them ribald cuckolding folktales and others
more loftily literary (most famously the myth of Cupid and Psyche).

Or, if you make Cervantes rather than Apuleius your representative early
novelist, throughout the first book of *Don Quixote* the hero keeps encounter-
ing beautiful young maidens and forlorn youths who appear to have wandered
into the novel from **romance**; these characters tell Don Quixote their self-
contained stories, leaving the main narrative of Cervantes's novel temporarily
suspended. Or, going forward to the early *English* novel, **embedded narratives**
show up in the work of the self-consciously Cervantic Henry Fielding, as when
Tom Jones meets a misanthropic hermit, the Man of the Hill, and pauses in
his journey to listen to his story over the course of some chapters. Perhaps
needless to say, the use of the embedded text subsequently informs *Tristram
Shandy*, as in, for example, the incorporation of Parson Yorick's sermon, as

well as Sterne's other widely read novel, *A Sentimental Journey* (1768), a fictional journey through France and Italy told from Yorick's perspective. You can still see traces of this early novel tradition – the fragmentary journey narrative, episodic and anecdotal – in the compellingly strange fiction of the late twentieth-century German novelist W. G. Sebald, whose novels are like series of curious encounters with unpredictably connected people and things, held together by the narrator's wanderings across England and the continent.

But there's a distinction to be made between the episodic and/or journey novel incorporating distinct stories – as in these examples of Apuleius, Cervantes, Fielding, Sterne, and Sebald – and a novel structured as a multiperspectival cluster or compilation. As the example of *Wuthering Heights* suggests, nested, multiple, and mediated perspectives have a radically destabilizing effect, prompting the reader to ask the essentially epistemological question of *how do we know what we know?* Is this true? How do we know it's true? And what if we cannot decide? Although the form was surely indebted to the epistolary novel, Wilkie Collins thought he had pioneered the device of structuring a novel as a "compilation" of separate documents in his **sensation novel** *The Woman in White* (1859–60), a gripping story of poisoning, adultery, illegitimacy, madness, and false imprisonment, narrated as separate legal testimonies from all the novel's characters. As if to draw attention to the problems of authenticity, trustworthiness, and truth raised by the departure from reliably omniscient narration, the plot turns on the destruction of written evidence.

And then there is the "found manuscript," a common device in gothic novels going at least as far back as Walpole's *The Castle of Otranto* (1764), which was first published purporting to be a translation from the Italian of a medieval text discovered in the home of an ancient Catholic family. The upcoming interchapter discusses a novel that purports to be a found manuscript, James Hogg's dark *The Private Memoirs and Confessions of a Justified Sinner* (1824), but other famous examples of nineteenth-century gothic novels structured as texts-within-texts include Mary Shelley's *Frankenstein* (1818), Charles Maturin's *Melmoth the Wanderer* (1820), Bram Stoker's *Dracula* (1897), and Robert Louis Stevenson's *The Strange Case of Dr. Jekyll and Mr. Hyde* (1886). Shelley's iconic story of how the ambitious young scientist Frankenstein makes a monster that destroys his life is relayed in letters to his sister from a polar explorer, Captain Walton, who has met the dying Frankenstein as he pursues his monster across the globe, and embedded within the tale that Frankenstein tells Walton is the tale that his monster has told Frankenstein. Maturin's *Melmoth the Wanderer*, the story of a seventeenth-century Irishman who has sold his soul to the devil and can be released from his wanderings only when he finds someone willing to take his place, deploys embedded narratives to an almost vertiginous extent. After Melmoth's descendant first encounters his terrifying ancestor in a manuscript found in the decayed mansion of his dying grandfather, he meets a shipwrecked Spanish sailor who describes his encounters with the wanderer. The sailor then recounts the text of a manuscript about Melmoth that he once translated, and within that manuscript further stories are told, and within *these* stories are stories that the wanderer tells other characters.

Novels structured as composite texts rather than nested stories include Stoker's *Dracula* and Stevenson's *Jekyll and Hyde*. *Dracula* is composed entirely of separate pieces of writing: the journal of Jonathan Harker, the young lawyer lured by business to Dracula's castle; the letters and memoranda of his fiancée Mina Murray and her friend Lucy Westenra; diaries, letters, telegrams, and notes from the other vampire-hunters Arthur Seward and Dr. Van Helsing; newspaper articles and phonograph recordings pasted or transcribed by the characters. One of the things that makes the first part of *Dracula* so enjoyable is the multiple points of view afforded by the splintered narration: we're at Dracula's castle with Jonathan and in Whitby with Mina and Lucy, and know much more than any individual character does. Underlining the work the reader intuitively does in putting the parts together, around halfway through the novel Mina tries to reshape all the different texts chronologically into "a whole connected narrative."[28] *Jekyll and Hyde* is also fascinatingly self-conscious: partly told from an impersonal omniscient perspective – this is a "strange *case*," remember, the title mimicking juridical and medical authority – it turns into a series of more partial, less authoritative documents by the end: letters, confessions, and eyewitness accounts. Initially we might be tempted to suppose that these documents make a strong claim to truth because they're written from the perspective of those who saw at first-hand what happened, and yet, paradoxically enough, they convey none of the impersonal authority of the third-person narration that frames them.

Framed and composite narratives are an open invitation to the reader's interpretative talents: we have to judge the reliability of and relations among different scraps of evidence, and there are gaps that we have to bridge in order to reach a conclusion. Is *Jekyll and Hyde*, for instance, the "strange case" its title promises or a plain case of social and sexual repression? In another celebrated late nineteenth-century exploitation of the indeterminacy generated by the story-within-a-story-within-a-story, Henry James's **novella** *The Turn of the Screw* (1898) has an unnamed narrator recount a friend's retelling of the testimony of a young governess in a remote English country house who comes to believe that the two children in her care are in communication with dead servants. A chilling ghost story? Or is the governess insane? When little

Miles's heart stops at the end of the story, are the ghosts or is the governess responsible? The story is radically ambiguous, its truth ultimately indecipherable. The character who reads the governess's story within the story appears to be helping us out when he speaks in warm praise of the governess, whom he knew personally. But can we trust *him*?

James Hogg, *The Private Memoirs and Confessions of a Justified Sinner* (1824)

The events of this gothic classic are narrated from two perspectives. In the first part of the novel, an editor contextualizes the document we read in the second part by recounting from "history, justiciary records, and tradition" the century-old story of how the Laird of Dalcastle's line ended with the murder of his oldest son George Colwan by George's brother or half-brother Robert Wringhim, who disappears before he can be brought to justice.[1] The story's "editor" then reprints a found manuscript in which we read the "private memoirs and confessions" of the likely murderer, the "justified sinner" of the novel's title. Robert Wringhim is named after the Calvinist minister who has assured him that he is "a justified person, adopted among the number of God's children ... and that no bypast transgression, nor any future act ... could be instrumental in altering the decree" (115), and his narrative recounts how, on the day on which he has become convinced of his salvation, he meets a mysterious stranger called Gil-Martin. Impressing upon him the truth of this Antinomian doctrine of a predestined "elect" status that Wringhim has learned from his minister (and possible biological father), and thus liberating him from the possibility of jeopardizing his salvation through wrongdoing, Gil-Martin encourages Wringhim to consider himself exempted from such moral prohibitions as would prevent his murdering of his worldly (half-?) brother George Colwan. At an early stage in the confession, the reader realizes – though Wringhim perhaps never will – that Gil-Martin is the devil.

"I have been conversant this day with one stranger only, whom I took rather for an angel of light," Robert tells his parents after the momentous meeting with Gil-Martin (121). His mother's reply that "It is one of the devil's most profound wiles to appear like one" is quickly hushed, but the reader sees what Wringhim cannot: that appearances are no reliable guide to anything in *Justified Sinner*, not when it is at the very moment when he becomes convinced of his salvation that Wringhim ensures his damnation. No surprise, then, that Wringhim's account is wildly unreliable. Even if we don't hear the alarm sounded by Wringhim's admission that he was "particularly prone to lying" in his younger days (108), we never doubt that Hogg wants us to see the limits of Wringhim's vision, as when, comically, he takes Gil-Martin's talk of loyal subjects to mean that Gil-Martin is foreign royalty traveling incognito: "I asked, with great simplicity, 'Are all your subjects Christians, prince?' 'All my European subjects are, or deem themselves so,' returned he; 'and they are the most faithful and true subjects I have.' Who could doubt, after this, that he was the Czar of Russia?" (136). And we recognize the devil to be telling the ironic truth – not even his prevarications are exactly lies. Asked why he refuses to disclose his origins, Satan/Gil-Martin responds that "I have no parents save one, whom I do not acknowledge" (129). Everything he says is *true*, according to the religious world of this novel, but also completely ambiguous.

Ambiguity is at the heart of *Justified Sinner*, its double telling reflecting its concern with undecidability: good might be evil, and salvation damnation. Gil-Martin himself is a shape-shifter, able to assume the perfect likeness of anyone he chooses: at different points he resembles Wringhim ("You think I am your brother," he tells Wringhim on their first meeting, "or that I am your second self" [117]); and the good minister Blanchard whom Wringhim will murder; and the innocent man framed for Blanchard's murder; and Drummond, whom he will frame for the murder of George Colwan; until, finally, he takes the shape of the dead heir himself. The prostitute Bell Calvert has witnessed the fratricide and knows that Drummond did not kill Colwan; however, she has been watching from a window with someone who believes that the murderer *is* Drummond, and that witness "never mistook one man for another in his life" (79). The reason she has never come forward with testimony that would implicate Wringhim and exonerate Drummond is that her companion's "evidence would have overborne mine" (79): two irreconcilable eyewitness accounts, and no way to decide between them.

Aptly enough, a matter of identification is what brings Bell Calvert into the editor's narrative in the first place. After a burglary, the old laird's mistress, Mrs. Logan, is called as a witness against the woman, Bell Calvert, who is in possession of her stolen goods, valuable silver marked "C" for Colwan (or Calvert?). Mrs. Logan refuses to testify because she wants to save Bell Calvert's life; her maid Bessy Gillies refuses to identify the stolen goods because, as behooves any character in this novel, she won't take likeness for identity:

> "Did you ever see this gown before, think you?"
> "I hae seen ane very like it."
> "Could you not swear that gown was your mistress's once?"
> "No, unless I saw her hae't on, an' kend that she had paid for't. I am very scrupulous about an oath. *Like* is an ill mark. Sae ill indeed, that I wad hardly swear to ony thing." (67)

"Like" is indeed "an ill mark" in *Justified Sinner*. In the novel's other judicial inquiry, the editor tells us that not even the people present on the night of

Colwan's murder can agree on what they saw in the preceding hours: some do and some do not remember a quarrel with Drummond; some remember a quarrel but not what it was about; none could swear Drummond came to the door, though all had the impression that he did.

"We have nothing on earth but our senses to depend upon," says Bell Calvert: "if these deceive us, what are we to do?" (80). A fair point, except that immediately after saying so she and Mrs. Logan see the deceased George Colwan, whose very corpse Mrs. Logan dressed for the grave. Empirical knowledge, the evidence of the senses, is all they have, and yet it is not enough to account for what they are seeing – or, compounding the complexity, what *Mrs. Logan* is seeing, since Bell Calvert has not recognized George Colwan, either despite that or because she witnessed his murder. So Mrs. Logan prompts Bell Calvert into seeing the dead George and then, absurdly, their vision communicates itself to the landlady of the inn: "Oh, it is he! it is he!" the landlady screams along with them, even though she has no idea who they are screaming about (83). In pursuit of a real-world explanation, Mrs. Logan proposes that the reappearance of the dead man is "a phantasy of our disturbed imaginations" (84). The problem, though, is that once you allow for mental disorder ("phantasy … disturbed imaginations"), the evidence of the senses is nowhere near as stable as Bell wants to believe.

And this psychological turn on Mrs. Logan's part when she dismisses her vision as fantasy speaks to the interpretative split so characteristic of these framed narratives. On the one hand, this is a horror story: a series of supernatural events leads up to the moment when a man is finally lured to his damnation by the devil, who offers to "save" him, at the last, with "an ejaculatory prayer … *equivocal*, and susceptible of being rendered in a meaning perfectly dreadful" (238, my emphasis). But Hogg's editor returns at the end of Wringhim's narrative to tell you that it would be ludicrous to give the confession the supernatural reading it seems to solicit: Wringhim's narrative must be "either dreaming or madness" (254). That real-world reading would be supported by Wringhim's own sense of internal division, which is entirely explicable in secular, psychological terms: "I was a being incomprehensible to myself," Wringhim writes: "Either I had a second self, who transacted business in my likeness, or else my body was at times possessed by a spirit over which it had no controul, and of whose actions my own soul was wholly unconscious" (182). Gil-Martin is not the devil, then, but the wicked side of Wringhim himself – *Justified Sinner*, according to that interpretation, anticipates the parable of psychological splitting that Hogg's compatriot Robert Louis Stevenson would later present in *Jekyll and Hyde*.

The problem with this naturalistic or real-world reading is that the editor's perceptions may be no more reliable than those of the justified sinner himself.

At best, the editor resembles Lockwood in *Wuthering Heights*, incapable of understanding the world he describes; at worst, he is not simply ignorant but willfully blind, as the novel's many polarizations imply. These are the political and cultural schisms between low-church dissenters (the Wringhims) and high-church Episcopalians (the Colwans); between Whig and Tory; between middle-class and aristocratic values; between Puritanism and libertinism. When the once-lovely Arabella Calvert describes to Mrs. Logan how she was driven into prostitution when "the vile selfishness of a lordly fiend ruined all my prospects, and all my hopes" (59), we should be reminded, first, of her description of the old laird Colwan ("your old unnatural master" whom she knew "and never for any good" [60]), and, second, of the radical disparity between this selfishly pleasure-seeking villain and the good old boy of the editor's account. It would not be a stretch, though, to be reminded also of an earlier novel deploying a double perspective, Richardson's *Clarissa*, with its "lordly fiend," Lovelace. We know that the sympathies of Hogg's editor are all with the Colwans, and we know that, culturally speaking, the Colwans are akin to Richardson's Lovelace: free-living aristocrats. Writing from the other side of a culture as cloven as the feet of Satan in one of the novel's embedded narratives, our editor is no unbiased interpreter of Wringhim's memoir.

And if there were ever any danger of our taking the editor at face value, Hogg distances himself entirely from him by assuming a cameo role at the end of his novel. Approached by the editor, he refuses outright to help him dig up Wringhim's corpse, the corpse on which the manuscript will be discovered; the editor has approached him for help because of a letter about an ancient suicide that Hogg wrote to the Edinburgh magazine *Blackwood's* on August 1, 1823 (this letter really appeared). So *Justified Sinner* is a text composed not only of texts – Wringhim's printed confession and handwritten journal, and the editor's narratives of first the legend and then the exhumation – but with a real-world **paratext** attached, Hogg's real-life letter to a real-life journal. Is this an authenticating gesture? On the contrary: at the end of the novel, the editor wonders aloud if Hogg's letter is to be trusted. "For my part I never doubted the thing," an acquaintance tells him: "But, God knows! Hogg has imposed as ingenious lies on the public ere now" (246).

Chapter 4

Character and the novel

And there, for the time being, let us leave Vic Wilcox, while we travel back an hour or two in time, a few miles in space, to meet a very different character. A character who, rather awkwardly for me, doesn't herself believe in the concept of character. That is to say (a favourite phrase of her own), Robyn Penrose, Temporary Lecturer in English Literature at the University of Rummidge, holds that "character" is a bourgeois myth, an illusion created to reinforce the ideology of capitalism.

David Lodge, *Nice Work* (1988)[1]

This passage from David Lodge's *Nice Work* raises the two main issues that this chapter explores: our readiness to imbue with both individuality and reality entities that we know do not exist (we "meet" Robyn as we would a living person), and twentieth-century criticism's erosion of our investments in novelistic character, as something to be questioned rather than taken for granted (Robyn "doesn't believe in the concept of character"). Clearly having read her Ian Watt (see Chapter 2), Robyn believes that character represents an "illusion" of a self-motivating individual invented in the eighteenth century to serve the interests of an emergent capitalist society; by this she means that the novel is both a product and a conduit of capitalist ideology because it imagines human beings only as competitive, acquisitive individuals and then makes this view of selfhood seem naturally and self-evidently true. It is less clear that Robyn's author agrees. "Character is arguably the most important single component of the novel," Lodge proposed in *The Art of Fiction*, and, as both a successful novelist and a distinguished scholar of the novel, he brings a double perspective to bear on the matter.[2] That is to say (Robyn's favorite phrase is also mine), even if he shares Robyn's knowledge that our beliefs about selfhood have a cultural and social history, how, he seems to ask, do you write a novel without character, without that belief in the coherent and autonomous self that Robyn dismisses so loftily as just another "bourgeois myth"?

Constructing and construing character

Beginning with the most familiar sense in which character is a constructed thing, once you pay attention to particular narrative strategies you start to see how fictional subjectivities are constituted through language, or, in short, how literary characters are *made*. It could be said that such novelistic techniques as those discussed in Chapter 3 – omniscient narration, free indirect discourse, interior monologue, and so on – explain how we come to "know" characters, but it would be truer to say that they explain how characters come to exist in the first place. The conjuring tricks that novelists perform are often so convincing that we forget the obvious point that the words used to describe a character typically don't refer to some person who exists or has existed in the world that you and I inhabit, but rather bring that character into existence for the first time.

By way of reviewing quickly how particular narrative tactics create character, let's pause on the famous opening of *Pride and Prejudice*, in which the parents of the novel's heroine argue about the desirability of paying a visit to a rich gentleman incomer (remember that "truth universally acknowledged" in the novel's opening line?). The mother of five unmarried daughters, Mrs. Bennet is dying to meet the eligible Mr. Bingley but decorum dictates that her reluctant husband visits first. What do we learn here about the prospective heroine Elizabeth ("Lizzy") Bennet and her parents, and *how* do we learn it?

> "I dare say Mr. Bingley will be very glad to see you; and I will send a few lines by you to assure him of my hearty consent to his marrying which ever he chuses of the girls; though I must throw in a good word for my little Lizzy."
>
> "I desire you will do no such thing. Lizzy is not a bit better than the others; and I am sure she is not half so handsome as Jane, nor half so good humoured as Lydia. But you are always giving *her* the preference."
>
> "They have none of them much to recommend them," replied he; "they are all silly and ignorant like other girls; but Lizzy has something more of quickness than her sisters."
>
> "Mr. Bennet, how can you abuse your own children in such a way? You take delight in vexing me. You have no compassion on my poor nerves."
>
> "You mistake me, my dear. I have a high respect for your nerves. They are my old friends. I have heard you mention them with consideration these twenty years at least."[3]

So here is Elizabeth Bennet characterized in absentia, and characterized relationally: although neither the most beautiful (Jane) nor the most cheerful (Lydia) of the girls she is her witty father's favorite, the cleverest of his offspring, and the least favored daughter of an appalling mother. We're already ready to like her when she comes onstage for the first time in the following chapter. All the while, dialogue characterizes Mr. Bennet as clever, entertaining, irresponsible, and tells us nothing good about Mrs. Bennet, with her hypochondriac claim to bad nerves (a habitual complaint, her husband's riposte tells us), and her inability to understand Mr. Bennet's sense of humor (*of course* he isn't going to write to offer a stranger whichever daughter he chooses!). Soon Austen's omniscient narrator will confirm what we just figured out: "Mr. Bennet was so odd a mixture of quick parts, sarcastic humour, reserve, and caprice, that the experience of three and twenty years had been insufficient to make his wife understand his character. *Her* mind was less difficult to develop. She was a woman of mean understanding, little information, and uncertain temper."[4] So there are numerous strategies of characterization in operation here: Elizabeth Bennet is characterized by other characters, and in relation to how we feel about them; Mr. and Mrs. Bennet come into being through their "own" words, and then Austen's report confirms our impressions. Rather tellingly, "First Impressions" was the novel's working title; this is not only a novel about particular characters, but a novel about how we *infer* character from what is in front of us.

So omniscient narration creates a character through what we take to be an authoritative summary of an imaginable person, while dialogue, like free indirect discourse, interior monologue, first-person narration, and so on, represents subjective thoughts and values and asks the reader to infer a human consciousness "behind" them. Importantly, these techniques for constructing personhood are historically contingent, and we can learn to understand a culture better from how it imagines the fictional human being. For example, the character summary provided by omniscient narration by definition assumes the explicability of the self – even Austen's admittedly complex characters can usually be summarized. In contrast, the emergence of psychoanalysis in the early twentieth century would present a challenge to the idea of the coherent, integrated individual, dissolving any belief in the coherence and transparency of the person at the same time as literary modernism was doing the same to the fictional character. Indeed Virginia Woolf claimed that the reason her generation's fiction presented difficulty for the reader was that it was trying for the first time to investigate "the dark places of psychology," a project requiring and producing new fictional techniques.[5] In her view, the task of seeing human consciousness anew meant rejecting older conventions for portraying character, conventions which made novels easy to read (the thing about conventions is that their familiarity makes us forget that they *are* conventions), but which ultimately falsified the human experience that they aspired to document.

In her famous essay "Mr. Bennett and Mrs. Brown," an argument with the bestselling Edwardian novelist Arnold Bennett, Woolf proposed that the fictional people of **realist** novelists are formulaic products, no longer matching our sense of what constitutes selfhood. Here she invents a character called "Mrs. Brown," a string of speculations about a stranger seen on a train:

> I asked them [the Edwardian realists] – they are my elders and betters – How shall I begin to describe this woman's character? And they said: "Begin by saying that her father kept a shop in Harrogate. Ascertain the rent. Ascertain the wages of shop assistants in the year 1878. Discover what her mother died of. Describe cancer. Describe calico. Describe – " But I cried "Stop! Stop!" And I regret to say that I threw that ugly, that clumsy, that incongruous tool out of the window, for I knew that if I began describing the cancer and the calico, my Mrs. Brown, that vision to which I cling though I know no way of imparting it to you, would have been dulled and tarnished and vanished forever.
>
> That is what I mean by saying that the Edwardian tools are the wrong ones for us to use. They have laid an enormous stress upon the fabric of things. They have given us a house in the hope that we may be able to deduce the human beings who live there. To give them their due, they have made that house much better worth living in. But if you hold that novels are in the first place about people, and only in the second about the houses they live in, that is the wrong way to set about it.[6]

Woolf's charge is that realist novelists can construct a character only by accumulating social, material, and economic detail – imagining a house so that we can infer the person who lives in it – and in doing so they misrepresent human consciousness by devaluing the significance of the interior life, of how the world looks from the inside out.

Of course, Woolf's own fiction is famous for doing the opposite, for constructing a character by replicating what he or she sees, feels, and thinks in the course of her ordinary day. Trying to pinpoint the difference between nineteenth- and twentieth-century methods of characterization, the novelist and critic Robert Liddell proposed that we know Austen's characters as we know our friends but know Woolf's characters as we know ourselves: summarizing a Woolf character is almost as hard as summarizing your *own* character, he thought, because you're standing too close to be able to sum up.[7] "It is no use trying to sum people up," Woolf wrote in her novel *Jacob's Room* (1922);

indeed, she would go further in *Mrs. Dalloway* and say that summing up a person is not only impossible but undesirable: Clarissa is almost certainly speaking for her author when she claims that she would not say of herself or anyone else "I am this, I am that."[8]

Because we live, as Woolf did, after the psychoanalytic revolution, we may also feel that the interior life is the real life, and might even be tempted to agree with her that focusing on inner consciousness rather than outward circumstances gives a "truer" view of character than earlier novels accomplished. Nonetheless, it is not remotely surprising to find that Woolf's novelistic practice was less hard-line than her manifestos: after all, it's virtually impossible to imagine a fully naked subjectivity, a self that is in no way dependent on or determined by its material contexts. It would be hard to read *Mrs. Dalloway* and *not* notice the extent to which wealth and class, for example, matter for how we read this story of a politician's hostess wife and a shell-shocked war veteran who refuses to compromise as she has with the expectations of a repressive society. (Indeed, Woolf wrote in her diary that her intention for *Mrs. Dalloway* was to show the *social* system at work at its most intense.)

But what Woolf was trying to get away from was our habit of reading exclusively on the basis of the "outsides" of other people, as we have to do in real life. "There is no such thing as an isolated man or woman; we're each of us made up of some cluster of appurtenances," the worldly wise Madame Merle tells the young Isabel Archer in Henry James's *The Portrait of a Lady* (1881):

> "What shall we call our 'self'? Where does it begin? Where does it end? It overflows into everything that belongs to us – and then it flows back again. I know a large part of myself is in the clothes I choose to wear. I've a great respect for *things*! One's self – for other people – is one's expression of one's self; and one's house, one's furniture, one's garments, the books one reads, the company one keeps – these things are all expressive."[9]

Mrs. Dalloway's house in Westminster, the brown stocking Mrs. Ramsay knits for the lighthouse keeper's son in *To the Lighthouse*: "these things are all expressive." The treacherousness of James's cultured, graceful, and utterly corrupt Madame Merle lies in her ability to "express" quite a different self from the one which Isabel Archer, horrified, will come to reconstruct, but her comments capture very effectively the condition of the reader interpreting character in real life: what we call a self is the *expression* or rendering outward of a self that, circularly, we presume exists "behind" or "inside" that exterior. Ironically enough, the least realistic thing the novel does in the pursuit of "truth to life" is to make the insides of characters accessible.

Flat/round, major/minor, transparent/opaque

The fictional mind that we collaborate with the author in inventing when we extrapolate a human subjectivity from the signs on the page may be more or less complex. Our evaluations of these degrees of complexity are still shaped by the distinctions proposed by early twentieth-century novelists: Henry James, for example, distinguished between characters of primary significance, of interest for their own sake, and those puppets he called "*ficelles,*" instrumental characters written to advance the plot or illuminate the main character. More famous still are the categories of **"flat" and "round" characters** that E. M. Forster invented in *Aspects of the Novel* (1927), where he defined *flat* characters as those shaped by a single quality, unchanging in the course of the novel, and *round* characters as those that develop, change, or act surprisingly as the narrative proceeds.[10] To go back to my earlier example of *Pride and Prejudice*, Mrs. Bennet is a flat character, while her daughter Elizabeth (who begins as the "flat"-sounding embodiment of "Prejudice" in the novel's title) quickly becomes a "round" character. But what of Mr. Bennet? In fact, what makes Austen such an interesting example is that she has many characters less easy to categorize. Mr. Bennet sounds complicated even from Austen's summary ("a mixture of quick parts, sarcastic humour, reserve, and caprice"). He seems to "flatten" into a charming but irresponsible father as the novel goes on, and "rounds" when forced to confront the consequences of his disengagement (given free rein to follow her own bad judgment, the youngest Bennet daughter nearly ruins them all).

One important reason for using the categories of flat and round cautiously is that not even Forster himself thought them definitive: in fact, he also used Austen to indicate the instability of the distinction (in the example he gives from *Mansfield Park* Lady Bertram goes from flat to round to flat again in the space of a single sentence!). It's often simply a question of narrative emphasis: in the novels of the socially panoramic French realist, Balzac, characters who are "round" in one novel may be "flat" in another, while even in Woolf's novels (and Woolf might be considered an exemplary writer of "round" characters) you can see the same phenomenon at work when you look back at the first appearance of Mrs. Dalloway. Clarissa Dalloway is the complex heroine of the novel that bears her name, but she began her fictional life as a minor character, the brittle, snobbish society hostess in Woolf's debut novel, *The Voyage Out* (1915), where her sole purpose is to form an anti-role-model, a negative exemplar, for the novel's young heroine, Rachel Vinrace. Critics have long since been uncomfortable with the "flat and round" distinction, but, most recently, James Wood has suggested that the customary spatial metaphors of flat/round and deep/

shallow would be better substituted with the metaphor of transparency: some characters can be seen through more easily than others (corresponding to the old "flat" or minor character); some remain relatively opaque (the "round" or major character).[11] It seems to me that this division works much better with some writers than others: more helpful for reading, say, Henry James, whose protagonists, especially the women, can remain extraordinarily mysterious, than George Eliot, whose characteristic narrative and moral interests are in sympathetic demystification, in explaining why people do what they do.

What is potentially productive about the distinction between flat and round (or transparent and opaque) characters is that it helps the reader to focus on questions about the *function* of characters within a novel. If the character is confused and even confusing, chances are that we are dealing with the kind of character ("round," "opaque") that allows an author to explore the complexities of human motivation in a socially and psychologically believable way. Why, to go back to Eliot and James, does George Eliot's ambitious Dr. Lydgate unconsciously destroy his own career in *Middlemarch*? And why, at the end of *The Portrait of a Lady*, does Isabel Archer return to the man who has ruined her life? Conversely, if a character is, as the cliché has it, one-dimensional, it must be there for some other reason. What is the concept or quality for which this character stands, and why is it so significant for the novel as a whole? How does this character advance the plot? How does this character reflect on the novel's protagonist? Because it can generate questions that drive us to think more deeply about the structure, objectives, and worldview of a novel, distinguishing between the purposes that different modes of characterization serve can be helpful so long as the distinctions are used descriptively rather than evaluatively (the very worst way to read a novel is with the assumption that flat is bad and round is good), and with an eye to the points at which they collapse (these are invented categories from 1927 rather than universal facts about fictional character) – or, in short, only as a starting point for analysis rather than as its conclusion.

Character as text

Perhaps the reason why we are so enthralled by metaphors of surface and depth is that, with its origins in writing itself, the word "character" has inbuilt connotations of writing and symbolism, of signs and meanings. Etymologically, a character – from the Greek *kharakter*, an engraved mark – is something to be interpreted, to be taken as standing for something else (we retain this much older sense of the word when we speak of typographic "characters"). In a fascinating study of eighteenth-century fiction, Deidre Lynch reinstates those older connotations of character in order to explain how we actually managed to forget them in the first place: "individuated, psychological meanings did not come naturally to British writers and readers in the long eighteenth century," she argues: "They do not come naturally to us either."[12] Our habit of reading character as complex individuality rose with the novel itself, Lynch argues, and offered a way for readers to accrue "cultural capital," prestige, in priding themselves on their own individuality and their refined ability to recognize the individuality of fictional characters.

Many novels provide overt reminders of these older meanings of "character" as text, and so ask us to keep in mind that a character is an entity actively to be read and interpreted. "The women one meets – what are they but books one has already read? You're a whole library of the unknown, the uncut," Merton Densher tells the beautiful and sinister Kate Croy in James's *The Wings of the Dove* (1902); she, meanwhile, looks at him as if he were a guidebook.[13] In this novel about people pretending to be what they are not – Densher and Kate masquerade as lover and best friend of a dying heiress in the hope of marrying on her money – the conspirators see each other as the reader sees them, as puzzles to be explained, texts to be deciphered. And George Eliot assigns us a similar challenge more playfully in *The Mill on the Floss* (1860) when she has Mr. Tulliver, the heroine's self-destructive father, encounter his soon-to-be enemy, Mr. Wakem:

> You have never seen Mr Wakem before, and are possibly wondering whether he was really as eminent a rascal, and as crafty, bitter an enemy of honest humanity in general, and of Mr Tulliver in particular, as he is represented to be in that eilodon or portrait of him which we have seen to exist in the miller's mind ...
>
> But it is really impossible to decide this question by a glance at his person: the lines and lights of the human countenance are like other symbols – not always easy to read with a key. On an *a priori* view of Wakem's aquiline nose, which offended Mr Tulliver, there was not more rascality than in the shape of his stiff shirt-collar, though this too, along with his nose, might have become fraught with damnatory meaning when once the rascality was ascertained.[14]

The face becomes a text, and by virtue of being thought legible is vulnerable to prejudiced misreading and false retroactive certainties; only when Mr. Wakem acts viciously will his viciousness be "conveyed" in his features. In a self-fulfilling prophecy, one man reads another for indications of a cruel character, only to ensure that the enraged object of his scrutiny will respond by mistreating him.

Perhaps the most celebrated writer of novelistic character, Charles Dickens constantly plays tricks with the textuality of character. What a character *is* might be written all over him, but that doesn't mean we know how to read it. Here is the first description of the bank messenger Jerry Cruncher in his historical novel *A Tale of Two Cities* (1859). Asked to convey the coded message that a man has been "recalled to life," he finds himself completely at a loss:

> His message perplexed his mind to that degree that he was fain, several times, to take off his hat to scratch his head. Except on the crown, which was raggedly bald, he had stiff, black hair, standing jaggedly all over it, and growing down-hill almost to his broad, blunt nose. It was so like smith's work, so much more like the top of a strongly spiked wall than a head of hair, that the best of players at leapfrog might have declined him, as the most dangerous man in the world to go over.[15]

The mysterious message, "recalled to life," will soon be explained: it refers to the secret release of a political prisoner after eighteen years of imprisonment. The other mystery of this passage, why Jerry Cruncher is so discomfited by the message, will be explained when yet another code is cracked: his utterly bizarre physiognomy. What the churchyard appearance of his hair ("a strongly spiked wall") alludes to is, first, his nighttime occupation as a body-snatcher, a so-called resurrection man, and, second, the horrible practice of displaying malefactors' severed heads on spiked prison railings. No wonder the thought of bodies being "recalled to life" worries him so much! Both his crime and his likely punishment are plainly visible, but the reader can't interpret them yet. Of course, everyone familiar with Dickens will recall other occasions in his fiction on which physiognomy is used as a means of characterization, but *A Tale of Two Cities* is especially fascinating because its story hinges on the purely physical resemblance of two men, the conscience-stricken French aristocrat Charles Darnay and the debauched English lawyer who will famously do a far, far better thing than he has ever done by taking his place on the guillotine. The novel derives its comedy from characters that are precisely what they look, and its pathos from characters that prove to be more than they seem.

One final example of the relationship between the two meanings of character as person and as text is the illuminating in-joke that opens *Great Expectations*. Pip has just introduced himself as an orphan:

> As I never saw my father or my mother, and never saw any likeness of either of them (for their days were long before the days of photographs), my first fancies regarding what they were like, were unreasonably derived from their tombstones. The shape of the letters on my father's, gave me an odd idea that he was a square, stout, dark man, with curly black hair. From the character and turn of the inscription, "*Also*

Georgiana Wife of the Above," I drew a childish conclusion that my
mother was freckled and sickly.[16]

The young Pip is conflating the two meanings of "character": from the *characters* on his parents' headstones, he derives the *characters* of his parents. You will notice that there's a third meaning of character ominously missing – character in the sense of, roughly, moral interiority, as when someone is described as having a "bad character" or as being of "good character," or when you write someone a "character reference." Pip's inability to read beyond surfaces in this story of fakes and forgers will be his undoing.

In an important sense, Pip's deduction of characters from text puts him in the position of any novel reader. To be sure, it isn't literally on the typeface that (we hope) we base our judgments, but nonetheless we should be conscious that characters are textual entities, words to be interpreted as well as hypothetical persons to be identified with or reprehended. Reminding us of the essentially *textual* status of character has been important to many twentieth-century critical efforts to sever what they consider readers' sentimental and anti-intellectual attachments to characters. We should be concerned, they propose, with characters' functional and structural status in the novels in which they appear, and not with their (allegedly irrelevant from the literary point of view) emotional or moral interest. Or, as the critic Joel Weinsheimer so memorably put it, "Emma Woodhouse is not a woman nor need be described as if it were."[17] It perhaps goes without saying that characters in a novel need not be literally human: think of the children's classics *Black Beauty* (1877) and *Watership Down* (1972), or of that odd subgenre of eighteenth-century fictions following the fortunes of an object, as in Charles Johnstone's *Chrysal, or The Adventures of a Guinea* (1760–5). Nonetheless, fictional animals and animated objects are clearly being anthropomorphized, given psychological reactions akin to that of a human character. What Weinsheimer was protesting through that shock tactic of calling Austen's adorable heroine an "it" is our tendency to think less critically about character than we do about other rhetorical and formal aspects of the novel.

Character as function and person

Accounts of character that stress its status as a function of narrative often start with the analysis of the folktale undertaken by Soviet critics in the 1920s. In his *Morphology of the Folktale* (1928), Vladimir Propp condensed folktale personae into seven variations, defined solely by their actions: the Villain, the Donor, the Helper, the Princess and her Father (he thought the two functionally indistinguishable), the Dispatcher, the Hero, and the False Hero. The names may change but the functions remain the same. Focusing on analogous structural functions performed by novelistic characters would later become commonplace as critics tried to get away from what they considered naïve readings of fictional characters as real people. As Alex Woloch writes, it is as if "the decoupling of literary characters from their implied humanness becomes the price of entry into a theoretical perspective on characterization" – in other words, you can't speak analytically or abstractly about characterization unless you skim off the most intuitive aspect of character, that sense we have of characters as hypothetical human beings.[18]

This habit of discussing fictional characters as if they were people with an existence outside the text is usually categorized with a derogatory inflection as "humanist." "It is as if succumbing to the illusion that a 'character' in a book is a person implies losing your critical faculties," John Mullan writes of the academic embarrassment about novelistic character: he gives the example of an eminent narrative theorist who proposes with the most sober caution that "the character is not a human being, but resembles one."[19] You have already encountered the humanist account of the novel in my first chapter's discussion of the Leavises, who thought great fiction taught us how to live better, but exemplary humanist accounts of novelistic character, specifically, would include John Bayley's *The Characters of Love* (1960), and W. J. Harvey's *Character and the Novel* (1965). To a structuralist critic, their concerns with human freedom, autonomy, and possibility, would sound, along with the questions I asked earlier about why James's Isabel Archer and Eliot's Dr. Lydgate act the way they do, critically irrelevant, even simple-minded.

So for a time the issue of character polarized modern critics: on one side were the structuralist critics, concerned, as the labeling suggests, with the impersonal structural qualities of the novel; on the other, the humanist critics, who focused on the "**mimetic**" or reality-imitating qualities of fiction. For the one group, characters are just another function of narrative; for the other, characters can be spoken about as plausible imitations of human beings. In their extreme forms, each is probably as unattractive as the other: impressively rigorous though they are, the chilly taxonomies of structuralist and formalist criticism have little to say to readers drawn to the novel by its human content, psychological, cultural, and historical; meanwhile the humanist account of character, more sensitive to the emotional rewards of fiction, ultimately risks leaving out the ways in which fiction is art rather than life, constructed rather than given. If we take seriously W. J. Harvey's humanist claim, on the face of it rather sympathetic, that "most great novels exist to reveal and explore character," we might well find ourselves committed to a kind of criticism that is not very interestingly descriptive (how the novel "reveals and explores" a character) and evaluative ("most *great* novels …"), rather than complexly analytical.[20]

Quite different from both the functionalist and humanist accounts of character is the distinction the mid-twentieth-century critic Northrop Frye advanced between novelistic and romance characters: where the former are plausible social beings, the latter are more like "psychological archetypes … Jung's libido, anima, and shadow reflected in the hero, heroine, and villain respectively"; marked by passionate intensity and a hint of allegory, the characters in romance are more like emotional conditions than social realities.[21] This distinction is helpful in explaining why it feels inappropriate, even absurd to speak of the monomaniacs of, say, Herman Melville and Emily Brontë in the same way as you'd speak about the fully socialized, meticulously psychologized characters of George Eliot and Henry James. Lambert Strether in *The Ambassadors* can be judged by normal social and moral codes; Captain Ahab simply is what he is. However, the Jungian underpinnings of Frye's theory perhaps ensured its critical obsolescence in an era increasingly distancing itself from ideas of universal archetypes and fundamental essences (witness how pejoratively modern critics use the term "essentialist"). In practice, it was the humanist and structuralist accounts of character that proved most influential.

But given the stark choice between character-as-function and character-as-real-person, you might throw your hands up: would you prefer to write with cool impersonality about the helper function "Mr. Micawber" in *David Copperfield* or with sentimental effusion about how inspiring you find his buoyant optimism about how something will always turn up? The good news is that most of us don't have to choose, managing to keep both versions of character in mind at the same time. Thus we can attend to the plot function served by Mr. Micawber at the same time as we take his predicament seriously: he is simultaneously a comic and self-conscious acknowledgment of a novel's artful fictionality (something usually does turn up) *and* a bleaker reflection on the arbitrariness of capitalist fortune (what if nothing turns up?). If you consider how the novel uses the artifice of plot (in which Micawber is a narrative instrument) to compensate for the far bleaker realities of mid-Victorian life (Micawber as a down-at-heel husband and father), you'll see that formalist and humanist insights into the nature of fictional character needn't be thought of as mutually exclusive.

Although the argument between the humanists and the formalists is very much a twentieth-century dispute, novelists themselves have often been conscious that the role of character is both structural and affective, a matter of both form and feeling. When the eighteenth-century novelist Tobias Smollett put character at the very center of his definition of a novel, he was thinking *both* about the architecture of a novel *and* about the attachments readers form to invented people.

> A Novel is a large diffused picture, comprehending the characters of life, disposed in different groupes, and exhibited in various attitudes, for the purposes of a uniform plan, and general occurrence, to which every individual figure is subservient. But this plan cannot be executed with propriety, probability or success, without a principal personage to attract the attention, unite the incidents, unwind the clue of the labyrinth, and at last close the scene by virtue of his own importance.[22]

Notice how Smollett describes novelistic organization as "a uniform plan … to which every individual figure is subservient": the plan is the important thing, and "every individual figure" "subservient" to it. The protagonist is an expedient "to attract the attention, unite the incidents, unwind the clue of the labyrinth, and at last close the scene by virtue of his own importance." Even the main character, then, is primarily a *rhetorical* dimension of the novel, something to hold it together, and yet Smollett knows that he or she is needed in order to make the reader care about everything else ("by virtue of his own importance").

Embedded in Smollett's initially confusing use of the word "character" are instructive traces of the term's older meanings. When he speaks of a novel "comprehending the characters of life," I think he means something like "a novel's list of characters includes all the different types of people you encounter in the real world." While we think of "character" as a question of individuality, the term actually carries the connotations of "type." I've already mentioned this feature in Austen: Elizabeth Bennet as "Prejudice" to Fitzwilliam Darcy's "Pride," Elinor Dashwood as "Sense" to her sister's "Sensibility." Characters often come even more definitively labeled than this, a name being in all senses an identity: think of the good and evil struggle represented by Richardson's beautiful, martyred Clarissa ("most radiant") and the vain rake Lovelace ("loveless"). Or of the aptness of Scott's choice of "Waverley" for the vacillating hero of a novel that begins with a long disquisition on the problem of novelistic naming. Waverley is "an uncontaminated name," Scott disingenuously writes in his preface, "bearing with its sound little of good or evil, excepting what the reader shall hereafter be pleased to affix to it": on the one hand, Scott is distinguishing himself from the trite conventions of romance naming (he has, he says, rejected "chivalrous" and "sentimental" names); on the other, he's pretending that "Waverley" is an innocent name for a character who can't decide which of two warring factions he ought to side with.[23] Scott's minor characters often have wonderfully descriptive names – among *Waverley*'s cast are the cowardly Macwheeble and the spurious heir Inchgrabbit.

That character conveys ideas of "type" ("type" is a writing metaphor, of course, from printing) probably sounds intuitive enough with reference to the kinds of character that Forster designated "flat," but, to go back to my earlier examples of round characters, James's Isabel Archer is a marriageable young woman, an heiress, a betrayed wife, an adulteress, an American in Europe; Eliot's Lydgate an ambitious young doctor, an unhappy husband, a wrongfully suspected man. Part of the preliminary work we do as readers is to "place" characters in the context of what we already know about real and fictional types, if only so that we can see how particular characters ultimately conform to or overturn the expectations we had in mind. Talking in terms of types and expectations implies that we read these fictional characters in relation to *other* fictional characters as much as we read them in relation to real-life people, but examining these types and expectations can also tell us something about our own culturally constructed and inherited beliefs, values with real-world implications: why, for example, should we have made categories of person called "adulteress" (signifying disapprobation of women who breach the conventional boundaries set around sexual desire) and "ambitious young doctor" (signifying approbation of middle-class advancement)?

Lodge's Robyn Penrose, to go back to where we started, is ultimately concerned with those very beliefs and values, what we might call real-world *fictions* by virtue of the fact that they are *made* things, constructions rather than natural, universal, timeless, or transcendent categories. Robyn, you'll remember, "doesn't ... believe in the concept of character." This is why:

> According to Robyn ... there is no such thing as the "self" on which capitalism and the classic novel are founded – that is to say, a finite, unique soul or essence that constitutes a person's identity; there is only a subject position in an infinite web of discourses – the discourses of power, sex, family, science, religion, poetry, etc.[24]

What you or I might call an individual, a character, or a self, Robyn would call "a subject position," a place where the multiple strands of culture intersect. The metaphor is a political one: instead of imagining the self as *sovereign*, master or mistress of his or her own destiny, the self is *subjected* to **ideological** forces – to how, for example, your culture understands gender, family, sex, science, religion, and the rest. And yet even though Robyn's jargon is clearly a **satirical** target for her author, Robyn's view is borne out by her very characterization (or, if you like, subject position) as a middle-class person, as a woman, as a late twentieth-century literary critic. If you look at character in this way, you see that to examine even a single character in a sustained way – whether you are thinking about Isabel Archer, Dr. Lydgate, or even Robyn Penrose herself – is to be forced to move far beyond the character itself, and toward understanding the cultural forces out of which it is made.

Nathaniel Hawthorne, *The Scarlet Letter* (1850)

This rag of scarlet cloth, – for time, and wear, and a sacrilegious moth, had reduced it to little other than a rag, – on careful examination, assumed the shape of a letter. It was the capital letter A.

Nathaniel Hawthorne, *The Scarlet Letter* (1850)[1]

In the frame story of *The Scarlet Letter* Hawthorne discovers a package containing an ancient piece of embroidery that he identifies as the letter "A," along with a brief narrative, written by a predecessor in the Customs House where he works, about the woman who created and wore that "character." By beginning with the *character* A, Hawthorne reminds us that the foundations of literary character, the fictional person, are in the written and the interpretable. *The Scarlet Letter* is a novel about *a* character, the intensely memorable character of Hester Prynne, but it's also a novel about what character means.

The long Customs House prologue introduces the first of many meanings of "character." Conversationally, a "character" is an eccentric, an oddball, known by sight throughout a community, and the prologue takes the form of a "gallery of Custom-House portraits" (21), a description of the odd people with whom Hawthorne works, among them the man who has lost his entire family but thinks of nothing but cheerful gourmandizing. These are indeed "characters" in the colloquial sense. And this first meaning of character matters because the narrator initially imagines Hester Prynne as a character of this type. According to Surveyor Pue, whose manuscript supplies the outline of her story, Hester was a woman notable for her charitable works in her community "doing whatever miscellaneous good she might; taking upon herself, likewise, to give advice in all matters, especially those of the heart, by which means, as a person of such propensities inevitably must, she gained from many people the reverence due to an angel." And here Hawthorne dryly intervenes, "but, I should imagine, was looked upon by others as an intruder and a nuisance" (32). Two things are important here: first, the way in which "character" – being "a character" – conveys an ambivalently *social* role, because it rests on your community knowing you at the same time as it marks your oddity within it (and, with its simultaneously ostracized and indispensable Hester, *The Scarlet Letter* is very much a novel about this duality); and second, the way in which that role might be looked at from multiple angles, because even though Surveyor Pue thinks Hester must have been revered as a ministering angel, Hawthorne supposes that she might as plausibly have been resented as a pestering busybody.

The double perspective – what looks like one thing can be interpreted as its opposite – immediately becomes central to Hester's story. As she stands on the pillory scaffold to be publicly shamed in the opening chapters of the main story, the narrator will turn the character her neighbors see as a "fallen woman" into a painter's image of the Virgin Mary. In this substitution of one archetype for another – whore turned holy virgin – you see the substantially communal element of characterization, the way in which character emerges out of the stock images we bring to it. At this early stage in the novel, the reader knows little of Hester, and Hawthorne emphasizes how we interpret character through what we already know and what we want to see: a beautiful unmarried woman standing above the crowd with her baby in her arms may be the very *emblem* of sin – "a living sermon" (58) and "the figure, the body, the reality of sin" (72) – or "the image of Divine Maternity" (53).

This duality of perspective is closely connected to another meaning of character that the novel examines: character as reputation. When Hester and her illegitimate child, Pearl, return at the end of the novel to the scaffold they occupied in the opening chapters, they will be accompanied by Pearl's tortured father, the Reverend Arthur Dimmesdale. In this climactic scene Dimmesdale denounces himself as the worst of sinners, ripping open his shirt to show the assembled congregation the "A" emblazoned on his own chest: a self-inflicted wound, some onlookers claim, while others think it witchcraft. But there are still other spectators who refuse to see anything at all except that a dying minister has embraced the pariah adulteress in order to draw the holy moral that the godly and the outcast are sinners alike:

> Without disputing a truth so momentous, we must be allowed to consider this version of Mr. Dimmesdale's story as only an instance of that stubborn fidelity with which a man's friends – and especially a clergyman's – will sometimes *uphold his character*; when proofs, clear as the mid-day sunshine on the scarlet letter, establish him as a false and sin-stained creature of the dust. (224, my emphasis).

Dimmesdale's guilt has fully externalized itself in a copy of the "A" that Hester has been forced to wear, and yet his friends "uphold his character," or defend the public version of Dimmesdale even in the face of what proves it manifestly false. Insofar as character means reputation, then, it is an external matter, the specifically public version of a self even in the face of what proves it inauthentic.

And through the inwardly divided Dimmesdale, Hawthorne foregrounds what to us is a more familiar way of thinking about literary personhood:

character as deep psychology. It is because of our habitually metaphorical understanding of selfhood as somehow "interior" or "within" that Hawthorne plays with ideas of surfaces and depths, with what is externally visible and what can legitimately be inferred from it. The Puritans of Boston misread Dimmesdale as a saint, and refuse to read the outward signs of his guilt for what the reader knows they are: when he doubles Hester's shameful badge with a hand over his heart, the community sees bodily weakness where spiritual weakness is indicated; when he denounces himself from the pulpit, the congregation hears not abject confession but holy humility. Perversely enough, their mistake is in reading too "deeply."

Only two of the novel's characters are adept "readers": Hester and her estranged husband Roger Chillingworth. Whether through the supernatural powers of the emblem on her breast or through her own subconscious wish, Hester believes that the scarlet letter gives her "knowledge of the hidden sin in other hearts":

> Sometimes, the red infamy upon her breast would give a sympathetic throb, as she passed near a venerable minister or magistrate, the model of piety and justice, to whom that age of antique reverence looked up, as to a mortal man in fellowship with angels. "What evil thing is at hand?" would Hester say to herself. Lifting her reluctant eyes, there would be nothing human within the scope of view, save the form of this earthly saint! (78)

The former lover of the revered Dimmesdale (himself publicly a "model of piety and justice" and an "earthly saint"), Hester sees her judges as hypocrites, no more innocent than she is. Ominously, the sinister Chillingworth is another skilled reader of hearts, and, though his eyes may be spoiled by a life of scholarly reading, "those same bleared optics had a strange, penetrating power when it was their owner's purpose to read the human soul" (55). Only Chillingworth guesses that Dimmesdale's bodily infirmity speaks of mental troubles, and he pursues his secret "like a treasure-seeker in a dark cavern" (109), "like a miner searching for gold" (113), and, ultimately, "like a sexton delving into a grave" (113). But while Chillingworth seeks Dimmesdale's dark secret, his own guilt is being written across his face, which grows uglier and more misshapen until he himself becomes a physical embodiment – a sign, an emblem, a *character* – of his evil obsession: "striking evidence of a man's faculty of transforming himself into a devil, if he will only, for a reasonable space of time, undertake a devil's office" (148).

But Hawthorne's anti-fundamentalist point is that a *character* can never mean just one thing. That written character "A" was supposed to stand for

Adulteress but by the end of Hester's story it could equally mean "Able" or "Angel." And, in the humanistic sense of character, fictional people won't stay put in the roles assigned them. For the greater part of the novel, Chillingworth is changing from "a man thoughtful for others, craving little for himself, – kind, true, just, and of constant, if not warm affections" (151) into a symbol of demonic antagonism, and yet at the very end he leaves Pearl his fortune, refusing to turn Pearl into a symbol of the marital betrayal from which she was conceived – saving her, and saving himself.

Chapter 5

Plotting the novel

"If you judge by appearances in this place," said Mme de Chartres, "you will often be deceived, because what appears to be the case hardly ever is."

Madame de Lafayette, The Princess of Clèves (1678)[1]

"Hale knew, before he had been in Brighton three hours, that they meant to murder him."

Graham Greene, Brighton Rock (1938)[2]

These lines from two very different novels remind us, first, that a "plot" is a conspiracy as well as the organization of a narrative, and, second, that fictional plots, like their criminal counterparts, depend on secrecy and withholding. Although it takes the form of a declarative statement, the crisp opening of *Brighton Rock* works only to elicit questions; it doesn't so much inform us of what's going on as it reminds us of what we don't know yet: Who is "Hale"? Who are "they"? And why do they want to murder him? One of the pleasures of reading novels is the detective work of piecing information together to see below surfaces ("what appears to be the case hardly ever is"), with the confidence that we will end the novel having achieved some form of clarity and revelation. When critics speak of readerly investment, they're describing how we are motivated to keep reading, how we "invest" in a novel in the expectation of a later reward. This chapter describes the tactics through which novels ask us to defer our gratification, to give our time and attention in the assurance of future disclosure. Plot arouses, sustains, and satisfies our interest, the promise of enlightenment keeping us reading to the finish.

Suspense, interruption, and delay

There is an amusingly self-conscious exploitation of our plot addictions in Italo Calvino's **postmodernist** *If on a winter's night a traveler* (1979), a novel about readers whose big quest is (like ours) to finish the novel they've started. "You are about to begin reading Italo Calvino's new novel, *If on a winter's night a traveler*," reads its opening line, and there follows a list of suggestions – smokers should have their cigarettes to hand, readers who need to go to the bathroom should go now ("All right, you know best") – as you and your fictional alter ego, "Reader," settle down with the new Calvino.[3] And then the story commences: this looks to be a **thriller**, opening with a missed encounter at a foggy railway station. But just as you (and Reader) have become engrossed, something goes wrong. A defective copy? Reader returns to the bookstore to learn that a printing error has combined the new Calvino with a Polish novel; Reader asks for what he believes to be the Polish book instead, which he was just beginning to enjoy (not minding that it wasn't Calvino after all), but what he then starts reading proves to be a completely different novel; Reader becomes engrossed in that one, only to be unable to find the next chapter, but becomes absorbed by the novel someone else incorrectly believes it to be. And so it goes on, because *If on a winter's night a traveler* is a series of ten embedded "chapters" of ten different "novels," its frame story an espionage narrative as Reader tries to unravel the international book fraud conspiracy that connects all these fragments. This ironic novel of intrigue makes central the intrigue that novels generate, novels of all kinds, from works of grimly descriptive northern realism (the second of the novel's "novels") and Belgian gangster fiction (the fifth), through the erotic adventures of a Japanese acolyte (the eighth).

Postmodernist fiction thus thwarts what Calvino terms our "invincible tendency to passivity, to regression, to infantile dependence," even as it exploits so knowingly that capacity to care what happens next.[4] From the earliest times, fiction has worked through **suspense**. To be suspended, literally, is to be left hanging – an apt enough description of the feeling of immersion that novels elicit, when you know that every judgment you make is provisional until you can finally see the design to which all the individual parts of a novel will conform. Typically, though, the condition of being "suspended" applies to the narrative itself. On the face of it, we might think that uninterrupted absorption is the key to our enjoyment of fiction and yet *If on a winter's night a traveler* shows how suspense always requires interruption and delay. In building his novel around this insight, Calvino gives himself a very distinguished lineage.

That is, Calvino recalls the most important model for all storytellers: the famous Scheherazade, heroine-storyteller of the anonymous collection of

Middle Eastern folktales known as *The Arabian Nights* or *One Thousand and One Nights*. The frame story describes how a king, betrayed by his first wife, resolves to take future wives for one night only, and has each killed the following morning rather than be cuckolded again. But his vizier's brilliant daughter Scheherazade resolves to save the other women of the kingdom by marrying the king and preventing him from killing her (and thus future wives) by telling him nighttime stories that he will want to hear through to their conclusion – a conclusion that must necessarily be deferred. Night after night Scheherazade tells stories, spinning them out by having characters within the stories tell further stories, and when each morning comes she promises the king that he will hear something more marvelous still if he allows her to live another day. The example of *The Arabian Nights* suggests that plot works through the deliberate frustration of the reader's need to know how it all works out: reading word-by-word and page after page we move toward the distant revelatory conclusion, wanting – and yet in another sense *not* wanting – to get to the end.

In thinking about the mechanics of interruption and suspense we should remember that we experience many classic novels quite differently from how their first readers did. For us, the first experience of reading Richardson's *Clarissa* will likely be a matter of spending a month with an elephantine paperback reprint, but her first readers spent a whole year with her. In contrast with our intense but comparatively short-lived reading experience, these readers had *Clarissa* integrated into a year of their lives – which helps to explain why so many readers felt they had come to love Clarissa Harlowe, and why some resisted the tragedy Richardson scripted for her ending. Or, if you think forward to the nineteenth century and to another famous heroine-victim, knowing that Dickens's *The Old Curiosity Shop* was serially published in no fewer than forty-five weekly parts – again, the best part of a year – the legendary sentimentality of readers pleading with Dickens to spare the life of Little Nell Trent starts to become a little more accountable. When you read these books in a single volume you start to feel (and even in spite of the serialization-induced false start of *The Old Curiosity Shop*) that they couldn't have ended any other way, that the ending has been worked into everything that precedes it.

Serial publication, whether in monthly numbers or as the star turn in a weekly magazine, helps to explain the characteristic plot structure and much of the reading pleasure of the nineteenth-century novel, which is on the one hand episodic and interruptive, and, on the other, unites all its episodes in a genuinely gratifying wrap-up in the final pages. Serial publication also explains the page-turning suspense of nineteenth-century fiction, with its plot twists that encourage you to come back for the next installment. The term "cliffhanger" asks you to imagine a character in grave peril – as in the irresistible, classic, chapter-ending "cliffhanger" in Thomas Hardy's *A Pair of Blue Eyes* (1873), where Stephen Knight faces certain death as he hangs over the deadly "cliff without a name," hoping against expectation for a miraculous rescue. The cliffhanger is the convention with which Calvino plays when he cuts off his ten novels just when they're getting interesting, and you can skip forward to the discussion of John Fowles's *The French Lieutenant's Woman* in Chapter 9 of this book to see another postmodernist twist on the Victorian cliffhanger. But the cliffhanger generally isn't the same in the era of the non-serialized, single-volume novel; if you want to know how it all works out you need now wait no longer than the time it takes to turn the page.

Which brings me to another important feature of the novel's publishing history with important plot implications: the three-volume novel, or "three-decker." In a time when novels were expensive, many acquired their reading material from commercial circulating libraries. In the case of the most famous of these, Mudie's, a subscription fee of a guinea a year allowed readers a volume at a time, which could be exchanged as often as the borrower wanted. The three-volume novel proved advantageous for the circulating libraries because it could be read at the same time by three borrowers, and the dominance of these libraries must have played some part in both the Victorian novel's content and its shape: respectable and middle-class, compendious enough to run to multiple volumes, and divisible into three substantial parts (and, remember, you'd need to be gripped enough after the first or second volume to make the effort to get hold of the next part rather than start over with another book).

When it comes to plot, then, the material circumstances of how novels have been published have a bearing on what we're otherwise tempted to think of as a purely "aesthetic" matter, a matter of authorial artistry: how a book feels, how its story unfolds. And writing shortly after the collapse of the three-decker, the critic George Saintsbury memorably described the aesthetic problems of a form that had to stretch to three volumes: with a tendency toward padding and a dull middle volume, the three-decker frequently turned into "a sort of preposterous sandwich with meat on the outsides and a great slab of ill-baked and insipid bread between."[5] Yet even the master aesthetician Henry James – writing around the same time – acknowledged that some of the artificial conditions under which he and his predecessors had worked could also be considered formally *enabling*: "a tax on ingenuity," was how he referred to the artistic demands imposed by serial publication: "that ingenuity of the expert craftsman which likes to be taxed very much to the same tune to which a well-bred horse likes to be saddled."[6]

Early twentieth-century writers would deplore the artifices of plot, with its clunking coincidences, its falsification of ordinary, uneventful human experience, and the enslavement of the writer to the audience's desire for a tidy conclusion. The events of modernist fiction are typically psychological rather than in a more conventional sense "actual," and the endings of these novels may be rapturously affirmative (Molly Bloom's "yes I said yes I will Yes" the most famous of them all[7]) but they're seldom conclusive. (So what *does* happen to Bloom and Molly the next day? The next year? The rest of their lives?) It's essential to remember, though, that the devaluation of plot could be put into practice only after the late nineteenth-century demise of serialization and the three-decker. The modernist reluctance to gratify the desires for plot that the **Victorian novel** had both fuelled and fulfilled could possibly be construed as an advance in aesthetic integrity – and that's certainly how some of these writers saw it – but it also marked the sharp stratification of the novel into commercial and high-art spheres. In view of its resistance to what novel readers wanted or perhaps (as the rebels thought) had been *trained* to want, it was probably not incidental that literary modernism reintroduced into the literary landscape the pre-novelistic publication mechanisms of patronage and subscription.

Consequentiality and meaning

Unlike the "loose baggy monster," as James notoriously characterized the Victorian novel, the modernist novel makes *pattern* its plot. With its use of the *Odyssey* as its parallel text, Joyce's *Ulysses* is an extreme but not unrepresentative example of modernist fiction's will to design; this use of an ancient parallel was one reason why the poet T. S. Eliot praised the novel for finding "a way of controlling, of ordering, of giving a shape and a significance to the immense panorama of futility and anarchy which is contemporary history."[8] The key phrase here is "a shape and a significance": an implied "thus" bridges the two, with "significance" following from "shape." Even if modernist fiction breaks away from Victorian plotting (reward/punishment, inheritance/marriage), it's as true of modernist fiction as of the fiction it thought itself superseding that there is a *design* into which local details will fall, and that it is in the design that meaning is made.

Even the earliest and least shapely English novels are full of active speculations on the overarching pattern to which apparent accidents and contingencies will ultimately be subordinated. What invisible hand shapes the lives of fictional characters? In this passage from *Robinson Crusoe* the stranded protagonist is amazed to find genuine English corn growing on his island off the coast of South America:

> I had hitherto acted upon no religious foundation at all, indeed I had very few notions of religion in my head, or had entertain'd any sense of any thing that had befallen me, otherwise than as a chance, or, as we lightly say, what pleases God; without so much as enquiring into the end of Providence in these things, or his order in governing events in the world: But after I saw barley grow there, in a climate which I knew was not proper for corn, and especially that I knew not how it came there, it startled me strangely, and I began to suggest, that God had miraculously caus'd this grain to grow without any help of seed sown, and that it was so directed purely for my sustenance on that wild miserable place.[9]

Seeing that corn has risen unplanted in a climate where it should never have grown, the formerly irreligious Crusoe replaces his casual old idea of "chance" with the belief that God has performed a miracle for his benefit. The miraculous corn cannot be a random or freak occurrence but something that assures Crusoe of God's care for him, and which will help bring him back into the spiritual fold. It is as if the great plotter of Crusoe's life is God himself, and Providence another name for the plot.

But arbitrary supernatural power won't do for a novel. Suddenly, Crusoe remembers that the corn is growing in the same spot where he shook out an empty corn sack some months earlier. The power that made the corn grow is not God's but that of the novelist who constructs those chains of causes and effects, acts and consequences, out of which plots are made. Plots require causality – this happened because this happened – and an invisible controlling intention that makes contingency read like predestined necessity. Defoe's protagonists look back on their lives and see God's hand shaping local circumstances into a grand plan that is only retrospectively visible, but, importantly, the events that constitute that plan are always susceptible to real-world explanation, and even if these are sometimes improbable events, they are seldom impossible. Although, say, gothic or **magical realist** novels sometimes provide exceptions to this general rule, novelistic plots typically do not violate or suspend the laws of nature.

Still, even if novelistic plots do not rely on supernatural interventions, they frequently depend on credulity-stretching coincidences from the author doing for the fictional world what God might be supposed to do for the real one – wickedness is punished, virtue rewarded. Although there are many novels in which plausibility gets stretched in the interests of justice, perhaps the best example of novelistic plot modeling itself on providential order comes in

Oliver Goldsmith's *The Vicar of Wakefield* (1766), a rewriting of the scriptural story of Job. Gentle Dr. Primrose loses his vicarage and his fortune; has his daughter Olivia taken from him by a wicked seducer; watches everything he owns destroyed by fire; is cast into prison for debt, where he learns of Olivia's death; falls ill; has his younger daughter Sophia kidnapped; and, finally, has his oldest son arrested on a capital charge. Only once he has lost everything but his faith does the tide of his fortune turn, when the abducted Sophia is rescued by a former recipient of Primrose's charity, the vagrant Mr. Burchell. Mr. Burchell turns out to be a rich, titled eccentric who will now put Primrose's world back to rights like a fairy godmother (even the dead Olivia returns to life). Here, as in many other eighteenth-century novels, the novel administers a wish-fulfilling compensatory justice, plot serving not only the structural function of holding discrete components of the novel together but also the extra-literary function of underwriting a moral order. Perhaps paradoxically, the characteristic "providential" plot is also highly visible in its overturning, as in those eighteenth-century persecution narratives that place the protagonist at the mercy of an evil human plotter and then *refuse* to put things right. *Caleb Williams* (1794), by the political radical William Godwin (father of Mary Shelley), is polemically explicit about the social implications of refusing fictional justice: Falkland may be evil but his aristocratic wealth and status guarantee his triumph over the novel's lower-class hero. "Things as They Are" is the telling alternative title of *Caleb Williams*.

When, a century later, Oscar Wilde joked of Miss Prism's sentimental novel in *The Importance of Being Earnest* that "the good ended happily and the bad unhappily. That is what Fiction means," he was recalling the novel's long tradition of quasi-providential restitution and readers' willingness to buy into a system of punishment and reward in which they never *really* believe.[10] The mid-twentieth-century writers Graham Greene and Muriel Spark (both converts to Roman Catholicism) would make explicit that relationship between Christian providence and the novelist's acts of plotting. The narrator of Greene's *The End of the Affair* (1951) is the successful novelist Maurice Bendrix, who is forced to confront the limits of his powers in determining his relationship with his lover, the married Catholic Sarah. Like the fascistic fiction-making heroine of Spark's *The Prime of Miss Jean Brodie* (1961), who wrongly "thinks she is Providence … she sees the beginning and the end," Bendrix must come to learn the limits of plot's controlling, shaping power.[11] The demands of plot coexist with an interest in the contingent and the accidental, with what human beings *can't* know and *can't* control.

What the implied parallel between plot and providence helps to show is that plot is to do with *consequentiality*. Nothing is irrelevant, and nothing is arbitrary, and even the most trivial-seeming of details becomes meaningful once it is recognized as part of an overarching general plan – as the Russian critic Boris Tomachevsky once famously put it, if a character hammers a nail into the wall in the first act of a play, someone will have to hang himself from it in the third. Many critics have found the idea of the *consequential* a helpful way of distinguishing between story and plot, between chronology and causality. In *Aspects of the Novel*, Forster gives a nicely economical example when he explains that: "'The king died and then the queen died' is a story. 'The king died, and then the queen died of grief' is a plot."[12] His example of a *story* conveys chronology by the stringing together of two events, one following the other; in contrast, his example of a *plot* conveys causality because one event results in the other. For Forster, plot is more sophisticated than story because it is in the idea of causality that readers find their rewards.

Connectivity and social order

"Nothing, I daresay, has been farther from your thoughts than that there had been important ties in the past which could connect your history with mine," the Evangelical banker Nicholas Bulstrode tells the free-spirited Will Ladislaw in George Eliot's *Middlemarch*.[13] Late in the novel we are now learning that Bulstrode was the first husband of Will's grandmother, and knowingly responsible for the death in poverty of his parents, a twist that will help to bring the novel's two seemingly separate storylines (Will belongs to the Dorothea Brooke narrative and Bulstrode to the Lydgate story) to their convergence and climax. That the reader has been kept in the dark about Ladislaw's relationship to Bulstrode is an important reminder that, when it comes to plot, omniscient narration may "know" all but doesn't necessarily reveal all – or not all at once. And this hitherto withheld connection between the two characters of Bulstrode and Ladislaw speaks to a wider interest, evidenced here as in many other Victorian novels in the relationship between atomization and coherence, between the accidental and the meaningful. Final shape and explicability come out of an initially random-seeming profusion, an "apparently unruly superfluity of material gradually and retrospectively revealing itself as order," writes Gillian Beer of the nineteenth-century plots of Charles Dickens *and* Charles Darwin: "The sense that everything is connected, though the connections may be obscured, gave urgency to the enterprise of uncovering such connections."[14]

Plot, then, can be made to enact a model of social coherence, a social ecology. Eliot, "watching keenly the stealthy convergence of human lots," is interested in how people come to see that they actually have something to do with one another.[15] In this respect, plot works in *Middlemarch* as it does in Charles Dickens's *Bleak House* (1853) to model a society in which what seems irrevocably separate can and should be brought together. Having introduced all his major characters in their places, from elegant townhouse to country manor, Court of Chancery to abject slum, Dickens calls readers' attention to the extraordinary breadth of his social panorama, rhetorically asking them to speculate on what might hold together the radically different social spheres occupied by a smart manservant (nicknamed "Mercury") and a destitute street-sweeper ("Jo the outlaw"):

> What connexion can there be, between the place in Lincolnshire, the house in town, the Mercury in powder, and the whereabout of Jo the outlaw with the broom, who had that distant ray of light upon him when he swept the churchyard-step? What connexion can there have been between many people in the innumerable histories of this world, who, from opposite sides of great gulfs, have, nevertheless, been very curiously brought together![16]

And then the plot of the novel is going to demonstrate precisely what those connections are, showing that the poor have to matter to the rich, as the acts and whims of the rich shape the lives of the poor. In the best-known passage of his novel *Sybil* (1845), the future Prime Minister Benjamin Disraeli had a character speak of a Britain divided into "two nations" of rich and poor, "between whom there is no intercourse and no sympathy; who are as ignorant of each other's habits, thoughts, and feelings, as if they were dwellers in different zones, or inhabitants of different planets."[17] The Victorian plot that brings these groups together symbolically redresses the grim effects of social atomization and stratification in the non-fictional mid-nineteenth-century world.

Nineteenth-century novelists often had massive social range, but in his book on two of the most capacious and inclusive of them, Scott and Dickens, Ian Duncan points out that the more "realistic" the novel became in terms of its social *content* the less "realistic" it became in its commitment to shaping that material into tightly plotted *forms*. This "elaborate commitment to plot" itself has essential social implications, he explains, because plot imagines "a transformation of life and its conditions, and not their mere reproduction."[18] So if the defining quality of plot is *consequentiality*, causes having effects, you can see here how that technical quality can be used to articulate a moral or political point. For example, the plot of *Bleak House* makes the social outsider, the absolutely marginal Jo, *consequential*. He matters because he helps to resolve the mystery of the heroine's birth, and he matters because the squalid poverty in which he lives breeds the sickness that kills him and disfigures her.

The connective power of plot bridges social division, and the very worst evils in Victorian novels are crimes of egotism, refusals to acknowledge the ties that bind us to other people. Dickens gives this refusal a name in his late masterpiece *Our Mutual Friend* (1865): "Podsnappery" is the arrogant complacency of a self-insulating prosperous bourgeois adamant that he will not be touched by the suffering of others. "I don't want to know about it; I don't choose to discuss it; I don't admit it!" is Mr. Podsnap's refrain, and with these words he is "clearing the world of its most difficult problems, by sweeping them behind him."[19]

"Mr. Podsnap settled that whatever he put behind him he put out of existence," Dickens writes, but plot works to ensure the return of whatever you think you have put "behind" you. In spatial and social terms, this means that the upper-class constituents of Dickens's London have to be brought face to face with those fellow citizens with whom (they like to think) they have nothing in common, and the plot of *Our Mutual Friend* brings together the slick *nouveau riche* Veneering family with those who make their living from fetid bodies pulled from the Thames, and exorbitant wealth is forced to confront the tragic human wastage that has made it possible.

But plot connectivity makes temporal and psychological shapes as well as spatial and social ones. The past is never really past in these densely plotted novels – the drowned John Harmon (the "mutual friend" of Dickens's title) apparently returns from the dead; the illicit repatriation of Magwitch destroys Pip's new life as a gentleman; Bounderby's mother returns to prove him a fraud in *Hard Times*; Eliot's Bulstrode is ruined by the reemergence of the shady Raffles; Lady Dedlock's hauteur is shattered by the return of her illegitimate daughter Esther Summerson. Perhaps no novelist is as insistent on plot as the return of the past as Thomas Hardy. At one point in *Tess of the D'Urbervilles* (1891), the return of the disappeared Alec D'Urberville destroys all possibility of happiness with Angel Clare; at another, the return of the disappeared Angel destroys any possibility of happiness with Alec D'Urberville. *The Mayor of Casterbridge* (1886) also uses such returns to create ironic effects: a character presumed dead returns alive; the character presumed alive proves to be only the namesake of a character long-since dead.

Plots and masterplots

The classic Victorian plot is predicated on the *return*, on the hold of the past over the present. Sigmund Freud identified the "compulsion to repeat" with the death drive, the death drive with an instinctual desire to return to a prior state of being: we head toward death as the closest approximation of the condition of not yet having been born. If *story* implies chronology, linearity, and succession – this happens, then this happens, then this – it could be said that the backward orientation of *plot* entails a form of regression that brings the protagonist back to what had been left behind. Hardy's *The Mayor of Casterbridge* ends with the hero dying in a hovel, having become once again the hay-trusser he was at the start of the novel. In Eliot's *The Mill on the Floss*, the young Maggie's fate is "like the course of an unmapped river," but "for all rivers there is the same final home."[20] Eliot's comments recall the riverside mill from which Maggie has been expelled and anticipate the flooded river that will finally bring her back in death to the point at which she started.

I mention Freud because so many critics have sensed that there is an affinity between psychoanalysis and narrative, not least because psychoanalysis is already a plotting form because it organizes our formless experience in such a way as to make it mean something. "The plotting of the individual or social or institutional life story takes on new urgency when one no longer can look to a sacred masterplot that organizes and explains the world," argues Peter Brooks in his book on plot's nineteenth-century apotheosis.[21] On this model, novelistic plot and the plots created by psychoanalysis and other explanatory narratives ("masterplots") take on a particular compensatory power in a postreligious world (if that's indeed what we are living in) in which providential meaning is no longer self-evident. Living in time and, like all other biological beings, bounded by it, we respond to plot's capacity to wrest form and thus meaning out of our otherwise shapeless experience. Novelistic plot is pattern and implies a governing intention, and, in its capacity to make sense and order out of the meaningless flux of time, it speaks to our deepest human desires for meaning.

If you recall Forster's distinction between "chronology" (story) and "consequentiality" (plot) you can see what Brooks means by making such strong claims for plot: recounting the events of your life one after the other ("and then we got married, and then we got divorced, and then I changed jobs … ") does not give them coherence and meaning; identifying the relationships among these events, explaining *how* each follows from the other, gives them both. Meaning inheres in the retrospective narrativizing and interpretation of events and not in the events themselves.

We read and live looking forward but understanding is necessarily retrospective and retroactive, and we imagine an ending that will let us understand the beginning and middle. The German cultural theorist Walter Benjamin argued in the 1930s that novelistic plotting allows us to live symbolically beyond our own deaths, to survive the end point from which chains of cause and events, and thus their meanings, become retrospectively visible. The novel reader, Benjamin argued, finds a version of "the meaning of life" in living through the deaths of characters, whether their literal deaths within the pages of the novel or the figurative deaths that come with a novel having always to end. Thus, Benjamin writes, the reader consumes a novel as a fire consumes fuel, and the fire that is the novel radiates some comfort to readers, who obliterate (in the sense that we "finish" a novel) what they feed on:

> The novel is significant, therefore, not because it presents someone else's fate to us, perhaps didactically, but because this stranger's fate by virtue of the flame which consumes it yields us the warmth which we never draw from our own fate. What draws the novel to the reader is the hope of warming his shivering body with a death he reads about.[22]

Written in solitude, read in isolation, wholly distinguished from the oral story by being a non-transmissible, non-communal form, novels cannot offer us what Benjamin speaks of as "wisdom" but only whatever comfort we can find in extrapolating the meaning from the fictional deaths we survive.

I'll return in the final chapter to fictional endings, but this sense that death, literal and narrative, is what confers meaning seems woven into the idea of all plotted fiction, from the pre-modern – Scheherazade's survival depends on the infinite continuation of her stories – to the postmodern. "All plots tend to move deathward," declares the hero of Don DeLillo's *White Noise* (1985), his death-haunted novel about the exorbitant consumerism of the 1980s, about the fears and inevitabilities capitalist postmodernity won't name and can't assuage: "This is the nature of plots. Political plots, terrorist plots, lovers' plots, narrative plots."[23] Or, as Calvino writes on the penultimate page of *If on a winter's night a traveler*, "In ancient times a story could end only in two ways: having passed all the tests, the hero and the heroine married, or else they died. The ultimate meaning to which all stories refer has two faces: the continuity of life, the inevitability of death."[24] You will have to read the final page of his novel to discover which of those two "ancient" possibilities Calvino chooses.

Gustave Flaubert, *Madame Bovary* (1857)

> Before her wedding-day, she had thought she was in love; but since she
> lacked the happiness that should come from that love, she must have
> been mistaken, she fancied. And Emma sought to find out exactly what
> was meant in real life by the words *felicity, passion* and *rapture*, which
> had seemed so fine on the pages of books.
>
> Gustave Flaubert, *Madame Bovary* (1857)[1]

Emma Bovary is the second wife of a provincial doctor characterized by plod-
ding decency and his love of a wife he does not understand. When, after her
willing seduction by the shallow Rodolphe, Emma suddenly announces to no
one "I have a lover! A lover!" we know why she is so happy: for the first time
this avid reader has managed to make her disappointingly ordinary existence
conform to the conventions of fiction (150). Famously, marriage is the final
destination toward which the story of a fictional heroine traditionally tends,
but Emma's story begins only after hers. *Madame Bovary* works by literalizing
the symbolism of the traditional female plot that makes marriage a kind of figurative death, the conclusion to the heroine's existence on the page, the point
at which her story ends. The outcome of all plots is, you might say, plotlessness,
and death is the plotless condition *par excellence* because it is where nothing
else can happen. Emma's "failing" is that she cannot see that marriage is supposed to be, death-like, an end to all adventures.

But even if Emma's fantasy life is treated ironically, the social and psychological conditions that make it necessary are not. This is why the pregnant
Emma longs for a boy:

> A man, at least, is free; he can explore each passion and every kingdom,
> conquer obstacles, feast upon the most exotic pleasures. But a woman is
> continually thwarted. Both inert and yielding, against her are ranged the
> weakness of the flesh and the inequity of the law. Her will, like the veil
> strung to her bonnet, flutters in every breeze; always there is the desire
> urging, always the convention restraining. (82)

Men's capacity for experience need not stop with marriage, but women's must;
and a life that has no further plot or design, a life that is pure persistence, is no
life at all. When her mother-in-law forbids Emma her novels, we're reminded
of the scene in *Don Quixote* when the priest burns the hero's romances, but
one vital difference between the two novels is that Flaubert "genders," as critics

would say, the problem in such a way as to let us see that Emma's reading is as much a symptom as the cause of her dissatisfaction.

After all, *Don Quixote* may have provided the original cautionary tale of literacy misused, but there's a good reason why the most famous self-destructive fictional readers who followed were women characters like Emma Bovary and Anna Karenina. When Sheridan's novel-reading Lydia Languish complains in *The Rivals* of being "made a mere Smithfield bargain" by marriage – Smithfield is literally London's fleshmarket, where meat is bought and sold – we see why she heads toward fiction for something different.[2] Charlotte Lennox likewise proposed that women's use of fantasy to mitigate real-world expectations is an attack on and consolation for those expectations: having read the seventeenth-century romances of her emotionally isolated mother, the heroine of Lennox's *The Female Quixote* (1752) expects her life to be as interesting as fiction. Scolded by an older woman character for her unrealistic expectations, Lennox's Arabella is told that she must learn to want more than "those few and Natural incidents which compose the History of a Woman of Honor": birth and christening, a modest education, marriage to someone recommended by her parents.[3] With his fear that novels give girls false ideas about their future, Lennox's mentor Samuel Johnson might well have thought this enough, but it isn't obvious that Flaubert would agree.

"Familiar with the tranquil, she inclined instead to the tumultuous," we are told of the young, unmarried Emma, who is already using the vicarious pleasures of fiction as a means to resist the socially idealized but emotionally deadly serenity of middle-class women's lives (34). Indeed, her fantasy life as a reader leads her to the perverse but understandable conviction that the normal is abnormal, that "her immediate surroundings, the imbecile petit bourgeois, the general mediocrity of life" is "a kind of anomaly, a unique accident that had befallen her alone" (55). The fantasies inspired by fiction give you simultaneously the illusion of freedom, or the belief that this life you have is an accident but there might have been others, *and* the illusion of entrapment, or the sense that your unrewarding life was forced upon you.

Emma is a consumer of industrially produced fantasy, of novels about "love, lovers, loving, martyred maidens swooning in secluded lodges, postilions slain every other mile, horses ridden to death on every page, dark forests, aching hearts, promising, sobbing, kisses and tears, little boats by moonlight, nightingales in the grove, *gentlemen* brave as lions, tender as lambs, virtuous as a dream, always well dressed, and weeping pints" (35). Flaubert's mockery of junk fiction is clear in his comic redundancies ("love, lovers, loving"), his hyperbolic plots ("horses ridden to death on every page"), the absurd mixture of literary inflation ("brave as lions") and everyday cliché ("weeping pints"), and the amusing reminder of how fiction conflates moral and social aspiration ("virtuous as a dream, always well dressed"). What's not so obvious on a first reading, though, is how Flaubert will go on quietly to reuse these discredited conventions in such a way as to make them sound not conventional at all: there are many "aching hearts" and much "promising, sobbing, kisses and tears" in *Madame Bovary*; there is a seduction scene in a "dark forest"; there is even a horse ridden to death while Emma lies dying at the end of the novel. Emma's fantasies dictate the form the novel takes, right up to her end when, heroine-like, she poisons herself with arsenic – it has "an awful taste of ink," as if print itself is what kills her (295).

But, crucially, the end of Emma Bovary isn't the end of the novel. Flaubert clearly exploits many of the novelistic expectations he mocks – love, passion, betrayal, drama, death – but it is important that the dramatically plotted story of his heroine is surrounded by stories that are almost the opposite of plot: tangential rather than necessary, everyday rather than exceptional, anticlimactic rather than consequential. As many readers have noticed, the novel opens not with Emma but with Charles Bovary, and with a long description told in the voice of a nameless classmate of an amazingly ugly hat he wore on his first day of school. It is difficult to make this hat *mean* anything – and that's the point. In a novel about a woman who cannot bear life's refusal to be artfully organized, shapely, and significant, this opening passage is a triumph of comic irrelevance and inconsequentiality.

And then consider the bathetic aftermath of Emma's death, of the priest and pharmacist snacking on cheese in the room where her poisoned body lies. Hippolyte clonking around the village on his wooden leg after the botched surgery that might have made Charles Bovary's reputation seems an apt image of the novel's insistence on how embarrassing, ordinary persistence triumphs over the well-formed excitements and catastrophes of plot. Or you might think not of Hippolyte but of the sexton Lestiboudois planting his potatoes in the village graveyard ("to this day, he is still cultivating his tubers, and ... maintains quite calmly that they grow naturally" [68]), a wonderfully grotesque way of illustrating the ways in which life, defiant of fiction's efforts to impose a shape on it, just goes on.

With even her adoring husband relieved to see his wife buried, Emma retains just one midnight mourner, the young servant Justin who silently adored her all along. This is how the chapter ends:

> On the grave, among the pine-trees, a boy knelt weeping, and his poor heart, cracked with sorrow, was shaking in the darkness, under the burden of an immense regret, softer than the moon and fathomless as night. The gate suddenly gave a squeak. It was Lestiboudois; he'd come

to fetch the spade he'd left behind. He recognized Justin scaling the wall, and now he knew the name of the malefactor who had been stealing his potatoes. (318)

Pathos collapses into bathos, tragedy into farce, and a plot catastrophe into village comedy. As the Irishman Joyce knew when he had his everyman hero carry one around Dublin, there is nothing in the world less romantic but more life sustaining than a potato.

Chapter 6

Setting the novel

Space is not the "outside" of narrative, then, but an internal force, that shapes it from within. Or in other words: in modern European novels, *what* happens depends a lot on *where* it happens.

Franco Moretti, *Atlas of the European Novel* (1998)[1]

It does not seem to me to be enough to say of any description that it is the exact truth.

Charles Dickens[2]

Nathaniel Hawthorne begins his preface to *The House of the Seven Gables* (1851) by distinguishing between the novel and the romance: when an author calls his book a romance, as Hawthorne has, he "wishes to claim a certain latitude, both as to its fashion and material, which he would not have felt himself entitled to assume, had he professed to be writing a Novel."[3] He wants us to treat as pure invention his cursed New England house as well as the old Puritan Pyncheons who guiltily live there: "the Author ... trusts not to be considered as unpardonably offending, by laying out a street that infringes upon nobody's private rights, and appropriating a lot of land which had no visible owner, and building a house out of materials long in use for constructing castles in the air."[4] What I want to suggest in this chapter, though, is that novelistic setting always collapses the boundaries between the *realistic* and *romantic*: to write a place is to imagine a place, to call a new place into being around even an old signpost. Bakhtin was surely right to propose that the concrete specificity of setting is one of the most important features distinguishing the novel from preexisting forms of fiction.[5] Nonetheless, and as Dickens says and Hawthorne implies, the "exact truth" is not the point.

Improving your estate

The significance of situation in the novel is perhaps best attested to by the fact that so many novels take the form of a journey narrative.[6] "A novel: it's a mirror carried along the highway," writes Stendhal as a chapter epigraph in his novel *The Red and the Black* (1830), offering a definition of the novel that captures very well the importance of location and relocation to the novel (physical mobility means social mobility in *The Red and the Black*).[7] Telling the story of the British novel from its origins to the present day Patrick Parrinder has recently pointed out that novels betray their debts to the chivalric romance by making the journey motif so prominent; in view of the hero's knightly obsessions, *Don Quixote* would certainly support this argument.[8] When Quixote hit the road on Rosinante, he famously established a shape for the novel to come, a bold outward journey and a final homecoming. Or, as Austen playfully writes of her Quixotic Catherine Morland when she leaves her quiet country home for the town of Bath, "if adventures will not befal a young lady in her own village, she must seek them abroad."[9] To leave home is to be made ready for the seemingly contingent but ultimately fateful encounters and experiences that all novels require.

"Give me something to desire," pleads the title character of Johnson's *Rasselas*. In what would become a typical novelistic maneuver, Johnson and Voltaire opened their contemporary fables by driving their heroes out of Eden. Forcibly exiled from his Westphalian castle, the title character of Voltaire's *Candide* (1759) journeys across Old and New Worlds before being reunited with friends in Constantinople; they, too, are displaced persons, and their wanderings have given them adventures and misadventures to recount. And just as Candide and his companion find themselves eager to leave the mythical utopia of Eldorado they discover on their travels ("the two happy men resolved to be happy no longer"[10]), Johnson's *Rasselas* opens with the hero's efforts to get out of the bland bliss of the Happy Valley: "I fancy that I should be happy if I had something to pursue," Rasselas tells his tutor: "I have already enjoyed too much; give me something to desire."[11] Only when paradise has been lost – or renounced – can novels really begin. Voltaire and Johnson's books may be bad examples because they're too plainly philosophical in their objectives to be comfortably categorized as novels; nonetheless, you can see the same pattern in *Tom Jones* when the protagonist is unjustly driven from Squire Allworthy's estate as Candide is driven from the Baron's castle, and in *Robinson Crusoe*, which begins with the hero rejecting what you might term the "happy valley" of middle-class life in favor of a riskier fortune.

That the novel's protagonist is a restless adventurer is most visible in the Spanish **picaresque** tradition of novels in which a low-class hero (a *pícaro* is a rogue) makes his rascally way through life with nothing but his own street-smart wits to depend on. This form is usually said to begin with the anonymous *Lazarillo de Tormes* (1554), in which the illegitimate young Lazaro, more sinned against than sinning, learns from his exploitation how to exploit others. You can see its influence on English prose narrative in early fictional works like Thomas Nash's *The Unfortunate Traveller* (1594), which recounts the pranks and scrapes of its protagonist Jack Wilton as he journeys through Europe, through early eighteenth-century novels like *Moll Flanders*, whose heroine, forced to make her own disreputable way in life, gets as far as colonial Virginia and back. Sometimes you see the designation "picaresque" deployed without such strong connotations of roguishness as it originally had to describe highly episodic novels structured by a journey (which is to say, a series of adventures). Loosely structured eighteenth-century novels like Smollett's *Roderick Random* and *Peregrine Pickle* are often referred to in this way (a translator of Cervantes, Smollett was well versed in Spain's early novel tradition).

His epistolary *Humphry Clinker* represents a journey away from the more familiar kind of setting for the British novel, the country estate, when Squire Bramble leaves behind his orderly home in Wales to undertake his tour of mainland Britain. Reacting against the metropolitan sociality that had, J. Paul Hunter writes, come to define the eighteenth-century nation itself, Squire Bramble's letters from London are jeremiads against urban commodity culture and its new "vile world of fraud and sophistication"[12] "Shall I state the difference between my town grievances, and my country comforts?" he asks his correspondent Dr. Lewis.[13] There follows a long set of contrasts between town-bought food and the products of his own estate; between constriction and space; between filth and cleanliness; between interruption and peace; between claustrophobic sociability and chosen intimacies; between luxury and good sense. The good life is the life of the good squire, improving his farm and watching his tenants thrive – a familiar eighteenth-century ideal, the rural estate would provide one of the English novel's most characteristic settings. Different novelistic settings make possible different kinds of novel, Franco Moretti argues in the book I quoted at the head of this chapter; they also dramatize different social and moral values.

The classic statement of the social values underpinning the estate novel is Austen's *Mansfield Park* (1814). Sir Thomas and Lady Bertram's niece Fanny Price has been brought up at Mansfield Park, the country estate of which she will come to be mistress once she has driven off her town-bred competitor, Mary Crawford. What the country estate means becomes apparent when Fanny returns after a long absence to her impoverished parents in the naval town of Portsmouth: the Prices' home is "the abode of noise, disorder, and impropriety. Nobody was in their right place, nothing was done as it ought to be."[14] But it isn't simply that the Portsmouth house is messy and noisy compared to Mansfield Park, but that the literal disorder that shocks Fanny so much on her arrival portends a disregard for the interpersonal civilities that make domestic coexistence tolerable. Even on her first night home Fanny is ignored, whereas at Mansfield Park "there would have been a consideration of times and seasons, a regulation of subject, a propriety, an attention towards every body which there was not here," Fanny nostalgically recalls. "The elegance, propriety, regularity, harmony – and perhaps, above all, the peace and tranquility of Mansfield, were brought to her remembrance every hour of the day, by the prevalence of every thing opposite to them *here*."[15]

At the end of *Pride and Prejudice*, Jane Bennet asks her sister how she came to change her mind about haughty Mr. Darcy: "I believe I must date it from my first seeing his beautiful grounds at Pemberley," Elizabeth replies.[16] Although Jane supposes that Elizabeth is joking when she implies that she has ulterior motives for changing her mind about Darcy, there is also an important truth in her confession. (To a less dramatic extent than Fanny Price, she is also the product of a cash-strapped, chaotic household.) Consider her conclusions after she has seen Pemberley for the very first time: "She had never seen a place for which nature had done more, or where natural beauty had been so little counteracted by an awkward taste. They were all of them warm in their admiration; and at that moment she felt, that to be mistress of Pemberley might be something!"[17] The attractions of wealth have been transfigured into the allure of taste, sense, and reasonableness, and Darcy's *moral* virtue is confirmed when Elizabeth hears from his housekeeper that he is "the best landlord, and the best master ... that ever lived."[18] Austen's treatment of Darcy's well-run country estate as a model society implies the generally conservative political orientation of the estate novel: wealth, always un-conspicuous, comes from land rather than commerce ("the best *landlord*"), and the estate is run along benignly paternalistic lines ("the best *master*").

Critics have become increasingly attuned to the ideological work performed by this traditional country house setting. Why does fiction present country life as having a moral, even spiritual dimension? Why should fiction imagine landed wealth, "old money," as somehow cleaner than money made through trade? The great cultural critic Raymond Williams put it best when he wrote that ideas of a "traditional order" are "mystifying" and "misleading":

> For there is no innocence in the established proprietors at any particular
> point in time, unless we ourselves choose to put it there. Very few
> titles to property could bear humane investigation in the long process
> of conquest, theft, political intrigue, courtiership, extortion and the

power of money. It is a deep and persistent illusion to suppose that time confers on these familiar processes of acquisition an innocence which can be contrasted with the ruthlessness of subsequent stages of the same essential drives.[19]

Property is typically acquired by discreditable means, Williams suggests, and the novel is one of the cultural artifacts fostering the "deep and persistent illusion" that the length of time for which property, wealth, and status have been held has somehow rendered their origins innocent.

For Williams, then, what writers like Austen understand as established county families and "ancient stock" are simply "those families who had been pressing and exploiting their neighbours rather longer."[20] However, the legitimizing function of the country house ideal is not simply of interest in terms of domestic class questions, as the **postcolonial** critic Edward Said demonstrated in his classic discussion of space in *Mansfield Park*.[21] The money sustaining what Fanny comes to think of as the decorous harmony of Mansfield Park comes, in fact, from one of the most brutal forms of human exploitation: Sir Thomas's slave-worked plantations in Antigua. While this kind of money-making requires a degree of forgetfulness that keeps Antigua on the margins of the novel, imaginatively as well as literally distanced from the English country house, Mansfield Park itself is, Said argues, like a colonial estate in miniature: the orderliness that Fanny admires has its ironic but entirely historical counterpart in the force required to maintain the offstage colonial plantation that makes the country house possible in the first place.

The monster at the margins

But the orderly imagined center of the English novel has what you might call other "others." Disabused of her belief that the country house of Northanger Abbey is home to horrors like those she has read about in the gothic novels of Ann Radcliffe (here, murdered or incarcerated women), and having learned from Henry Tilney how to appreciate the quieter landscapes of southern England, Catherine Morland has a telling epiphany:

> Charming as were all Mrs. Radcliffe's works, and charming even as were the works of all her imitators, it was not in them perhaps that human nature, at least in the midland counties of England, was to be looked for. Of the Alps and Pyrenees, with their pine forests and their vices, they might give a faithful delineation; and Italy, Switzerland, and the South of France, might be as fruitful in horrors as they were there represented. Catherine dared not doubt beyond her own country, and even of that, if

> hard pressed, would have yielded the northern and western extremities. But in the central part of England there was surely some security for the existence of a wife not beloved, in the laws of the land, and the manners of the age.[22]

What makes this moment of seeming clarity and revelation so delicious is that Catherine still fails to grasp the essential fictiveness of the gothic novel, and mistakes for realism the stylized, conventional descriptions of sublime Pyrenean mountains and ancient Italian castles, and the plots they make possible ("with their pine forests and their vices"), occupying the greater part of books like Radcliffe's *The Mysteries of Udolpho* (1794). In Catherine's purportedly more mature mind, it is not that the secret murder or immuring of Mrs. Tilney could never really happen, but that it could never happen *here*.

Importantly, Catherine will vouch for neither Europe's Catholic countries nor for Britain's own "northern and western extremities." These are essential locations for the gothic novel: Charles Maturin exploited both when he set the frame story of *Melmoth the Wanderer* in a decrepit mansion on a remote coast of Ireland and the main action in the monasteries, dungeons, prisons, and secret underground passageways of Inquisition-era Spain. The English Protestant association, often paranoid and sometimes vaguely pornographic, of Catholicism with the gothic is both hinted at and exploded in Charlotte Brontë's *Villette* (1853), with its continental setting, its seductive priests, spectral nuns, dwarfish crones, and perpetual surveillance – all of which titillating trappings turn out to be, as in *Northanger Abbey*, covering up all-too-worldly cupidity. In these debunking novels, the insistently foreign proves curiously familiar. But what, precisely, are they debunking?

In her preface to *Frankenstein*, a novel famously conceived on a reading party in the Swiss Alps (conventionally gothic, as Catherine Morland's comments record), Mary Shelley implied that her gothic imagination should be attributed to a childhood spent substantially in the Scottish countryside, as if she could count on her readers' assumptions about the contagion of remote places. Geographical isolation is also essential to the novel itself: "Prepare to hear of occurrences which are usually deemed marvelous," Frankenstein tells Captain Walton aboard the Arctic ship: "Were we among the tamer scenes of nature, I might fear to encounter your unbelief, perhaps your ridicule; but many things will appear possible in these wild and mysterious regions, which would provoke the laughter of those unacquainted with the ever-varied powers of nature"; and it is to the Orkney Islands off Scotland's northern coast ("some obscure nook in the northern highlands of Scotland") that Frankenstein retreats to make his aborted second monster.[23]

It is as if in Scotland, Switzerland, or the North Pole, anything is possible and everything is believable. Bram Stoker shifts the location but not its fundamental meaning in *Dracula*, which opens with Jonathan Harker's journey from Munich to the Romanian city of Bistriţa ("The impression I had was that we were leaving the West and entering the East," Harker records in his diary[24]). These remoter parts imply a kind of boundary crossing, from civilization into barbarism, from society into the asocial. As in *Frankenstein*, the shifts of setting act out the figurative transgressions of *Dracula*, where boundaries are dangerously crossed between the human and the inhuman, the creator and the creature, the living and the dead. Perhaps it goes without saying, though, that all of this presupposes a more-or-less metropolitan reader, since you would have to suppose that a reader from the Balkans, say, or the Scottish islands, would be as little inclined to think themselves outside the pale of "humanity" and "civilization" as would African readers of *Heart of Darkness*.

The dark, decayed castle in which Stoker's Jonathan Harker finds himself is the *locus classicus* of the gothic novel. Here, as in the original of its type, Horace Walpole's *The Castle of Otranto*, the doomed "house" is a dwelling and a dynasty, a total conflation of people and their places. However, gothic fiction tends to destabilize that feudal conflation (a conflation central to the estate novel) by having the horror plot emerge precisely out of longstanding but fundamentally illegitimate ownership. In *The Castle of Otranto*, the tyrant Manfred knows that his claim to the castle rests on the crime now being supernaturally avenged before his eyes, while, a century later, supernatural happenings in Hawthorne's *The House of the Seven Gables* originate with the crime that first put the wizard Maule's land into the hands of the Pyncheons. You can hear echoes of this gothic trope of illegitimate ownership, stripped of its full-blown supernaturalism, in many twentieth-century novels. The creepy decayed plantations of William Faulkner's novels about the aftermath of the American Civil War imply the illegitimacy of the aristocratic white south, while, with its powerless orphan heroine and its doomed, decrepit mansion, Elizabeth Bowen's novel about the Irish Civil War, *The Last September* (1929), invokes the gothic as a way of writing about the end of English power in Ireland, here exposing the fragile foundations on which Anglo-Irish power had been built. The thoroughly un-homely gothic home is like a distorted reflection of the feudal country estate: where the latter is reassuringly static, a source of enduring values, the other is in a terrible and unstoppable – but deserved – decline.

Land, sea, and labor

The idea of "land," then, has traditionally been important to the novel, but it has set very precise limits to its social range. I think this is implied in the famous passage from his 1879 study of Hawthorne where Henry James uses setting to contrast the situation of the nineteenth-century American novelist with that of his British counterparts:

> No sovereign, no court, no personal loyalty, no aristocracy, no church, no clergy, no army, no diplomatic service, no country gentlemen, no palaces, no castles, nor manors, nor old country-houses, nor parsonages, nor thatched cottages, nor ivied ruins; no cathedrals, nor abbeys, nor little Norman churches; no great Universities nor public schools – no Oxford, nor Eton, nor Harrow; no literature, no novels, no museums, no pictures, no political society, no sporting class – no Epsom nor Ascot! Some such list as that might be drawn up of the absent things in American life … The American knows that a good deal remains; what it is that remains – that is his secret, his joke, as one may say.[25]

James proposes that the American novel lacked the ready-made settings that came with Britain's long "civilized" history and cultural accomplishments. But, he goes on to say, "a good deal remains" – and what you notice as you read this list is that these "lacks" refer mainly to a very narrow band of society: the traditional educational, clerical, military, and educational hierarchies; the leisure activities of the titled and wealthy ("no Epsom nor Ascot!"); and Britain's architectural and cultural monuments to wealth and status. The American "joke" is a democratic one: that only a British novelist could look at this list and suppose that American writers have nothing to write about.

Dedicated to Hawthorne, the author whose fiction prompted James's remarks, the American classic *Moby-Dick* (1851) has a different kind of setting altogether, a Nantucket whaling ship on the hunt for the white sperm whale to which the godless but godlike captain lost his leg on an earlier expedition. Instead of the contingent social particularities that James associated with the British novel – Epsom, Ascot, and the rest of it – we have a bid for the timelessly, transcendently universal made through the novel's seascape: the pursuit of what Melville calls "landlessness," or a willingness to lose the comfortable earth-bound orthodoxies of social existence, becomes the highest human virtue in the novel.[26] In an ironic departure from the social and class categories that (James implied) give their orderliness to the British novel, *Moby-Dick* is a novel about the *failure* of categorizations, an encyclopedia of whaling that admits at every turn the limits of its own encyclopedic mode. Chapter after chapter of this novel tackles an individual aspect of the whale and whaling, but not even the most dogged accumulation of facts can shed light on the predestined, fated act of self-destruction that the novel describes. Captain Ahab will destroy himself, his ship, and all but one of his men in this quest and yet will not call off the hunt for the white whale that has become for him a material, tangible embodiment of the metaphysical evil that lurks unseen everywhere and at all times.

So while this novel about work and workers seems to propose an almost encyclopedic factuality, all its explanatory detail is put ultimately into the service of what you might call a mythology, or an overarching way of thinking about the place of human beings in the universe. You can see its influence in the modernist Conrad's use of the ocean in *The Shadow-Line* (1917), his autobiographical novel about a ship's captain tormented by deadly illness, madness, guilt, and malevolence of a quasi-supernatural order; and you can see its influence very clearly, too, on Ernest Hemingway's novella *The Old Man and the Sea* (1952), about a Cuban fisherman, the Christ-like Santiago, and his struggle with a giant marlin. More generally, though, it would be true to say of many realistic-seeming novels that what initially resembles a scrupulously particular attention to the details of laboring life proves to be driven by some further-reaching and more metaphysical interest.

You can see this yoking of the particular and the abstract later in the nineteenth century when Thomas Hardy advances a whole view of human existence through his documents of working-class life in England's rural West Country, a way of life so specific that it would have been unfamiliar even to metropolitan contemporaries. Like *Moby-Dick*, Hardy's *The Mayor of Casterbridge* (1886) has an almost archival quality, from its recording of West Country dialect and folk customs to its cataloguing of sheer *stuff*, as when we learn what can be found in the shop windows of Casterbridge:

> Scythes, reap hooks, sheep-shears, bill-hooks, spades, mattocks, and hoes at the ironmonger's; beehives, butter-firkins, churns, milking-stools and pails, hay-rakes, field-flagons, and seed-lips at the coopers; cart-ropes and plough-harness at the saddler's; corn-drills and winnowing machines at the wheelwright's and machinist's; horse-embrocations at the chemist's; at the glover's and leather-cutter's hedging-gloves, thatcher's knee-caps, ploughman's leggings, villager's pattens and clogs.[27]

This almost ethnographic list of objects reveals a town dominated by agricultural labor, the town within which the hero has risen from poverty and drunkenness to a position of local eminence. Even though this social ascent is plausible enough (by Hardy's standards, anyhow), the novel is essentially concerned, again like *Moby-Dick*, with what defies plausibility, with the malignant unreason of human motivation. In the course of the novel, Michael Henchard will compulsively, obliviously annihilate everything he has achieved, from his professional and social reputation to his romantic and familial affections, before finally willing even his own death. "Nature" is to blame – in the sense of Henchard's own nature but also that it is in the nature of things to go wrong. At one telling moment in the novel, Henchard's pessimistic daughter, a passive victim of his self-destructive actions, is described as having "that field-mouse fear of the coulter of destiny despite fair promise" – Hardy is evoking Robert Burns's famous poem about contingency, which uses the harvest-time destruction of a field-mouse's nest to speculate on the futility of the best laid plans o' mice and men.[28] Giving a novel a natural setting, whether it is Melville's ocean or Hardy's fields, is part of a rhetoric of determinism and fatality; the universe is as inexorable as the tides, as oblivious to human suffering as the sun and the rain.

One of Hardy's most important twentieth-century inheritors, D. H. Lawrence would also imaginatively return to his working-class rural childhood in his major novels, which are set in the farming and coal-mining countryside of the English Midlands. His characters work within nature, too, raising livestock or wresting coal from the earth. The farming men in *The Rainbow* (1915), his novel of passionately destructive marriages, are part of nature itself: "So much warmth and generating and pain and death did they know in their blood, earth and sky and beast and green plants, so much exchange and interchange they had with these, that they lived full and surcharged, their senses full fed, their faces always turned to the heat of the blood, staring into the sun."[29] Lawrence's most approbated characters are like this: as inhuman as foxes, driven not by reason but instinct; the cerebral and intellectual, in contrast, are associated with deathly insensibility. His best-known delineation of this polarity comes in the contrast between the wounded intellectual Clifford Chatterley and the vital gamekeeper Mellors in *Lady Chatterley's Lover* (1928). As with the working seascapes of Melville and Conrad, the provincial landscapes of Hardy and Lawrence seem to resemble a form of realism, carefully documenting the realities of laboring life, and yet imply a whole view, deeply spiritual but seldom religious, of the relationships between people and the cosmos.

Cityscapes

To be sure, not all rural settings subordinate the social to the metaphysical in this way. "Do you expect passion, and stimulus, and melodrama?" Charlotte Brontë asks early in *Shirley* (1849). "Calm your expectations," she cautions: "Something real, cool, and solid, lies before you; something unromantic as Monday morning, when all who have work wake with the consciousness that they must rise and betake themselves thereto."[30] As the comparison between the appropriate expectations to bring to her novel and a Monday morning implies, *Shirley* is, like the novels discussed in the preceding paragraphs, a novel about work, but it declares its refusal to mythologize. More precisely, this novel is about industrial unrest, a "condition of England" novel; what is slightly unusual about it as an industrial novel is its rural setting (the title character, Shirley Keeldar, is the heiress to the estate where the hero's mill is located).

In contrast, and more typically, Brontë's first biographer Elizabeth Gaskell used industrial life as a contrast to rural life in mid-nineteenth-century England. Margaret Hale in *North and South* (1855) is a vicar's daughter forced to leave her beloved home in the Hampshire village of Helstone ("like a village in a tale … like a village in a poem"[31]) for a northern manufacturing town, Milton-Northern, in the distant county of – no equivocation here – Darkshire. Whereas the South stands for leisure, the North represents labor; and whereas pseudo-aristocratic gentility and hierarchy dominate the South, commercial and manufacturing life in the North means modernity and the struggle for a democratic relationship between masters and men; ultimately the Southerner Margaret will come to embrace the North in the shape of the self-made man Thornton. That geography in *North and South* means shaping concrete places into seemingly incommensurate worldviews is what allowed David Lodge to rewrite it in *Nice Work* – the Robyn Penrose discussed in Chapter 4 is a modern Margaret Hale, cultured, humane, and unknowingly snobbish, whom the enduringly awful academic job market forces to work in the industrial town of "Rummidge" (Birmingham) where she is thrown into the company of the rough-and-ready factory manager Wilcox. As in *North and South*, a learned mutual appreciation allows Lodge's characters to surmount the limitations of their individual ways of looking at the world.

Gaskell's novel was first published serially under Dickens's editorship of *Household Words*, and forms a telling contrast with the superficially more denunciatory but stylistically very different treatment of industrialism Dickens presented in *Hard Times*. This is how Dickens describes the northern manufacturing city of "Coketown":

> It was a town of red brick, or of brick that would have been red if the smoke and ashes had allowed it; but, as matters stood it was a town of unnatural red and black like the painted face of a savage. It was a town of machinery and tall chimneys, out of which interminable serpents of smoke trailed themselves for ever and ever, and never got uncoiled. It had a black canal in it, and a river that ran purple with ill-smelling dye, and vast piles of building full of windows where there was a rattling and a trembling all day long, and where the piston of the steam-engine worked monotonously up and down, like the head of an elephant in a state of melancholy madness.[32]

In keeping with this novel's story of the necessary triumph of fantasy and feeling over Gradgrind-style utilitarianism, Dickens has imaginatively transformed the drab and prosaic setting of an industrial town into something as unfamiliar ("a river that ran purple"), exotic ("the painted face of a savage"), and exorbitantly fanciful ("an elephant in a state of melancholy madness") as the circus that brings the redeeming Sissy Jupe into the lives of the wretched Gradgrinds. On the one hand, then, Dickens's argument requires that the industrial setting be hideous – the river is poisoned, the buildings are filthy, and the factory machinery is vast and ugly – but, on the other, the *description* of the setting has already been viewed through the sensibility that will save the place from itself. It is almost as if to present Coketown *realistically* would be to collude with the fact-worshiping utilitarianism that has made it possible.

But not even the most "realistic" of urban realisms is ingenuously descriptive, and there is an intimate relationship between *documentation* and *argumentation* in fiction. Think of the determinisms of nineteenth-century French novelists like Honoré de Balzac and (at the later end of the century) Émile Zola, with their not so much anthropological as *zoological* approach to the places where people live. Although the very famous vignette that opens Balzac's *Père Goriot* (1834–5) is too long to quote in full, the description of Madame Vauquer and her seedy boarding house is a deservedly well-known example of the interdependence of human beings and their places in Balzac: "her whole person is an explicit comment on the boarding house," Balzac summarizes, "just as the boarding house is implicitly suggestive of her."[33] People and their places are one and the same in Balzac, and it's never clear in this deeply deterministic kind of "realism" whether human beings make their habitats or their habitats make them.

A still more extreme instance of the perverse *un*-realism of hyperrealism is the "**Naturalist**" novel of the late nineteenth and early twentieth centuries, with its avowedly dispassionate investigations of the social margins, of underworlds of sex and crime – in intention as "realistic" as you could get. When Zola, its most famous proponent, argued for "the *experimental* novel" (my emphasis), in a famous essay of that title, he meant quite literally *experimental*, as if a novel were a laboratory in which hypotheses could be tested. In the preface to his scandalous *Thérèse Raquin* (1867), a novel of adultery, murder, and suicide in a lower-class home, he wrote that his "objective was first and foremost a scientific one": "given a powerful man and an unsatisfied woman, to seek within them the animal, even to see in them only the animal, to plunge them together into a violent drama and then take scrupulous note of their sensations and their actions. I simply carried out on two living bodies the same analytical examination that surgeons perform on corpses."[34] So far, so scientific, you might say, but when you open the novel you find something quite different. The novel begins with a long, detailed description of the backwater alley where the main characters live above their haberdashery shop, and the description concludes with a wall that looks as if it is "covered with leprous sores and zigzagged with scars."[35] These bodily similes are less than neutral, to say the least, because we have already been moved to disgust rather than clinical observation. Description conditions our readerly expectations; it is, as the narrative theorist Mieke Bal puts it, "generative of narrativity."[36] So, looking again at that corrupted wall of Zola's we start to anticipate possible stories – what has happened here? – and re-reading the novel we notice how its opening has turned moral corruption into a circular kind of environmental corruption: the consequences ("sores" and "scars") of the characters' crimes are written all over the squalid setting that the deterministic Zola seems to believe elicited these crimes in the first place. The story's end is built into this opening description, "realistic" only if you believe that the relationship between people and the places in which they live is wholly and reciprocally determining.

Cities make particular *kinds* of story possible. Part of the appeal of the city for novelists is that, especially in Europe, its population density brings the ruling class, the underclass, and all classes in between into close physical proximity to one another. This setting has crucial implications for their plots. Think of how novels like Oscar Wilde's *The Picture of Dorian Gray* (1891) allegorize psychic division through geographical boundaries that prove fragile and inadequate. A bright young thing by day, by night the rich and beautiful hero frequents the slums, wrongly believing that the city confers anonymity upon him even as reports of his subterranean crimes make their way into high society. The anonymity of the city typically proves no more than theoretical, and no city becomes big enough to render invisible the perpetrators of its crimes: the plots of mid-Victorian novels as different as *North and South* and *Great Expectations*, for example, hinge on a transported character returning to Britain on pain of death only to be recognized in the city by someone who knows him; while Conrad's *The Secret Agent* (1907) emphasizes London's appalling anonymity ("a monstrous town more populous than some continents"; "darkness enough to bury five millions of lives") only to have the crime pinned to the novel's title character within hours of its being carried out.[37]

But even if the cities of the Victorian novel would substantially be places of squalor and disgrace, many modern novels represent the connectivity of the city in a vastly more positive light. If the cities of Dickens, Gaskell, and Conrad are places where you try not to get found out, modernist novels like Joyce's *Ulysses* celebrate the opportunities the city affords for the casual encounter, and for a kind of fellow feeling that emerges from the unforced democracy of shared public spaces, whether you're talking about the cemetery or the pub, the library or the brothel. In the postwar novel, too, the city is imagined as a place where new communities can emerge out of the rubble of the old.

Take, for example, the Trinidadian-born Sam Selvon's *The Lonely Londoners* (1956): notwithstanding the hero's claim that "London is not like Kingston … it have millions of people living here, and your friend could be living in London for years and you never see him," and notwithstanding the pervasive racism and economic deprivation of postwar Britain, Selvon's anecdotal novel about the lives of Caribbean immigrants emphasizes the opportunities a city's public spaces afford for rewarding and more diverse forms of post-imperial community.[38] They may be "lonely," but these immigrants are emphatically *Londoners*, as Peter Kalliney points out when he reads Selvon's novel alongside Woolf's *Mrs. Dalloway*, an iconic work of metropolitan modernism, itself a novel that exploits and celebrates the new forms of community that urban life makes possible.[39]

Many mid-century British writers like Selvon, George Lamming, and even the white, upper-class Colin MacInnes wrote novels that, without underplaying the widespread racism of their time, celebrated urban collectivity on political grounds. Much of the best contemporary British writing, from James Kelman's and Irvine Welsh's representations of working-class and under-class sociability in Scotland's post-industrial cities to Hanif Kureishi's, Zadie Smith's, and Monica Ali's novels about the experiences of black and Asian Londoners, is about the sometimes unlikely solidarities made possible by the chance encounters of urban life. Nor is such redemption of even the least privileged of city lives a feature of contemporary British fiction alone. Don DeLillo's novel of the American millennial metropolis, *Underworld* (1997), ends with a "miracle" that draws hardened hundreds to the Bronx's hellish "inner ghetto" when the face of a murdered twelve-year-old girl from the ghetto, Esmeralda Lopez, supernaturally appears on an advertising billboard.[40] In DeLillo's tellingly titled *Cosmopolis* (2003), a billionaire asset manager in Manhattan has his view of a city he barely knew transformed when his limo gets stuck behind the funeral cavalcade of Brutha Fez – himself very much a cosmopolite, an unexpected hybrid, a Sufi rapper.

Nowhere and everywhere

As all these examples indicate, the novel is extensively implicated in particularities of social and historical context, tempting us to read novels as cultural documents: documents of conservative values in the case of the country house; of laboring life and industrialism; of immigrant experience, and so on. However, not all fiction has the categorizable kind of setting described in this chapter: the events of Franz Kafka's *The Trial* (1925) take place in an urban setting, certainly, but the city goes unnamed, as if what happens to K when the state indicts and executes him without either identifying his crime or allowing him to defend himself could happen anywhere sufficiently "advanced" – that's Kafka's irony – to have cities. Or think of Samuel Beckett's later fiction ("A voice comes to one in the dark," begins *Company*: "Imagine"), which is so alienating, so *world-deprived* that the only context you can imagine adequate to it is a live burial.[41]

A different kind of "nowhere" is *utopia*. The term comes from the fictional New World island of Sir Thomas More's *Utopia* (1516), and it means *good place* (the Greek *topos*, "place," preceded by the prefix *eu-*, "good") or *no place* (because the prefix may be *ou-*, "not"). As the pun on goodness and non-existence suggests, utopias offer the impossible standard by which real-world states of affairs can be measured. In practice, however, utopias in fiction are usually **dystopias**: unambiguously bad places. Famous modern examples would include Aldous Huxley's *Brave New World* (1932), George Orwell's *Nineteen Eighty-Four* (1949), and Margaret Atwood's *The Handmaid's Tale* (1985); in each the setting (the "topos") is not *geographically* elsewhere (More's Utopia is a remote island) but *temporally* elsewhere, in a monstrous future of mind-managed humanity in a totalitarian state: technocratic in Huxley, Communist in Orwell, and fundamentalist-theocratic in Atwood. Such skepticism about utopias is probably best understood historically, since the twentieth-century experience of totalitarian government and the twenty-first-century experience of religious fundamentalism have not exactly encouraged confidence in the benevolence and rationality of authoritarian regimes. Looking further back, though, and thinking again about Voltaire's Eldorado and Johnson's Happy Valley, it seems that from the novelist's point of view there isn't anything much to be said about human happiness, whereas there are positively endless permutations of human dissatisfaction and defeat.

What makes utopian and dystopian settings so relevant here is that even in all their fantastical extremity they help to cast light on the effects of "realistic" setting because they mark most clearly the duality of fictional worlds as something both ontologically distinct from and dependent on the real world. That is, they describe a world that does not exist and yet they make no sense unless you understand them in relation to the world we like to think we all know – consider, for instance, the clock that strikes thirteen in the famous opening of *Nineteen Eighty-Four* or the all-too-human animals of Orwell's beast fable *Animal Farm* (1945). This is essentially true of all fiction. But I would like to conclude by proposing that it is by virtue of their determined *otherness* that utopian and dystopian settings help to reveal what the settings of all novels do.

Consider, for example, Jonathan Swift's fantastical prose satire *Gulliver's Travels* (1726): in the four books of his journey Gulliver goes to countries run by tiny but vicious Lilliputians, gigantic and civilized Brobdingnagians, speculative and impractical Laputians, and impeccably rational horses, and each of these sojourns asks the reader to look from a different perspective at what he or she already knows. Suddenly taken-for-granted human corruptions and exploitations look unfamiliar and appalling: after reading Gulliver's account, intended to be patriotic and flattering, of Britain's recent history, we might be inclined to agree with the horrified Brobdingnagian king that Gulliver must belong to "the most pernicious Race of little odious vermin that Nature ever suffered to crawl upon the Surface of the Earth."[42] Centuries later, Kurt Vonnegut would recall Swift when he took his Martian view of the United States in *Breakfast of Champions* (1973). On the year of Columbus's "discovery," for example: "The teachers told the children that this was when their continent was discovered by human beings. Actually, millions of human beings were already living full and imaginative lives on the continent in 1492. That was simply the year in which sea pirates began to cheat and rob them."[43] American "icons" – guns, trucks, racism, the electric chair, and others – are all explained (with illustrations) as if to someone from another planet. The settings of utopian and dystopian novels are intended to make us look from a different angle at what we think we already know.

What these alienating fantasies seek to redress is the destruction of perception by familiarity and habit. "Automatization eats away at things, at clothes, at furniture, at our wives, at our fear of war," wrote the Russian critic Viktor Shklovsky: "If the complex life of many people takes place entirely on the level of the unconscious, then it's as if this life had never been."[44] Which is to say that seeing things all the time means that we are really not seeing them at all. And this is where literature comes in, because "in order to return sensation to our limbs, in order to make us feel objects, to make a stone feel stony, man has been given the tool of art": and art estranges or **defamiliarizes** familiar things to allow us to see them as if for the first time.[45] This, Shklovsky argued, is "the very hallmark of the artistic: that is, an artifact that has been intentionally removed from the domain of automatized perception."[46] As Dickens said, "the exact truth" is not enough: in making the world newly strange, fiction makes it newly visible.

Charles Dickens, *Bleak House* (1853)

Many novels are named after the house where the action takes place, and it is often said of novels like *The Castle of Otranto*, *Wuthering Heights*, and *The House of the Seven Gables* that the novel's main character is the house itself, the setting the principal agent of the narrative. But if you look at *Bleak House* in this light, the first thing you notice is how small a part is played by the two houses named "Bleak House." The first Bleak House is John Jarndyce's blandly serene Hertfordshire home where Esther Summerson lives with the wards of Chancery, Ada and Richard; the second is the equally peaceful Yorkshire cottage Jarndyce prepares for Esther and her husband Allan Woodcourt. Neither house appears in the novel for any length of time, and, of all the novel's many architectural spaces, they are the least bleak of all, and the ones of which least can be said. In keeping with the novel's interest in hypocrisy and secrecy, the truly bleak houses of Dickens's novel go by other names.

All the possible titles Dickens considered and rejected before he settled on "Bleak House" made some reference to the abject London slum Tom-all-Alone's, where Jo the crossing sweeper spends most of his miserable life. The slum is a contested legacy long since caught up in the Court of Chancery, and, in view of Dickens's concern with the casualties of the English establishment for which Chancery is made to stand, it makes sense that Dickens might have wanted to emphasize the symbolic significance of Tom-all-Alone's by making it the title of his book. Poverty and decay are the dominant characteristics of this "swarm of misery": "As, on the ruined human wretch, vermin parasites appear, so, these ruined shelters have bred a crowd of foul existence that crawls in and out of gaps in walls and boards; and coils itself to sleep, in maggot numbers, where the rain drips in; and comes and goes, fetching and carrying fever, and sowing … evil."[1]

"They dies more than they lives," the delirious Jo tells Esther on his deathbed: "they dies down in Tom-all-Alone's in heaps" (492). And then they are buried in heaps. The verminous horror of the slum is symbolically linked to the filthy cemetery where lies Nemo, the literal "nobody" who turns out to be Esther's father. This urban cemetery at the very heart of the imperial metropolis is "pestiferous and obscene … a beastly scrap of ground which a Turk would reject as a savage abomination, and a Caffre would shudder at":

> With houses looking on, on every side, save where a reeking little
> tunnel of a court gives access to the iron gate – with every villainy of

> life in action close on death, and every poisonous element of death in
> action close on life – here, they lower our dear brother down a foot
> or two: here, sow him in corruption, to be raised in corruption: an
> avenging ghost at many a sick-bedside: a shameful testimony to future
> ages, how civilisation and barbarism walked this boastful island
> together. (180)

Allusions to "heathen" Turks and Kaffirs mock the imperial hypocrisy of this "boastful island" and all its pretensions to Christian superiority: supposedly "our dear brother" – Dickens is using the language of the Anglican burial ser-vice – the newly dead man is buried under a thin sod riddled with decom-posed corpses that infect the living citizens of the overlooking streets. Never having known anything better than these horrors, the innocent Jo tells Nemo's solitary mourner, Lady Dedlock in disguise, that he'd be happy to uncover the corpse for her with his broom if she wished. "They put him wery nigh the top," he tells her, "They was obliged to stamp upon it to git it in" (262). On her first morning in London Esther remarks Jo's kindred as "extraordinary creatures in rags" (66), as if the residents of Tom-all-Alone's have nothing to do with her; she will learn at great personal cost that there is "not a drop of Tom's cor-rupted blood but propagates infection and contagion … through every order of society" (710).

If one symbolic double for the pauper's pestilential grave is Tom-all-Alone's, another is the moldy chapel at the Dedlock's country estate of Chesney Wold where on Sundays "the oaken pulpit breaks out into a cold sweat; and there is a general smell and taste as of the ancient Dedlocks in their graves" (21). The "cold sweat" of evaporation anticipates the vapors of putrefaction produced by the city cemetery, while that disgusting image of worshipers inhaling the corpses entombed in the church becomes more gruesome still when we real-ize, thanks to the parallel with the reeking city cemetery, that this is quite liter-ally what they're doing. No wonder the venal lawyer Tulkinghorn who learns Lady Dedlock's secret because he can bridge the world of high life and low life is characterized as a "noble Mausoleum" (23): an ominously leaky reposi-tory in a novel insistent that the stink of putrefaction is as uncontainable as the novel's fevers and fogs. Evoking the familiar metaphor of the hypocrite as a "whited sepulcher," where a façade of whitewashed purity denies the rot-ting cadaver within, the "noble Mausoleum" Tulkinghorn is an apt symbol of a society that refuses to recognize its own rottenness.

So the novel works by symbolically bringing together what its culture tries to keep apart: the dead from the living, the rich from the poor. Esther sees her mother for the first time in the church at Chesney Wold and for the last time by Nemo's appalling grave, and when the association of the pauper's grave and the Dedlock church collapses the boundaries between life and death, wealth and poverty, you can see how Dickens advances his argument about the interconnectedness of the society not only through the Chancery plot that brings everyone together (Chancery "has ... its dead in every churchyard" [15]), but through parallel settings. Perhaps the most overt example is in the nicknaming of Krook's disorderly rag and bottle warehouse as "Chancery" because like Chancery it is an incorrigible, intractable muddle of junk. And as the plot links Krook's filthy shop to another seeming opposite, Lady Dedlock's fashionable London world (her former lover Nemo will die in a room above Krook's shop), description does the same kind of work, because when her London house is introduced as "a deadened world, and its growth is sometimes unhealthy for want of air" (20) we might equally be hearing about either Krook's shop or Chancery. That these are all "things of precedent and usage" (20) doesn't sound so bad until you remember what happened to such un-adaptive dinosaurs as the lumbering Megalosaurus of the novel's famous opening paragraph.

The fossil Sir Leicester Dedlock admires Chancery as "a slow, expensive, British, constitutional kind of thing" (25). His own moribund Lincolnshire estate is an equally deadly institution: a dreary, stagnant, waterlogged place, Chesney Wold is evidently not a refuge from the foggy, muddy London streets but a parallel iteration of them: country and city are both implicated in Dickens's diagnosis of national malaise. On a conservative's view the custodians of the national heritage and tradition, Dickens's aristocrats are concerned only with maintaining their own ancient privileges: they represent a far less funny, because more socially powerful, version of the self-interest and nostalgia driving Caddy's father-in-law Mr. Turveydrop, the novel's master of deportment, and Esther's mother-in-law, a Welsh nationalist obsessed by her ancestry. Any talk of reform has Sir Leicester anticipating a bloody peasants' revolt.

Chesney Wold is a feudal country estate, but the estate is no longer the model of good governance and orderly stability it was in a novel like *Mansfield Park*. It is also a gothic mansion, where the figurative skeletons in Lady Dedlock's closet are heard literally to walk, hence the irony of the housekeeper Mrs. Rouncewell's belief that a ghost "is one of the privileges of the upper classes; a genteel distinction to which the common people have no claim" (112). The family tradition attributes the ghost to a woman who betrayed her Royalist husband by secretly passing information to the Parliamentarian revolutionaries in the English Civil War, and the modern counterpart to these revolutionary sympathies is the England of industrial labor: thus Mrs. Rouncewell thinks of her successful industrialist son "as if he were a very honourable soldier, who had gone over to the enemy" (108). In truth, the industrial north in

Bleak House resembles far more closely Elizabeth Gaskell's Milton-Northern in *North and South* than it does the Coketown of Dickens's own *Hard Times*. Associated with dynamism, energy, courage, self-making, and an emergent democracy, and thus presenting an essential contrast to the deadliness of the novel's southern regions, the industrial town in *Bleak House* reminds us that particular settings have to be understood in context and in relation to one another. Here is everything that Dickens considers missing – culturally, politically, and morally – from the country estate and the metropolitan center.

On the smaller scale, too, parallel settings abound. In ironic contrast to the "pleasantly irregular" (86) qualities of Bleak House are the novel's disorderly homes, among them the precarious residence of the selfish aesthete Harold Skimpole, a house full of children who have somehow "tumbled up" like those of Mrs. Jellyby at Thavies' Inn. Intent on "Telescopic Philanthropy," Mrs. Jellyby plans to export Britain's surplus population to establish coffee plantations in Africa; meanwhile her own home is "nothing but bills, dirt, waste, noise, tumbles down-stairs, confusion and wretchedness … like one great washing-day – only nothing's washed!" (219). Mrs. Jellyby nurtures grand ideas about "the Brotherhood of Humanity," but Esther Summerson's characteristically modest verdict that "it is right to begin with the obligations of home … and that, perhaps, while those are overlooked and neglected, no other duties can possibly be substituted for them" is almost certainly the novel's own (58, 83).

The novel begins at the heart of British Empire – its one-word opening sentence is "London" – and looks far outward: critically through the missionary energies of Mrs. Jellyby; heroically through the sea rescue undertaken off the shores of colonial India by Esther's beloved Allan Woodcourt; and redemptively through the comic Bagnets, with their children named for the imperial locations (Malta, Quebec, Woolwich) where their military father was stationed. The overarching argument, though, is that the globe cannot be put in order unless the house – quite literally the house – is put in order first. As when economists and politicians use the metaphor of the "domestic" to speak of the nation, the domestic spaces and places of Dickens's novels add up to a single bleak house. Dickens's England consists of many bleak houses: Tom-all-Alone's; the Dedlock homes in London and Leicestershire; the Court of Chancery and its ironic mirror image in Krook's shop. The reader is asked to reassemble all these parts into a national whole, to see that all these bleak houses are one house, and will stand or fall together.

Chapter 7

Time and history

For many scholars of the early novel, a distinctively new concern with place was accompanied by an unprecedentedly extensive attention to the temporal aspect of human existence: how people change over time, how one time differs from another. Although modern readers tend to take the time component in fiction for granted, "Shakespeare ... had been dead for thirty years before the word '**anachronism**' first appeared in English."[1] This was how Ian Watt argued that pre-novelistic literary forms prioritized what was understood as the timeless and universal over the time-bound and contingent, a hierarchy that the novel would completely reverse; Fielding had used an almanac to ensure historical accuracy in the treatment of 1745 (the year in which *Tom Jones* is set), while Richardson had meticulously dated Clarissa's letters as if to say that it matters when, very precisely, they were written. The novel's concern with human life in time and history is the subject of this chapter, which begins by looking at the panoramic and long-range historical novel and novel sequence, and ends by describing some of the important transformations of narrative time undertaken by twentieth-century writers.

History and story

The eighteenth-century critic James Beattie railed against how earlier romances conflated different historical modes for the sake of an exciting story:

> All facts and characters, real and fabulous; and all systems of policy and manners, the Greek, the Roman, the Feudal and the modern, are jumbled together and confounded: as if a painter should represent Julius Caesar drinking tea with Queen Elizabeth, Jupiter and Dulcinea El Toboso, and having on his head the laurel wreaths of antient Rome, a suit of Gothick armour on his shoulders, laced ruffles at his wrist,

a pipe of tobacco in his mouth, and a pistol and tomahawk stuck in his belt.[2]

That you can imagine this overthrow of historical decorum being attempted only by the comic novel (say, Mark Twain's *A Connecticut Yankee in King Arthur's Court* [1889]) or by a deliberately anachronistic work of postmodernism (a Starbucks-type coffee chain appears in Thomas Pynchon's "eighteenth-century" novel, *Mason & Dixon* [1997]) attests to the importance of modern forms of historical understanding in the novel.

It has often been said that up until the professionalization of history as a discipline, when history embraced a pseudo-scientific emphasis on documentary detail, there were "strongly interactive relations between novelistic and historical narratives, indeed at times an almost agonistic rivalry."[3] If you consider how extensively history even now remains a storytelling art – *this* happened, and then *this* happened, because *this* happened – you can see just how strong the connection between the historical and the literary imaginations, the telling of real-world and fictional stories, might be. The subtitle of Norman Mailer's autobiographical non-fiction novel *The Armies of the Night: History as a Novel, the Novel as History* (1968) suggests that "history" and "the novel" may be understood almost as interchangeable terms.

Leaving aside the "non-fiction novel," which typically tends toward the semi-journalistic "history" of the *present*, the novelist's ambition to meet historians on their own ground is most obvious in the "historical novel" or "historical romance." Although this type of fiction goes back at least as far as Madame de Lafayette's *The Princess of Clèves* (1678), set a century earlier, and Daniel Defoe's remarkable *A Journal of the Plague Year* (1722), a "documentary" account of the Great Plague of London in 1665–6, the invention of the genre is conventionally attributed to the Scottish novelist Sir Walter Scott, whose massively popular fiction influenced novel-reading and novel-writing cultures across the world throughout the nineteenth century. Scott's first and most influential novel *Waverley, or 'Tis Sixty Years Since* (1814) is a coming-of-age story set in 1745, the same year as *Tom Jones* and the year of a political uprising by supporters of the deposed Stuart dynasty, led by the character known in *Waverley* as "the Chevalier," Charles Edward Stuart ("the Young Pretender" or "Bonnie Prince Charlie" depending on which side you were on). The novel's hero, Edward Waverley, is forced to take sides in this conflict between supporters of the deposed Stuarts and the pro-Hanover establishment, and "wavers" between one side and the other, seduced to different sides at different moments by personal allegiances: his uncle's Jacobite (Stuart) loyalties must be measured against his father's role in a government committed to the Hanover succession; his admiration for the brilliant Jacobite Flora McIvor against her indifference to him; the integrity of the government soldier Talbot against the self-serving opportunism of the Frenchified Highlander Fergus.

By the time Scott is writing – sixty years later, the novel's subtitle announces – the national division has been safely sutured. The Jacobites lost this second uprising, and the brutal obliteration of the Highland culture that had shored it up ensured that there would be no third. This is surely what makes it possible for Scott to write in such an even-handed way: you see the glorious as well as the anachronistic qualities of Highland culture; and that, compared to the "backward" people they crushed, the winning Whigs may have had modern history on their side but had little to offer the imagination by way of myth and tradition. So this is a historical novel that is very much about *views* of history: the static, anti-historical traditions of the Stuart-supporting Highlanders versus the Hanover Whig's sense of history as progress and development. Even if Scott clearly subscribes to the latter, like his protagonist he surrenders for a time to the powerful imaginative allure of the former. (In truth even those novels Scott set in the present day are novels about history – see, for example, *The Antiquary*, a novel about the pleasures and pitfalls of a past knowable only in dubious fragments.)

In its relationship to history, *Waverley* is the very model of the nineteenth-century historical novel: it makes history a personal and deeply felt dilemma for its participants; it shows history at work shaping the lives of individuals; it uses historical events to reflect on the nature of historical representation itself; and it revels in the past even as it consigns it very forcibly *to* the past. With some important exceptions such as George Eliot's *Romola* (1865), which is set back in the 1490s, the nineteenth-century historical novel also typically followed Scott in addressing a period still within the range of living memory. This is the case with Leo Tolstoy's *War and Peace* (1869), which is set in the Napoleonic Era of sixty years earlier, the same period addressed in William Makepeace Thackeray's earlier *Vanity Fair* (1848). In both novels, characters' lives are affected (or ended) by the wars ongoing. Dickens's *Barnaby Rudge*, about the Gordon ("No Popery") Riots of the 1780s, and *A Tale of Two Cities*, set during the French Revolutionary terror of the 1790s, likewise follow Scott in tackling events of sixty or so years back, though these are perhaps less satisfying novels than Scott's because they personalize history *too* forcibly (the plot twist at the end of *A Tale of Two Cities*, where we find out what drives Madame Defarge's bloodlust, turns the French Revolution into a private vendetta) and because they tend not take the past as seriously as Scott does, treating it as a benighted precursor to a contrastingly enlightened mid-Victorian present that in less complacent moods Dickens was always ready to denounce.

The influence of Scott and the classic historical novel finds articulation in other ways and in sometimes surprising other places. In part what makes *Waverley* so absorbing is its discovery that different geographical spaces may represent different historical times, so to travel north with Waverley and the government soldiers from the English country estate of Waverley-Honour is to move further back into the history of the British Isles, until finally you get to the lochs, glens, and Gaelic-speaking bandits of the Scottish Highlands. Technically you've moved forward in time – obviously Waverley and the reader are older at the end of the journey than at the start – but symbolically you've moved backward in historical time. That intersection of space and time is what the novel theorist Mikhail Bakhtin was describing when he coined the neologism "**chronotope**," or "timespace," and it is a crucial component of novels that detail how traditional ways of life are lost to the processes of modern industrial homogenization. In Hardy's *Tess of the D'Urbervilles* (1891), for instance, the dairymaid Tess is of the first Wessex generation to be exposed to a modern, standardized education, which means that she and her mother represent "the Jacobean and the Victorian ages ... juxtaposed."[4] It may go without saying that there's potentially a patronizing and even racist dimension to that metaphor of moving "forward" or "backward" in history, as you can see in novels like James Fenimore Cooper's *The Last of the Mohicans* (1826), whose noble Native Americans owe much to *Waverley*'s exotic and obsolescent Scottish Highlanders. Still, nineteenth-century novelists and their readers were plainly interested by a fiction that could address the unevenness of historical development, the multiple temporalities coexisting until recently within a single country, consuming through the medium of the novel historical diversities that could safely be enjoyed only after their neutralization or annihilation.

Twentieth-century historical fiction on the Scott-style theme of a world necessarily but painfully lost ranges from the commercially popular to the critically revered. On the one hand there is Margaret Mitchell's sumptuously trashy *Gone With the Wind* (1936), a novel that inadvertently gave retrospective legitimacy to Mark Twain's witty claim that the pernicious influence of Scott's romantic sensibility on the American South had made the Civil War possible. On the other hand, there is the Italian Giuseppe di Lampedusa's much-admired *The Leopard* (1958), which describes the collapse of the Sicilian aristocracy during the unification of Italy in the nineteenth century. Perhaps di Lampedusa's own aristocratic genealogy helps to explain his sympathetic treatment of the capricious and sometimes tyrannical prince referred to by the novel's heraldic title, but the same cannot be said of the central European Jewish writer Joseph Roth, whose *The Radetsky March* (1932) describes the disintegration of Austro-Hungarian Europe. Roth's novel begins in 1859 with the ennobling of Joseph Trotta, a common soldier and the grandson of Slovenian peasants, for saving the life of the ominously reckless young emperor at the Battle of Solferino, and ends with the death of Trotta's own grandson in the (incomparably reckless) First World War. The haunting pathos of historical novels like this one comes from our knowing what the characters cannot: "still unaware that each of them, without exception, would have an assignation with Death within a couple of years," they cannot "hear the machinery of the great hidden mills that were already beginning to grind out the Great War."[5] The assassination of the Austrian Archduke Franz Ferdinand in Sarajevo late in the novel fills them with horrified disbelief, and yet is the single event for which the reader has been waiting all along.

The elegiac treatment of the deeply conservative Habsburg Empire on the part of the politically radical Roth offers an important reminder of historical fiction's power to illuminate the time of its own writing as well as the period it purports to reconstruct. Soon to take flight from a violently nationalistic, inherently anti-Semitic Nazi Germany that retrospectively made even the reactionary Austro-Hungarian monarchy resemble a beneficent power in central Europe, the Jewish Roth might well have been tempted to look back with regret to the polyglot cosmopolitanism and seeming stability of a pre-1914 Europe.[6] In that respect, it is as much an attack on its historical present as di Lampedusa's *The Leopard*, which, written while a newly republican postwar Italy was attempting to write out its recent fascist past, denounces what it perceives as the cynicism and deceit at the core of Italy's last transformation in the name of progress, under the self-proclaimed "dictator" Garibaldi.

Although di Lampedusa's historical panorama comes in the form of a single novel, modern fiction's historical engagements have often led to the "novel sequence" or *roman fleuve*, a format particularly popular in the first half of the twentieth century, perhaps in quiet resistance to the demise of the multivolume novel of the Victorians. In theory, a novel sequence could simply be two linked novels, as in D. H. Lawrence's *The Rainbow* (1915) and *Women in Love* (1920), which Lawrence had originally intended as a single novel. The two novels (a "dualogy"?) represent a family saga or the story of multiple generations, and though this could be done in a single novel, as, for example, Thomas Mann had shown in *Buddenbrooks* (1901), there's a strong connection between the multigenerational novel and the novel sequence. One of the most popular early twentieth-century examples was *The Forsyte Saga* (1906–34), which won one of Lawrence's near-contemporaries, John Galsworthy, the Nobel Prize for Literature in 1932. Or, later in the century and in an altogether different milieu, there's another Nobel Laureate, the Egyptian Naguib Mahfouz, whose *Cairo Trilogy* (1956–7) spans the period from the First World War through the early

1950s, telling the story of multiple generations of a Cairo family. However, as modern writers as different as John Dos Passos and Paul Auster have demonstrated, a novel sequence need neither represent a long temporal sequence nor be structured around a family, since the events of Dos Passos's "U.S.A. Trilogy" (1930–6) and Auster's "New York Trilogy" (1985–6) are largely synchronous and the characters often unknown to each other.

Among the rewards of the novel sequence are reading pleasures both sophisticated and populist. The most famous *roman fleuve* of all, Marcel Proust's multivolume modernist series *In Search of Lost Time* (1913–27) asks the reader to perform daunting feats of memory, assemblage, and interpretation to put the parts together. This demand led to the critic Joseph Frank's well-known argument that (notwithstanding Proust's title) the modernist novel deployed not a temporal but a "spatial" form because we read in such a way as to try and turn the work into a static pattern, almost like a visual image that can be apprehended in its entirety, rather than reading "forward" as we would more conventionally linear, end-directed novels. On the other hand, there are less rarefied pleasures to be had, as Anthony Powell's *A Dance to the Music of Time* indicates. Published across a staggering twenty-four years, from 1951 to 1975, Powell's series offers a panorama of English public life from the immediate aftermath of the First World War through the second half of the century. It works on the same addictive principles as real-life sociability – gossip, for one. As in Proust, characters from previous volumes return, and, deeply recognizable and yet much changed by time, they create in us the illusion of real-life aging. The illusion must have been doubly strong for those who read Powell's novels as they appeared, aging alongside his characters.

The immense popularity of the novel sequence in a postwar Britain coming to terms with the loss of its status as an imperial superpower speaks to the force of this form as a means of historical documentation. In Britain its public concerns are so dominant that in some respects its most obvious progenitor is not Proust but one of the first English authors he influenced, Ford Madox Ford, whose *Parade's End* tetralogy (1924–8) documented the transformation of Britain from Edwardian times through the First World War and its aftermath. Indeed, with its very sustained public concerns, the postwar English novel sequence may be looking back as far as the nineteenth-century "Barsetshire" novels of Anthony Trollope. Certainly, they have a strongly documentary quality in their detailing of "the way we live now," to borrow a Trollope title, as the lives of characters track the changing of the national culture through periods of geopolitical upheaval such as the Second World War (as in Evelyn Waugh's "Sword of Honour" trilogy and Olivia Manning's "The Balkan Trilogy") and the end of empire (as in Paul Scott's "The Raj Quartet"). The best known of the novels in C. P. Snow's eleven-volume "Strangers and Brothers" sequence (1940–70), is titled, revealingly enough, *Corridors of Power* (1964).

Transformations of time in the modern novel

Although major historical events such as the Dreyfus affair and the First World War certainly appear in Proust, what is so paradigmatically important about *In Search of Lost Time* is not its public but its private temporalities. After all, you need never have read Proust to know that "Proustian" denotes a concern with subjective involuntary memory. When, in the most famous passage of the entire work, Proust's narrator dips a madeleine into his cup of tea, the taste transports him back to infancy, and to an aunt sharing her tea and cake with him on Sunday mornings. That moment early in the sequence has come to seem emblematic of modernism as a whole, with its acute sensitivity to the reversibility and subjectivity of time, to the ways in which the past can make sudden incursions into the present.

There are other modernist moments that might work equally well if you wanted to choose a symbol for the early twentieth-century rejection of standardized linear time. Joseph Conrad's *The Secret Agent* (1907) hinges on a botched counter-terrorist plot to blow up the Greenwich Observatory in London, the point from which World Standard Time is measured, because "the blowing up of the first meridian is bound to raise a howl of execration!"[7] Figuratively speaking, modernist fiction blows up the first meridian all the time, understanding and representing time in unusual ways. You can see something of the change in fictional understandings of time when you notice that, unlike the big, panoramic historical novels that I discussed earlier, perhaps the most important modern novel of all, James Joyce's *Ulysses* (1922), covers only a single day in the life of a city and a citizen. The "day in the life" device had been used earlier (though Joyce didn't know it) in Andrei Bely's *Petersburg* (1913), and would subsequently be put to very various purposes by Virginia Woolf in *Mrs. Dalloway* (1925), Mulk Raj Anand in *Untouchable* (1935), Malcolm Lowry in *Under the Volcano* (1947), and, in our own time, Ian McEwan in *Saturday* (2005).

The cultural historian Stephen Kern has described an extraordinary transformation of time between 1880 and 1920, the period that saw the invention of World Standard Time as well as such distance-obliterating innovations as the telephone and the telegraph, the bicycle, motorcar, and airplane. Time-consciousness is everywhere in this era, Kern shows, and the gap between time as it is measured and time as it is experienced begins to become newly apparent: up until then no one but Sterne had "systematically questioned the homogeneity of time," Kern proposes: "The evidence for it was written on the faces of the millions of clocks and watches manufactured every year."[8] Indeed, it may well be our own ultra-modern experience of carved up schedules, of designated times to be in designated places, that underscores the sheer *heterogeneity* of time, the differences in how it may be subjectively experienced: a really boring two-hour appointment can feel half a lifetime long (to you), while a really engaging one passes before you know it (perhaps others found those same two hours deadly dull). Modernist fiction routinely distinguishes subjective time from time as it is chopped up and spatially recorded by clocks and calendars, and in the work of such innovators as Proust, Woolf, Ford, Faulkner, and Joyce, time may be reversible, fluid, and subjective.

One important caveat before more is said about time in modern fiction: the emphasis placed on modernist and postmodernist fiction in the rest of this chapter should not be taken to imply that the presentation of time in earlier fiction is wholly unremarkable. On the contrary, dealing with temporality has always made technical demands on the novel, which is one reason why such conventions as chapter divisions have proved almost indispensable because, like the changes of scene in the theatre, they can be used to mark the passage of time and bridge the gap between one temporal (or spatial) phase of the novel's action and another. And then there is the complicated business of negotiating between the two treatments of time known as *scene* and *summary*, when the novelist must decide whether to dramatize episodes or summarize *what happened or tended to happen* between one point in the story and another. In *Jane Eyre*, for instance, early "scenes" would include the blow-by-blow descriptions of her incarceration in the Red Room at Gateshead, her arrival at the Lowood School, and the death of Helen Burns. In contrast, you know you are dealing with summary when passages are prefaced by such formulations as: "November, December, and half of January passed away" (after the incarceration in the Red Room); "during January, February, and part of March, the deep snows … prevented our stirring beyond the garden walls" (after her arrival at Lowood); and, most explicitly of all, "I now pass a space of eight years almost in silence" (after the death of Helen Burns).[9]

Pseudo-autobiographies like *Jane Eyre* are told linearly, the protagonist and narrator never deviating from the chronological order in which things happened to her younger self, despite that she knows how it all worked out in the end. Because so many later novelists rejected that linearity, critics have often found it useful to distinguish the sequence of events described in a novel (the "*fabula*" or story content) from the order in which these events are presented to the reader (the "*syuzhet*" or narrative organization). The difference was first posited by Soviet critics in the early twentieth century, writing in the same period in which modernist novelists themselves were experimenting with time, and creating a wider and wider disjunction between the chronology (*fabula*) and the order in which we encounter them in our reading of the novel (*syuzhet*). In *Jane Eyre*, as in many other nineteenth-century novels, there is no conflict between *fabula* and *syuzhet*; in many modernist novels, however, the dissonance between the two is transformative.

In that respect William Faulkner's *The Sound and the Fury* (1929) is the exemplary modernist novel, deploying time shifts within and among its four dated sections. The first part, narrated by the mentally handicapped Benjy Compson, is dated April 7, 1928; the second part, narrated by his Harvard-student brother Quentin, takes us back to June 2, 1910; the third part, narrated by their embittered brother Jason, is dated April 6, 1928; the final section is narrated in the third person largely from the point of view of the Compson's African American servant, Dilsey, and takes place on April 8, 1928, two days after Jason's contribution and a day after Benjy's. So the novel does have a chronological progression to the extent that we end on a later date than the one on which we started, but what happens over three days in April 1928, isn't really the story, the *fabula*, which is almost over already when the novel opens: the characters' childhood and their family's financial ruin, Quentin's suicide, Caddy's disgrace and that of her daughter, all events that we have to reconstruct from their disordered telling. Complicating matters still further, the first two sections are full of unmarked time shifts as the characters relive their memories. Benjy is looking through a fence on to a golf course built on what was once Compson land, and a golfer calling for his "caddie" reminds him of his own long-gone Caddy. Quentin's narrative is also centered on memories of Caddy, replaying his conversations with her. Aptly enough, this second section opens with Quentin pulling his watch apart because "time is dead as long as it is being clicked off by little wheels; only when the clock stops does time come to life."[10] Woolf makes a similar point when she marks the passage of chronological time with the Westminster clocks that chime through *Mrs. Dalloway*. Even if it's the time that runs out on us in the end, linear time is not necessarily the time we live by.

"We agreed that the general effect of a novel must be the general effect that life makes on mankind," the modernist Ford Madox Ford wrote in a memoir of his friend and collaborator Joseph Conrad: "A novel must therefore not be a narration, a report."

> Life does not say to you: In 1914 my next-door-neighbour Mr Slack
> erected a greenhouse and painted it with Cox's green aluminium
> paint … If you think about the matter you will remember, in various

unordered pictures, how one day Mr Slack appeared in his garden and contemplated the wall of his house. You will then try to remember the year of that occurrence and you will fix it as August, 1914, because having had the foresight to bear the municipal stock of the City of Liège you were able to afford a first-class season ticket for the first time in your life. You will remember Mr Slack – then much thinner because it was before he found out where to buy that cheap Burgundy of which he has since drunk such an inordinate amount, though whisky you think would be much better for him! Mr Slack, again came into his garden, this time with a pale weaselly-face fellow, who touched his cap from time to time. Mr Slack will point to his house wall ...[11]

And so on until eventually you put together your story of how Mr. Slack built his greenhouse, a story full of associative reconstructions (the memory of your first-class season ticket helps to pin down the date), impressions (the weasel-faced builder), irrelevances (that cheap Burgundy), and flashes forward (Mr. Slack's weight problem): "And, if that is how the building of your neighbour's greenhouse comes back to you, just imagine how it will be with your love affairs that are so much more complicated."[12] Ford had followed his own advice in *The Good Soldier* (1915).

The Good Soldier is typical of modernist fiction in its "realistic" rejection of linearity *and* its recognition that chronological sequence is tied to our ways of making sense of events. "I have, I am aware, told this story in a very rambling way so that it may be difficult for anyone to find their path through what may be a sort of maze," explains the narrator John Dowell, who is only learning as he goes on what happened to destroy his own marriage and the marriage of his friends the Ashburnhams, but "when one discusses an affair – a long, sad affair – one goes back, one goes forward ... I console myself with thinking that this is a real story and that, after all, real stories are probably told best in the way a person telling a story would tell them. They will then seem most real."[13] Dowell's struggles with narrative ordering make for a demanding reading experience, and for a novel that, like so much fiction of its period, asks us to consider *how* we know what we think we know.

Temporally innovative novels constantly remind us that we organize information sequentially to trace causes and effects and so understand why things happen. But what if there *is* no "why"? The experiment with time at the heart of Martin Amis's *Time's Arrow* (1991) asks us to take this possibility seriously when it narrates all its events in exactly reverse chronological order. The magical realist Alejo Carpentier had pioneered this device in "Journey Back to the Source" (1958), and it appears briefly in Kurt Vonnegut's *Slaughterhouse-Five* (1969), when a war movie is played backward. The technique is not unique to *Time's*

Arrow, then, but this novel puts it to moral and political uses that are especially instructive because they point to the intersection of temporal experimentalism and historical representation in much of the best contemporary fiction. *Time's Arrow* is the life story of a Nazi eugenicist that begins with his death as an old man, a retired doctor, in the United States and works all the way back, via his arrival in America, via his escape, via Auschwitz, via medical school and marriage, to his birth in the German town of Solingen. "Here there is no why," Amis tells us when the protagonist reaches Auschwitz, alluding to the film-maker Claude Lanzmann's "hier ist kein warum" (literally "here there is no why") when he spoke of his monumental film of the Holocaust, *Shoah*: "There is an absolute obscenity in the very project of understanding the Holocaust," Lanzmann had argued.[14] With its realist-style social detail alongside its nightmarish reversal of reason and expectation – because when you watch events backward, doctors appear to be inserting rather than excising tumors, rapists to be healing rather than destroying their victims – *Time's Arrow* manages to convey both the historical reality of the Holocaust and its evil perversity.

As that last example implies, modern fiction may be every bit as concerned with the representation of textbook historical events as were its nineteenth-century precursors. What marks an important difference, though, is that the historical consciousness of modernist and postmodernist fiction is typically accompanied by fairly radical deviations from the linear temporality characteristic of historical narrative. That is, the "traumatic" has become the dominant paradigm for thinking about the impact of history on individuals, which is why so many of these novels should undertake disruptions of common sense understandings of time: trauma is, almost by definition, a deviation from linear time because it means reliving the past in the present. To offer just one recent example, the Haitian-American Edwidge Danticat's *The Dew Breaker* (2004) begins in the present-day United States with an artist travelling to Florida to deliver a sculpture of her father as the Haitian political prisoner she believes he was, but by the end we have been taken back decades to Haiti under the brutal regime which her father served as a "dew breaker," a torturer. Uncovering the past that you don't even realize you are reliving means going backward rather than forward in narrative time.

The literature of political crisis is full of such disruptions and reversals of linear time. The protagonist of Jorge Luis Borges's story "The Secret Miracle" (1944) lives a year between Nazi bullets leaving the guns of the firing squad he faces and their hitting him, while, to stay with the literary canon of the Second World War, throughout *Slaughterhouse-Five*, Vonnegut uses the narrative disruptions of prolepsis (**flashforward**) and analepsis (**flashback**) to describe the permanent effects on one American prisoner-of-war of his witnessing of the

Allied bombing of Dresden in the brutal last spring of the war. Vonnegut's veteran hero, Billy Pilgrim, has "come unstuck in time," so we never get the conventional "masterpiece" of reportage about Dresden the autobiographical narrator intended; rather, the novel declares itself "short and jumbled and jangled ... because there is nothing intelligent to say about a massacre."[15] It is as if to reorganize history into coolly sequential chronological narrative of causes and effects would be to rationalize what should never be rationalized.

One final example in support of my claim that the most historically conscious of modern novels are typically among the most innovative in their treatment of narrative time is W. G. Sebald's *Austerlitz* (2001), in which the main character, Jacques Austerlitz, comes to learn that he was taken as a Czech-Jewish child to Britain when Czechoslovakia was occupied by Germany in 1939. Austerlitz accompanies the narrator to the Greenwich Observatory, the arbitrary home of World Standard Time that Conrad's characters meant to blow up in *The Secret Agent*, where he explains his resistance to linear time, which says what is past is irretrievable:

> I have always resisted the power of time out of some internal
> compulsion which I myself have never understood, keeping myself
> apart from so-called current events in the hope, as I now think, ... that
> time will not pass away, has not passed away, that I can turn back and go
> behind it, and there I shall find everything as it once was."[16]

This novel is full of such time capsules ("everything as it once was"): a Belgian concentration camp preserved as a national memorial; a drowned Welsh village flooded to make a reservoir; a billiards room in an English country house left unopened for a century and a half; the forgotten waiting room at a London railway station, where Austerlitz falls into his past again; last, Austerlitz's old nanny's home in Prague, "where everything was just as it had been almost sixty years ago."[17] Less plausible, more wished-for than the permafrost-preserved body that shows up after seventy-two years in Sebald's *The Emigrants* ("so they are ever returning to us, the dead"), these time capsules remind us that fiction alone can make history revisitable, the devastating past "reversible."[18]

Virginia Woolf, *To the Lighthouse* (1927)

> Time the destroyer is time the preserver.
>
> T. S. Eliot, "The Dry Salvages" (1941)[1]

Woolf's *To the Lighthouse* is a novel in three parts. The first, "The Window," is set before the First World War in the house on the Hebridean island of Skye where the beautiful Mrs. Ramsay spends her summers along with her philosopher husband, her eight children, and invited guests. This is the longest of the novel's three sections and yet it covers the shortest period of "real" time, only a single afternoon and the long evening of a summer's day. In contrast, the novel's middle section "Time Passes," which describes what happens to the house after the Ramsays stop coming, spans ten years in a small fraction of the pages occupied by the novel's opening section. Also much longer than this middle section is the novel's conclusion, "The Lighthouse," which covers only a morning spent at the house by the survivors of the old family; here the painter Lily Briscoe, a longstanding summer guest of the Ramsays, assumes the central role that the now-dead Mrs. Ramsay played in "The Window." In total, then, the time spanned by the novel is more than ten years, but the bulk of the narrative is given over to the less than two days that occupy the novel's first and third sections. Narrative time is elastic, Woolf reminds us: you can write a hundred pages on what passes in the mind in the space of five minutes; you could cover a decade in twenty pages, or five, or one. Indeed, you could cover it in three words if you wanted to ("ten years later").

"Time Passes," the novel's short middle section, is about what Woolf's friend T. S. Eliot spoke of as "time the destroyer" in a poem set on the Atlantic's opposite coast. The temporal accelerations of "Time Passes" are the novelistic equivalent of time-lapse cinematography because what happens too slowly to be captured by human consciousness becomes painfully visible: ocean air peels the paper from the walls; tarnish covers the silver; wilderness reclaims the garden. Only human intervention can preserve objects from time, and yet, as we learn in Woolf's parenthetical asides, human beings cannot save even themselves from time:

> [Mr. Ramsay, stumbling along a passage one dark morning, stretched his arms out, but Mrs. Ramsay having died rather suddenly the night before, his arms, though stretched out, remained empty.]

> [Prue Ramsay died that summer in some illness connected with childbirth, which was indeed a tragedy, people said, everything, they said, had promised so well.]

> [A shell exploded. Twenty or thirty young men were blown up in France, among them Andrew Ramsay, whose death, mercifully, was instantaneous.][2]

Events that might take center stage – the deaths of major characters, one in the major world-historical event of the early twentieth century – are subordinated to clipped sentences in shockingly casual parenthesis. Narrative time, we realize through this stunning reversal of our expectations, is a form of prioritization: if something matters it gets lengthier treatment, while what is understood as trivial can be glossed over (thus ensuring its unimportance). These passages are so powerful because we know, and Woolf knows that we know, just how much these deaths matter, so the dramatic refusal to make them "matter" in narrative time is a powerful way of making us see anew the forces that wrongfully make them insignificant: trite, inadequate popular opinion (the "tragedy" of Prue's death; the "merciful" death of a blown-to-bits soldier); and a mechanized war that has treated human life with the most brutal disregard (were "twenty or thirty" boys wiped out in this explosion? No one's counting).

But, as Eliot put it, time the destroyer is also "time the preserver," and the other sections of the novel take an almost archival approach to consciousness, lavishing narrative space on the workings of time as they are subjectively experienced. This is especially true of the novel's first section, in which, at the same time as Mrs. Ramsay is conscious of what is happening around her – she is knitting socks for the lighthouse keeper's son, helping little James cut pictures from a catalogue, and listening to the older children playing cricket – she is also looking backward and ahead. A single moment encompasses not only the present but also melancholy retrospection and future-oriented feelings of hope and dread:

> But here, as she turned the page, suddenly her search for the picture of a rake or a mowing-machine was interrupted. The gruff murmur, irregularly broken by the taking out of pipes and the putting in of pipes which had kept on assuring her, though she could not hear what was said (as she sat in the window which opened on the terrace), that the men were happily talking; this sound, which had lasted now half an hour and had taken its place soothingly in the scale of sounds pressing on top of her, such as the tap of balls upon bats, the sharp, sudden bark now and then, "How's that? How's that?" of the children playing cricket had ceased; so that the monotonous fall of the waves on the beach, which for the most part beat a measured and soothing tattoo to her

thoughts and seemed consolingly to repeat over and over again as she
sat with the children the words of some old cradle song, murmured
by nature, "I am guarding you – I am your support," but at other times
suddenly and unexpectedly, especially when her mind raised itself
slightly from the task actually in hand, had no such kindly meaning, but
like a ghostly roll of drums remorselessly beat the measure of life, made
one think of the destruction of the island and its engulfment in the sea,
and warned her whose day had slipped past in one quick doing after
another that it was all as ephemeral as a rainbow – this sound which
had been obscured and concealed under the other sounds suddenly
thundered hollow in her ears and made her look up with an impulse of
terror. (19–20)

How long has all this taken? What lasts for one long paragraph on the page can
pass in the mind in a single revelatory second.

All that has "really" happened here is that the others have fallen silent,
allowing Mrs. Ramsay to hear what their voices obscure, the roll of the waves
on the beach, which occasionally she hears and finds consoling ("I am guarding you – I am your support"). The narrative mode here is iterative, recounting
habitual happenings ("for the most part … but at other times"), a common
way of representing time in essentially retrospective novels like those of Woolf
and Proust, perhaps because it is only after the fact that the repetitious quality
of huge swathes of a life becomes apparent. Here, iteration is interrupted by a
new "event," the non-event of sudden silence, and yet the events for which it
stands comprise Mrs. Ramsay's lifetime (because it makes her feel that she has
wasted her life in "one quick doing after another") and looks far, far beyond
her death, to the disappearance of even the ground on which she stands ("the
destruction of the island and its engulfment in the sea") as time and the waves
do their eroding work on the coastline. As Mrs. Ramsay sits in the window in
this present time, past and future find articulation in her thoughts, and "time"
itself can stand for something as private as time in the individual mind or
as global as the geological time brought into sight by the scientists working
during Mrs. Ramsay's Victorian childhood, the sweep of time that dwarfs the
human lifespan, and even human history altogether.

Perhaps because "The Window" is set in the lost era of Woolf's own distant
childhood, this is the part of the novel in which characters are most unre-
mittingly concerned with the future. "Children don't forget," Mrs. Ramsay
says over and over: "Never will they be so happy again" (66, 62). She tries to
manage the future by repeating the past, encouraging marriages between Paul
Rayley and Minta Doyle and between Lily Briscoe and William Bankes that
might extend into the future the kind of life she has had with her husband (we

later learn that the Rayley marriage hasn't worked out, that the Bankes marriage never happened). Her husband, an academic who fears for the resilience of his scholarly reputation, reads the then deeply unfashionable novels of Sir Walter Scott in order to reassure himself that a fall from public favor need not mean that a writer is bad, no longer worth reading. When in "Time Passes" Mr. Ramsay's mildewed books are thrown out of the crumbling house to be dried in the sun, Scott's novels alone are mentioned by name, as if to prove that everything is indeed as perishable, here literally perishable, as Mr. Ramsay fears.

Except it is not. After all, *we* remember those novels and what they meant to Mr. Ramsay, and we remember even when there's no one left in the world of the novel who still can. The Waverley novels thrown out on the lawn are among a number of objects that appear in multiple sections of the novel, drawing our attention to how objects move through time. Most revealing among them is the boar's skull introduced at the end of "The Window." James likes having it hung in the bedroom, but it terrifies his little sister Cam, so Mrs. Ramsay wraps a shawl around it, assuring James that the skull is still there, while telling sleepy Cam that it is "like a beautiful mountain such as she had seen abroad, with valleys and flowers and bells ringing and birds singing and little goats and antelopes" (117). Years later, housekeepers will encounter this skull as they try to put the house right after years of neglect, and wonder why the family hung it on the wall. Only the reader knows the answer. And when the skull returns at the end of the novel it is never named as such. Cam, dozing on the boat that will take her to the lighthouse, thinks of "a hanging garden; it was a valley, full of birds, and flowers, and antelopes … She was falling asleep" (207). In her drowsy state she is thinking back to her mother's improvised bedtime story from many years earlier, and we remember that story though Cam cannot. Though Mrs. Ramsay knew all along that "children don't forget," she leaves a legacy that only the reader can identify as such. In a novel so profoundly concerned with the depredations of time, memory preserves.

Chapter 8

Genre and subgenre

"Why pick up what literary history so resolutely discards?"
John Sutherland, *Bestsellers* (2007)[1]

"I adore stories that push on inexorably, frightening stories," Flaubert's Emma Bovary explains: "I detest common heroes and temperate feelings, the way they are in life."[2] In view of the incongruity of Emma's sensationalist reading matter with her unromantic provincial scene, she seems to have found herself in the wrong kind of novel, in one of those realistically muted novels she deplores ("common heroes and temperate feelings"), rather than in the formula fictions she likes to read, with their "frightening stories," their "stories that push on inexorably." I mentioned earlier that Emma's own story picks up the qualities of the books she reads as it rushes "inexorably" to abandonment and ruin, madness and suicide, rejected conventions of an older escapism sneaking into Flaubert's ultra-modern realism. As Flaubert implies, and for reasons I hope to outline in this chapter, the barrier dividing "**genre fiction**" from "literary fiction" is never really as stable as it appears.

Genre fiction/literary fiction

The difference is clearly considered great enough to warrant literary and genre fiction occupying distinct sections of bookstore and library shelves. Genres are separated from one another in categories titled "mystery," "romance," "fantasy," and the like, and all separated from the miscellaneous titles classified as "literature" or "literary fiction" or just "fiction." So if you were looking for one of Patricia Cornwell forensic mysteries, you would probably know not to look under "C" in the alphabetized literary fiction section, though if you went there anyhow you would find that some "genre" novels seem to have made it to that elevated position. Here, under "C," are some apparently misplaced **espionage novels** like Joseph Conrad's *Under Western Eyes* (1911), and some seemingly misplaced **detective novels,** like Arthur Conan Doyle's *The Hound of the Baskervilles* (1902). But these "finds" probably wouldn't surprise you one bit: the packaging of these novels as, say, Penguin Classics, World's Classics, or Modern Library volumes, tells you that these particular texts have attained "classic" status. Genre novels no more, they're now Literature.

So much for the prohibition on judging a book by its cover, the repackaging of these "classic" genre novels that distinguishes them from their like tells you that these novels are soliciting the attention of a group quite different from their first readers a little over a century ago, the era from which most of our "classic" genre novels date: such stories of adventure as Robert Louis Stevenson's *Kidnapped* (1886) and Rider Haggard's *King Solomon's Mines* (1885); **science fiction** novels like H. G. Wells's *The Invisible Man* (1897) and *The War of the Worlds* (1898); espionage novels like John Buchan's *The Thirty-Nine Steps* (1915), along with those novels of Conrad and Conan Doyle. If you are thinking about the implied audience of these works, that historical coincidence is extremely significant. In Britain, the Education Act of 1870 had made elementary education mandatory, leading to the birth of the mass-market daily newspaper and a potentially massive public for fiction. But the potential novel market fragmented as well as expanded: there would be something for everyone, but not all of it would be valued equally. That books initially addressing a populist audience now appear under prestigious publishing labels (Penguin Classics and so on) tells you at least as much about contemporary understandings of what constitutes the literary, and what constitutes literary *interestingness,* as it does about the books themselves. Who decides what makes a novel a "classic"? And who buys these books? If the "classic" status of these novels is evidenced in their repackaging as such, it is secured by their inclusion on college syllabi, and although teachers typically assign a novel only if it is easily available in print, it's only likely to stay in print because people choose to teach it.

This may be felt to represent a mechanical view of what constitutes the classic: Surely "classic" just means "good"? Surely the book has, as the common phrase has it, "transcended its genre"? Perhaps. But *prestige* is an institutional question rather than a qualitative one; like all teachers of the novel, I can think of many works of fiction I would assign if I could count on their availability.

Not all good novels are brought back into print or continuously reprinted (let alone as "Classics"); not all good novels can be assigned in time-bound English courses; and not all good novels speak to the interests of the literary critical profession at a particular historical moment.

Literary value and its arbiters

Any consideration of genre fiction must engage such institutional questions: questions of literary judgment not simply in the sense of "how good is this novel?" but in the sense of "who gets to decide?" For example, some critics have been concerned about a genre hierarchy that so forcefully marginalizes the novels that most readers of fiction actually read. Isn't this simply a form of snobbery, a way of making respectable this most democratic of literary forms by installing an artificial hierarchy within it? The literary canon, many critics have come to believe, is as much the product of political as aesthetic discriminations (so white, so male, so European) and in this regard it is worth considering how the novel, the only literary form that continues to command a huge audience, has to be stripped of its populist aspects in order to be considered worthy of serious attention.

Of course the hierarchy can work both ways, because even if "classic" fiction is very accessibly priced (out of copyright, these older novels can be cheaply reprinted), in another sense they're made inaccessible by virtue of their status as cultural monuments. By this I mean that even if "classic" connotes "worthwhile and improving," it also connotes dull, good for you in that cheerless sense in which cod liver oil and wheatgrass are good for you. This is surely what drove one British publisher of popular women's fiction to seize Jane Austen's novels from the passionless hold of the classic reprint publisher and to repackage them in 2006 as what's disparagingly categorized as chick-lit. The publishers presented this as a homecoming for the author they now designated the godmother of modern women's fiction, and, with their glossy pastel covers (pale peach for *Pride and Prejudice*, baby pink for *Sense and Sensibility*) the old Austens in new covers looked like all the other mass-market titles directed at young women, books about friendship, nice possessions, gorgeous men, and happy ever after.

In view of the endless cinema and television adaptations of Austen that keep her culturally present, the relatively low cost of reprinting older works, and the degree of free publicity this sort of venture was bound to attract, this was obviously a bright publishing idea. However, it raises an important point: that, in their extreme conventionality, genre novels allow us to see features of the so-called mainstream or literary novel that we wouldn't otherwise neces-sarily pay much attention to. As the great mid-century critic Northrop Frye explained, the point of thinking in terms of genre is "not so much to classify as to clarify … traditions and affinities, thereby bringing out a large number of literary relationships that would not be noticed as long as there were not context established for them."[3] If Austen is about more than female friendship, possessions worth having, desirable men, and happy ever after, it does her and her readers a disservice to say that she's not interested in these things at all, as if these matters are somehow beneath her dignity or ours. At least since Richardson's *Pamela*, the novel has been peopled by heroines who, albeit in their more modest way, are as keen on nice new clothes and rich handsome men who recognize their worth as those of any twenty-first-century romance. Typically you won't find anything in mass-market fiction that isn't primarily a monomaniacal amplification of interests to be found in the most canonical or "classic" of novels. Dickens's *Bleak House* and *Our Mutual Friend*, for instance, are police procedurals – among other things.

What makes the example of chick-lit particularly revealing, though, is that it is at just about the bottom of the novelistic hierarchy, in much the same relationship to the literary novel as the novel itself bore to the other liter-ary arts when it, too, was primarily associated with women. Writing in 1929, Virginia Woolf was among the first to point out that ideas of what constitute a subject worth writing about say less about literary importance than about its arbiters:

> It is the masculine values that prevail. Speaking crudely, football and sport are "important"; the worship of fashion, the buying of clothes "trivial." And these values are inevitably transferred from life to fiction. This is an important book, the critic assumes, because it deals with war. This is an insignificant book because it deals with the feelings of women in a drawing-room. A scene in a battlefield is more important than a scene in a shop – everywhere and much more subtly the difference of value persists.[4]

Here Woolf draws attention to the extent to which criticism of even the once-"feminine" novel is marked by patriarchal values that attribute importance *only* to fictional scenes that *only* men can write. Sport matters and clothes don't. Politics are serious; relationships are slight. Novels about men at war are prized; novels about ordinary life are not. Tolstoy matters more than Austen. By 1929 Woolf would also have known that, with their disempowered heroes, their reallocation of enemy status from those men fight to those who sent them out to fight, their anger and their black comedy, modern war novels can be in their own way as formulaic as romances.

Genre fiction as cultural text

So one way – though not the most satisfying way – to resist the hierarchies that distinguish genre fiction from literary fiction, and the different genres from one another, would be to say that these distinctions are arbitrary, elitist, and politically invested, and just leave it at that. Another would be to point out that good writers, writers like Conrad and Austen, wrote terrific thrillers or romances, while mediocrity isn't confined to the genre novel; and thus the only meaningful critical hierarchy is between good novels and bad novels, not between literary and genre fiction. These are all defensible positions. However, in at least one important respect literary criticism has rendered the literary fiction/genre fiction distinction less important than it once was. The word "criticism" comes from the Greek *krinein*, which means "to decide" or "to separate," but academic literary criticism is generally less concerned than it once was with aesthetic judgments, tending rather to see its object of study as one among many forms of cultural expression. The implicit question of "is this novel any good?" – which was never a real question when its presence on a syllabus had already presupposed the answer – is less relevant to many historically minded critics and students than "what does this novel tell us about the culture or cultures of which it is a part?" The bestselling novel may be "as short-lived as a camera flash," John Sutherland explains, but is also "as capable of freezing, vividly, its historical moment."[5] Nothing beats a popular novel for explaining the culture that made it one.

To read "symptomatically" is to ask yourself: "Of what in its culture is this novel, or aspect of the novel, a symptom?" This approach to literature cuts across the old distinction between high and low culture in order to let us see in new ways our object of study, which might well be either *Middlemarch* or *The Maltese Falcon*. "Symptomatic" is a really unfortunate term to the extent that it implies a sick or neurotic culture to which the critic assumes the superior position of physician or analyst, but, in practice, reading texts as articulations of historically and culturally specific concerns can allow us to think differently and more capaciously about both the text and the world of which it is a part.

And both genre fiction and the canon-to-be can be equally useful archives for thinking about particular cultural moments. For example, the golden age of the detective novel, the 1890s through the 1930s, was also the era of modernism, while the heyday of the espionage novel comes in the mid-to-late twentieth century at the same time as postmodernism. Now consider the highly influential definitions offered by the critic Brian McHale when he argues that modernist fiction is characterized by *epistemological* questions, questions of knowledge, and postmodernist fiction by *ontological* questions, questions of being.[6] You can see what McHale means by "epistemological" when you think about, for example, how modernist fiction deploys untrustworthy, limited, or shifting narrative perspectives that force you to weigh up the evidence, to consider how you know what you know: this is the work of "detection," with the reader as investigator. Sometimes the relationship between modernism and the detective plot is obvious: William Faulkner's *Sanctuary* (1931) is a brutal, sensationalist novel of rape and abduction, a confessed potboiler (Faulkner said he'd written it for money), but it also deploys many of the wrong-footing narrative techniques that made Faulkner's other novels modernist classics.

Likewise, McHale's sense of postmodernism's predominantly "ontological" interests becomes clearer if you consider how postmodernist fiction is concerned with the interchangeability of the fictive and the real, with the construction and multiplication of worlds; they, like the espionage novel, are driven in part by the paranoia induced by those half-glimpsed national and international systems that condition our lives. The world of intelligence is, Michael Denning argues in his study of spy fiction, "a shadowy figure for the social world of late capitalism where the opacities that surround human agency are cut through by projecting an essentially magical figure, the secret agent."[7] So McHale's distinction between the epistemological (problems of knowledge) and the ontological (problems of being) applies to formula fiction, too, responding in its more conclusive ways ("an essentially magical figure") to the same historical conditions. On this view, modernism and postmodernism, fictions of detection and espionage, are all "symptomatic" phenomena.

Reading for the ways in which a novel or kind of novel gives voice to the culture that produced it allows us to take seriously fiction read outside the academy – romances, mysteries, even children's literature. We can learn much about a culture from knowing what millions of its members read for pleasure. How do you explain the popularity of the Harry Potter novels? How do you explain the success of Dan Brown's *The Da Vinci Code* (2003), one of the bestselling novels of all time? You might well be correct in proposing that "everyone" read these novels only because everyone *else* was reading them – all commodities, literary and otherwise, benefit from hype – but the nature of their phenomenal popular appeal might tell us more than that: about contemporary attitudes toward Christianity, high culture, and history, for instance.

I imagine readers of the *Times Literary Supplement* and the *New York Review of Books* were less excited by, say, *The Da Vinci Code* and the publication of the fifth Harry Potter novel than by some of the other much-hyped novels being published around the same period: novels such as Mark Haddon's *The Curious Incident of the Dog in the Night-Time* (a comic murder mystery narrated in the first person by a severely autistic teenager), Monica Ali's *Brick Lane* (about a Bangladeshi woman removed to Britain in an arranged marriage, told from her point of view), Lionel Shriver's *We Need to Talk About Kevin* (an epistolary novel about a fictional high school massacre). These last three are all recognizably "literary" novels in ways that *The Da Vinci Code* and *Harry Potter and the Order of the Phoenix* are not. Nonetheless, if you put together the literary and popular novels of the same era, you get a fair snapshot of a culture's obsessions at that particular moment: Christianity and Islam and the relationships between them; anxieties about terrorism and other forms of orchestrated violence; the sometimes comic, sometimes redemptive, and sometimes tragic incomprehensibility of the young.

Originality and expectations

The reason I mentioned the narrative forms of the "literary" novels – free indirect discourse (*Brick Lane*), unreliable first-person narration (*The Curious Incident of the Dog in the Night-Time*), epistolary (*We Need to Talk About Kevin*) – is this: form matters for literary fiction in a way it typically doesn't matter for most genre fiction, which, however implausible its content, is usually traditionally "realist" in its narrative methods. It is because form matters that Haddon's *Curious Incident of the Dog in the Night-Time* is my favorite of the 2003 novels named above. Thanks to its limited narrative perspective we see much more of what's really going on than the narrator can (he suffers from Asperger's Syndrome), and yet it is these very "limitations" on his part that make it impossible for us to feel superior because they enable us to see familiar novelistic subjects (feelings, friendships, family relationships) in completely unexpected ways. In the context of genre, the most relevant point is this: the book both is and isn't "original." It takes the fairly conventional novelistic theme of domestic relationships and offers a slanted perspective on it (because what would "ordinary" relationships look like if you couldn't actually interpret them?). It is also a crime novel, the title announces, but the "crime" is quite other than in any conventional murder mystery: like Henry James's classic *What Maisie Knew* (1897) this turns out to be a story about adultery where information is filtered through a child's only ambiguously comprehending point of view, but, unlike *What Maisie Knew*, it is substantially a comic novel.

A sense of genre, of literary kinship, is potentially an aid to interpretation because when we are able to recognize the codes that a novel is deploying we readers find ourselves on common ground with its author – a *convention* is quite literally a "coming together." We tend to think of "originality" as a paramount value and devalue genre accordingly, but what the literary novel shares with its populist relatives is that it arrives in the world already in relationships with other novels. Of course, we all know that this is true of the genre novel, which relies on expectations formed from reading other novels of its type ("it was a dark and stormy night"), and some genre novels use these expectations in playful ways, as when Arthur Conan Doyle sets up *The Hound of the Baskervilles* as a gothic novel about a preternaturally massive ghost dog that haunts the Baskerville heirs, only to let Sherlock Holmes solve the problem in his characteristically rational way – as we always knew he would. But, crucially, we bring expectations to the literary novel, too, as the reader-response theorist Hans Robert Jauss showed when he wrote that all literary works assume a "horizon of expectations":

> A literary work, even when it appears to be new, does not present itself as something absolutely new in an informational vacuum, but predisposes its audience to a very specific kind of reception by announcements, overt and covert signals, familiar characteristics, or implicit allusions. It awakens memories of that which was already read, brings the reader to a specific emotional attitude, and with its beginning arouses expectations for the "middle and end," which can then be maintained intact or altered, reoriented, or even fulfilled ironically in the course of the reading according to specific rules of the genre or type of text.[8]

Seen in this light, the difference between genre fiction and literary fiction becomes a difference of degree rather than type because all novels are read in relation to one another. Where the relationship to other novels is most explicit, we either dismiss a book as "generic" or praise it for its "allusiveness" or "**intertextuality**" depending on how self-conscious and sophisticated we take those relationships to be. The critic Alastair Fowler suggests that even the most seemingly generic, the most slavishly imitative of literary works extends the genre to which it belongs; the relationship between text and gender is, he argues, "not one of passive membership but of active modulation."[9]

The idea of the "horizon of expectations" helps us to explain why a particular novel seems so *significant* an accomplishment, so "original." That is, a novel might actively *extend* the "horizon of expectations" that we brought to it. It might extend the horizon in formal terms, as when you read a novel that is doing something technically that you've never seen before. Or it might extend the horizon in social, political, or moral ways by raising a new cultural problem or question. So making *originality* the primary characteristic dividing the elevated literary novel from the devalued genre novel is rather more complicated than it seems. One the one hand, if a novel were truly original it could never have been written, let alone read, in the first place; on the other, only by understanding how a novel relates to others can we see why it's important and exciting (or not). Thus we get to see both the similarities and differences between formula and literary fiction when every new text "evokes for the reader (listener) the horizon of expectations and rules familiar from earlier texts, which are then varied, corrected, altered, or even just reproduced."[10] We pick up a novel and begin to speculate about what kind of thing we are dealing with: a true genre novel would prove us correct, according to Jauss's schema, where a really important novel would prove us wrong. There is certainly pleasure to be had in having your expectations fulfilled – but any novel reader knows the pleasure of having them overturned.

Graham Greene, *The Ministry of Fear* (1943)

"Let me lend you the History of Contemporary Society. It's in hundreds
of volumes, but most of them are sold in cheap editions: *Death in
Piccadilly, The Ambassador's Diamonds, The Theft of the Naval Papers,
Diplomacy, Seven Days' Leave, The Four Just Men ...*"

Graham Greene, *The Ministry of Fear* (1943)[1]

When the twentieth-century British novelist Graham Greene divided his fictions into "novels" and "entertainments," he implied a qualitative distinction
familiar to all students of the novel. So, to give the examples of two books
already mentioned, Greene's *The End of the Affair*, about an illicit wartime relationship ended by a religious conversion, was published as a "novel," whereas,
with its page-turning plot, its lowlife gangsters, and its seedy, sensational aura
of degradation and crime, *Brighton Rock* was "only" an entertainment. But all
readers of Greene know what's wrong with the distinction: that some of his
"entertainments" are at least as complex and rewarding as his "novels," rendering the terms useless for separating good fiction from bad. This interchapter
makes a case study of one of Greene's best-known "entertainments," *The
Ministry of Fear*, a spy novel that reflects explicitly on the nature of genre fiction. While it's tempting to say that what differentiates literary fiction from the
genre novel is that the former resembles life while the latter resembles only
other novels, this is the very distinction that *The Ministry of Fear* overturns.

Set during the bombing of Britain during the Second World War, *The
Ministry of Fear* opens at a fund-raising fete in London. The depressive Arthur
Rowe, newly released from a mental hospital after the mercy-killing of his ter-
minally ill wife, attends the fete because it reminds him of his idyllic upper-
middle-class childhood in rural Cambridgeshire, of a time when he had no
adult responsibilities and nothing to feel guilty about: "The fete called him
like innocence," Greene writes: "It was entangled in childhood, with vicarage
gardens and girls in white summer frocks and the smell of herbaceous borders
and security" (3). Mistaking him for someone else, an amateur fortune-teller
gives him the key to winning a prize cake, which the organizers of the fete then
try to make him give up. Though Rowe doesn't know it yet, the cake holds a
roll of film, images of government documents captured by a traitorous spy ring
and destined for Nazi Germany. First a misshapen dwarf from the spy ring
tries to poison him; then Rowe finds himself at a séance where he is framed for

the murder (a faked murder) of the implausibly named businessman "Cost" in order to get him out of the way; and, when that doesn't work, the spy ring tries to kill him with a bomb that leaves him safely amnesiac. In the second half of the novel, Rowe, liberated by amnesia from his guilt over his wife's killing, destroys the spy ring, and slowly comes to learn his true identity, by which time he has fallen in love with the Austrian refugee Anna Hilfe, mirror image of his dead wife, and the sister and unwilling accomplice to the leader of the Nazi fifth column.

Recounted thus, the novel's plot sounds absolutely preposterous – a charity ("Comforts for Mothers of the Free Nations") that is really a Nazi espionage ring; top-secret documents stashed inside a cake and delivered via a rigged competition at a fete; dwarves with poison; murders staged at séances; amnesia and self-reconstruction; the gorgeous woman sidekick (whose name means "help" in German!). But that is precisely Greene's point. At one point in the novel, Rowe dreams that he is back in his childhood home, telling his doting mother what has happened since her death:

> "This isn't real life any more," he said. "Tea on the lawn, evensong, croquet, the old ladies calling, the gentle unmalicious gossip, the gardener trundling the wheelbarrow full of leaves and grass. People write about it as if it still went on; lady novelists describe it over and over in books of the month, but it's not there any more."
>
> His mother smiled at him in a scared way but let him talk; he was the master of the dream now. He said, "I'm wanted for a murder I didn't do. People want to kill me because I know too much. I'm hiding underground, and up above the Germans are methodically smashing London to bits all round me. You remember St Clements – the bells of St Clements. They've smashed that – St James, Piccadilly, the Burlington Arcade, Garland's Hotel, where we stayed for the pantomime. It sounds like a thriller, doesn't it, but the thrillers are like life – more like life than you are, this lawn, your sandwiches, that pine. You used to laugh at the books Miss Savage read – about spies, and murders, and violence, and wild motor-car chases, but dear, that's real life: it's what we've all made of the world since you died … The world has been remade by William Le Queux." (54)

With that reference to William Le Queux, the popular, prolific, and wildly paranoid genre novelist of the early twentieth century, Greene proposes that what would once have seemed pure fantasy ("spies, and murders, and violence") is now, perversely enough, a form of historical record. The most falsifying kind of escapism, in contrast, comes in what *purports* to be realistic but is really just a seductive reconstruction of a way of life that no longer exists – if it ever did: "lady novelists describe it over and over in books of the month, but it's not there any more," he tells his mother in the dream. The rural idyll of "tea on the lawn, evensong, croquet, the old ladies calling, the gentle unmalicious gossip" really does sound like a fiction, the product of an evasive nostalgia analogous to those escapist desires that bring Rowe to the pseudo-fete in the first place, the desires for which he is punished by being dragged into the *unbelievable* present.

"Is life really like this?" Rowe asks the investigator unraveling the bizarre plot: "This is life," he responds, "so I suppose one can say it's like life" (145). The sense that genre fiction can tell you something essential about the non-fictional world that produced it ("thrillers are like life"), helps to explain not only the commercial popularity of *The Ministry of Fear* and the Fritz Lang film it almost immediately became, but also the high critical regard in which both are held as classic treatments of wartime Britain. The spy thriller format helps to articulate the hallucinatory strangeness of the experience of living in London in those times, when – to give examples from the novel – you couldn't know whether or not your street would still be there in the morning, or whether any telephone number you dialed would be answered in an undamaged building or ring out indefinitely into blitzed space. Waking up each morning requires "getting to know a slightly different London" (170). In *The Ministry of Fear*, a constantly shifting cityscape and the dreamlike displacements of the espionage plot ultimately become the same thing. "It's as if one had been sent on a journey with the wrong map," Rowe thinks, in a topographic comparison that identifies his frighteningly disempowered situation as victim of a bizarre conspiracy with the situation of all his fellow citizens trying to get around a city altered nightly by bombing (146). Like all wartime citizens, Rowe has to habituate himself to "life taking him up and planting him down without his own volition," even if it means being "directed, controlled, moulded, by some agency with a surrealist imagination" (69, 81).

With its concerns with obscure conspiracies, national belonging, disenfranchisement, and betrayal, the espionage novel speaks to the insecurities and uncertainties of living in a country at war: "Nobody's got a right to his life these days," Greene's detective tells an unwilling witness, "you are being conscripted for your country" (151). Writing around the same time, Elizabeth Bowen made a similar point about the contingency of knowledge and the limits of agency in wartime when she used the form of the espionage novel to write about the Blitz in *The Heat of the Day* (1949), a novel in which the heroine falls in love with a man who may be exploiting his intelligence work to convey state secrets to Nazi Germany. "The whole thing's so completely unreal," he protests when she finally voices her suspicions: "it's immaterial, crazy, brainspun, out of a thriller."[2] But the impossible proves all too true, and with this self-conscious insight about the *motivated* implausibility of the wartime spy novel, Bowen makes the same point as Greene: that extraordinary deviations from "common sense" expectations may be giving voice not only to genre formulae but to historical conditions.

Chapter 9

Novel and anti-novel

If the novel is truly no longer novel, then many of our critical procedures for discussing it will need revision; perhaps, even, we shall do well to think of another name for it.

> Bernard Bergonzi, *The Situation of the Novel* (1970)[1]

Or you can declare at the very start that it's impossible to write a novel nowadays, but then, behind your own back so to speak, give birth to a whopper, a novel to end all novels.

> Günter Grass, *The Tin Drum* (1959)[2]

As early as 1752 at least one critic of the novel had reached the amusingly premature conclusion that "all the variety of which this species of literary entertainment is capable, seems almost exhausted, and even novels themselves no longer charm us with novelty."[3] That everything had already been done in the novel would become a recurrent complaint, but it reached its apotheosis around the middle of the twentieth century, in the decades that followed the spectacular technical accomplishments of modernist fiction. As Bernard Bergonzi put it in 1970, the postwar novelist "has inherited a form whose principal characteristic is novelty, or stylistic dynamism, and yet nearly everything possible to be achieved has already been done."[4] What could be done in fiction that the generation of Joyce and Kafka, Woolf and Faulkner, hadn't already accomplished? "They're like cats which have licked the plate clean," conceded Henry Green, himself one of the most powerfully original novelists of the next generation: "You've got to dream up another dish if you're to be a writer."[5] As the narrator of Grass's *The Tin Drum* suggests in the passage I quoted above, claims about the depletion or obsolescence of the novel have typically been only the starting point for some of its most spectacular modern achievements.

Magical realism

Among those achievements is Grass's own most famous novel, *The Tin Drum*, the fictional autobiography of the demonic Oskar Matzerath from birth to the age of thirty. It is written from the mental asylum to which he has been consigned for a murder he never committed – though he accepts responsibility for other deaths, such as those of his "presumptive fathers," as he always designates them, Jan Bronski (caught by Nazis, thanks to Oskar) and Alfred Matzerath (fearing Red Army reprisals he fatally swallows the Nazi Party badge that Oskar hands him). Oskar's story is the story of Germany from the rise of Nazism through the so-called economic miracle of the postwar period, a historical chronicle of perhaps the darkest moment in modern European history. But it's a chronicle with a difference, and the difference resides in the fantastical Oskar himself: he claims to have arrested his own growth at the age of three (for most of the novel he is precisely three feet tall, though he grows thirteen inches and a fairytale hunchback toward the end); he has a voice that can carve inscriptions on glass; and at one point he successfully convinces a carved infant Jesus to take a turn on his famous tin drum. Incorporating such deviations from natural law and common sense expectation into its otherwise historical and real-worldly mode, and writing as if these wild impossibilities are every bit as factual as the Nazi rise to power, *The Tin Drum* isn't realism but magical realism, one of the most powerfully influential forms of writing in twentieth-century world fiction.

Although magical realism is a truly international form, other practitioners including such geographically diverse writers as the Indian-born Salman Rushdie, the Czech-born Milan Kundera, and the English Angela Carter and Jeanette Winterson, the term emerged in South America and is most closely associated with the Latin American "Boom" of the 1960s: with the Cuban Alejo Carpentier, who had coined "lo real maravilloso" ("the marvelous real") to describe the history of Latin America; with the hugely influential Argentine writer Jorge Luis Borges; with the Mexican novelist Carlos Fuentes; and, especially, with the Colombian Nobel-laureate Gabriel García Márquez. People return from the dead in Márquez's *One Hundred Years of Solitude* (1967), and the local priest can levitate. Some years the gypsies who visit remote Macondo bring natural wonders like magnets and ice; another year they bring a flying carpet and a man who has been turned into a snake for disobeying his parents. In the world of magical realist fiction, a flying carpet is no more remarkable than a magnet. Nor, indeed, is it any less real: this form of novel reminds you that all fictional worlds are indeed fictional, that realism is no less fabricated than the fantastical.

The famous fiction boom in mid-century Central and South America offers a crucial corrective to the postwar "death of the novel" argument, because superlatively original novels were clearly still being written. As Salman Rushdie pointed out, the postwar complaint about the novel being a defunct form betrayed all sorts of First-World, imperially nostalgic prejudices on the part of literary critics, prejudices that made it possible to speak of the perceived irrelevance of the contemporary Western European novel as if this were the condition of the contemporary novel in its entirety. Even supposing that the European novel were as tired out as these critics supposed (and Rushdie disagreed there too), "only a Western European intellectual would compose a lament for an entire art form on the basis that the literatures of, say, England, France, Germany, Spain, and Italy were no longer the most interesting on earth."[6]

Compounding the problem is that the "death of the novel" claim not only equated the novel with the *European* novel, but with the *realist* novel. In part, what drives magical realism and many other postwar fictional modes is a widespread sense that what purports to be realistic captures only the most consensual, limited versions of reality. In Muriel Spark's ingenious first novel, *The Comforters* (1957), the heroine is writing a literary-critical book titled, of all things, *Form in the Modern Novel*. Asked how her monograph is coming along, the heroine admits to "having difficulty with the chapter on realism" – as well she might in a novel in which she hears her own author typing out her thoughts in the very instant she is having them.[7] Spark would later speak for many postwar writers when she admitted to her own "difficulty with … realism," holding that "realistic novels are more committed to dogmatic and absolute truth than most other varieties of fiction."[8] Realism, on this view, pretends that reality is something stable, single, and wholly knowable; in fact, the mid-twentieth-century French theorist Roland Barthes went so far as to characterize it as "a totalitarian ideology of the referent."[9] (The "referent" is the thing to which a word is understood to refer.) The rejection of the realistic mode might be understood as a gesture toward pluralism and relativism, an embrace of multiplicity, uncertainty, and possibility.

The rise of metafiction

Spark's *The Comforters* identifies one common way in which postwar writers would rejuvenate the novel: by making the nature of a novel part of the story it tells. Novels like this we term metafictional, and metafiction is often considered a key component of the postmodernist novel. As Patricia Waugh explains in her invaluable introduction, metafiction is "fictional writing which self-consciously and systematically draws attention to its status as an artefact in order to pose questions about the relationship between fiction and reality."[10] This kind of novel "lays bare the device," as the Russian Formalists of the 1920s would put it; by openly exploring its own procedures it explodes the illusion of transparency, solidity, and actuality on which realist fiction relies.

Metafiction has been a vital component of the novel from its earliest days. I've already discussed a number of early novels that are acutely aware of their own status as fiction – novels such as *Don Quixote, Tom Jones,* and *Tristram Shandy* – and it's worth noting that works like these weren't necessarily "one-offs" but rather imagined themselves in a kind of tradition. Witness the genealogy declared in Denis Diderot's homage to Cervantes and Sterne in *Jacques the Fatalist* (1796). This is the story of a journey, à la *Don Quixote*, taken by the servant Jacques and his unnamed master, and it opens not with a description of the characters and their situation but by denying, like a more belligerent Tristram Shandy, the reader's request for that necessary context: "How had they met? By chance, like everybody else. What were their names? What's it to you? Where were they coming from? From the nearest place. Where were they going? Does anyone really know where they're going?"[11] Throughout the novel, the narrator constantly addresses – and frequently harangues – the reader, and by the end this willfully digressive, interruptive, ribald novel is not only plagiarizing Sterne ("I have a particular regard for Monsieur Sterne," Diderot tells us), but announces itself doing so ("absolutely no doubt that this is indeed plagiary").[12] Even if we think of the realist novel, fiction that maintains the illusion of its reality, as the "traditional" novel, there may be a case for saying that the *truly* traditional novel is in fact quite the opposite, as one scholar of the self-reflexive novel argues when she writes that "realism" is simply a period designation – roughly, the nineteenth-century novel – masquerading as the novelistic norm.[13]

The more conventional reading of the history of the novel says that only in the second half of the twentieth century did metafiction become the dominant novelistic mode, even as realist novels continued (and continue still) to be written. There are many reasons for this postwar predominance. Back in 1884 Henry James had complained that the problem with the novel was that it had "no air of having a theory, a conviction, a consciousness of itself behind it," but think of how much changed in the following decades, of how many modernist writers – James, Conrad, Woolf, Ford, and others – were also authors of classic statements, essays, and manifestos on the art of the novel (many of which I've quoted in this book).[14] This heightened self-consciousness about novelistic technique is surely one of the factors behind the rise of metafiction. And then there was also the modernist attraction to the *Künstlerroman*, the novel that traces the development of the artist, because it's a short step from prewar novels about novelists to the fully self-reflexive fiction of the postwar period: after all, the protagonist of André Gide's modernist *The Counterfeiters* (1925) is writing a novel titled – yes – *The Counterfeiters*. To these literary-historical explanations should be added such institutional factors as the emergence of literary theory in France during the 1950s and 1960s, and the postwar institutionalization of creative writing as a discipline in North American universities. This self-conscious kind of fiction is nothing if not a hybrid of the creative and the theoretical.

The French critic and novelist Alain Robbe-Grillet wrote in 1963 that "we seem to be tending increasingly toward an age of fiction in which the problems of style and construction will be lucidly considered by the novelist, and in which critical preoccupations, far from sterilizing creation, can on the contrary serve it as a driving force."[15] Robbe-Grillet was a key founder and spokesperson for what would become known as the *nouveau roman* or "New Novel." This was less a program for how the novels of the future should be written – "Each novelist, each novel must invent its own form" – than a rallying cry for the extension of modernism's exploratory impulses into the second half of the century: "no one would dream of praising a musician for having composed some Beethoven, a painter for having made a Delacroix, or an architect for having conceived a gothic cathedral," he wrote, arguing that nineteenth-century realism was still being upheld as the model for all novels.[16] But the nineteenth-century classic's chronological sequences, linear plots, and stable conclusions imply "a stable, coherent, continuous, unequivocal, entirely decipherable universe" that no one can believe in a century later, Robbe-Grillet explained, which is why, "by blinding us to our real situation in the world today," "the systematic repetition of the forms of the past is not only absurd and futile, but … can even become harmful."[17] Realism, he followed the prewar modernists in thinking, simply isn't *real* any more, a denial of the conditions under which we actually live.

Postmodernist fiction is also continuous with modernism in its demand that the reader collaborate in the making of meaning. One of Robbe-Grillet's contemporaries, Roland Barthes distinguished between what he called *lisible* and *scriptible* forms of fiction. A *lisible* – usually translated "readerly," though it means "readable" or "legible" – novel is the kind usually termed "realist," in which an omniscient narrator guides us through a story and directs our responses to it. In contrast, a *scriptible* or "writerly" text makes us almost co-authors because our participation is required. If *Middlemarch* is a read-erly text, Joyce's *Finnegans Wake* is the exemplary writerly text because mean-ing is never self-evident but something you have to labor to produce, with no expectation that the meaning you derive is anything like the meanings made by other readers. Indeed, one of the things that *Finnegans Wake* is a wake *for* is the traditional novel – perhaps not the most important casualty of 1939, but certainly one of the endings the novel implies.

Not least because the distinction between readerly and writerly tends to rest on such a caricatured version of realist "readerliness" – of course, all reading is *necessarily* collaborative, participatory – it is impossible not to notice the preference being given to the experimental "writerly" novel. The writerly text means democracy, as Barthes presents it, because it redresses the traditional power imbalance between the powerful author and the passive reader. The opposition is analogous to one he draws elsewhere between the "work" and the "text" to distinguish between ways of reading: whereas the literary work is the singular masterpiece of a genius, to be approached with timid reverence, the text is something we "play" as we'd play a musical instrument: it is plural, com-posite, and endless; as Barthes reminds us, the word "text" is derived from the Latin *texere*, to weave, and connotes a multiplicity of strands: for Barthes, texts are always and only constituted of quotations without quotation marks. You can see one fictional outcome of this insight that all texts are *by definition* intertextual, fundamentally citational, in the "index of plagiarisms" that mate-rializes toward the end of Alasdair Gray's novel *Lanark* (1981), when the hero meets his shambling, incompetent author.

By making paratextual apparatus such as an index part of the text itself, and in emphasizing the graphic surface of the text through the use of illustrations, varying fonts, and newspaper-style columns, *Lanark* is a typical postmodern-ist novel in emphasizing its own status as a material object in order to ref-use the reader the illusion of unmediated, transparent narrative on which the realist novel traditionally depends. Gray might have included on his index of plagiarisms one of the most striking experimental novelists of the 1960s, B. S. Johnson, who much earlier had performed a number of dramatic tricks with the materiality of the text: Johnson's *Albert Angelo* (1964) had holes in some later pages that allowed the reader to look through the cut-out to see what hap-pens next. His *The Unfortunates* (1969) is among the best-known "writerly" (if scarcely the most read) texts of the 1960s. A book-sized boxful of unbound chapters, *The Unfortunates* asks readers to shuffle the sections and read in any order they please, enforcing readerly participation by fighting against even the linear "beginning-middle-end" **codex** form of the bound book. Julio

Cortázar's contemporary *Hopscotch* (1967) works in a similar way, as its title suggests, by directing you to different, non-sequential chapters, making you move through the book in a non-linear way. As with the subsequent development of "Interactive Fiction" in the early years of the personal computer, postmodernism's 1980s heyday, these superficially participatory, game-like formal strategies soon teach you the limits of your apparent freedom. Not only does *The Unfortunates* come with its first and final sections marked as such, but you discover after a few attempts that if the novel doesn't have one "correct" order it certainly has an order that looks more like one than the others, while the treasure hunt style of *Hopscotch* directs your reading more visibly than any nineteenth-century **intrusive narrator** ever could.

In any case, it would be a mistake to treat the experimental novel as a wholly "writerly" project when, so much for the erosion of authorial power and the attendant empowering of the reader, many of the most radical postwar experiments leave you little to do except marvel at the novelist's virtuoso achievement. For example, the famous constraint operating in Georges Perec's *A Void* (1969) is its refusal to use words that contain "e," in French the most commonly appearing letter of the alphabet. The novel's original title is *La disparition* (which cannot be translated literally because there are three "e"s in "The Disappearance") and its plot recounts the sudden vanishing of the beautifully named Anton Voyl ("vowel" in French is *voyelle*) or Anton Vowl (in English editions). Though the novel's plot is absorbing enough, as mystery stories typically are, the reader's desire for immersion is denied by the substantiality and materiality attained by the very words on the page. We cannot *not* be aware of Perec's constraint, can never read the language as if it were transparent, a window looking on to the world of the novel.

Using the same metaphor of transparency, the American postmodernist John Barth presented the challenge to the postwar novelist schematically but handily when he asked: "Are you more interested in the thing said than in its saying (the Windex approach to language) or vice-versa (the stained-glass approach)?"[18] What makes *A Void* such fun to read is that it pulls the reader in both directions: language narrates the mystery plot but also narrates itself. Novels working around a verbal constraint are sometimes even more "stained-glass" than this. To take one extreme example, another novel more often read about than read, the first twenty-six chapters of Walter Abish's *Alphabetical Africa* (1974) are determined by the admission of a single letter of the alphabet (the first chapter is all "a" words, as in the title, the second all "a" and "b" words, and so on); in the next twenty-six chapters, letters are removed in the reverse order from that in which they were added ("z" disappears, then "y," and so on). Impressive? Certainly. Participatory? Not so much.

Writing and rewriting

In a more welcoming form, the novelist John Fowles made a similar argument to that of Barthes about the ideological dimensions of narrative form when he rhetorically renounced his authorial power in his bestselling *The French Lieutenant's Woman* (1969). Set in the 1860s, the story tells of an upper-class amateur paleontologist Charles Smithson, who, engaged to the bourgeois heiress Ernestina Freeman, finds himself attracted to Sarah Woodruff, a "fallen woman" known locally as "the French Lieutenant's whore." The early part of the story is told in the omniscient narrative style predominant during the period in which the story is set, but chapter 12 ends with what reads like an old-fashioned cliffhanger (again, common at the time of the novel's setting) as Sarah lingers by an upstairs window. Is she going to commit suicide? No, Fowles reminds us that we've seen her since. The real cliffhanger is the question, which we take to be rhetorical, at the end of the chapter: "Who is Sarah? Out of what shadows does she come?"[19] The next chapter opens thus:

> I do not know. This story is all imagination. These characters I create never existed outside my own mind. If I have pretended until now to know my characters' minds and innermost thoughts, it is because I am writing in (just as I have assumed some of the vocabulary and "voice" of) a convention universally accepted at the time of my story: that the novelist stands next to God. He may not know all, yet he tries to pretend that he does. But I live in the age of Alain Robbe-Grillet and Roland Barthes; if this is a novel, it cannot be a novel in the modern sense of the word.[20]

Fowles has "broken the frame," reminding us of the essential unreality of the world he has created with scrupulous attention to the illusion that omniscient narration serves: that what we are reading is (we collude by pretending) real. But "in the age of Alain Robbe-Grillet and Roland Barthes," that illusion won't do. Such narrative interventions underscore the perceived political implications of narrative forms. If "authorship" shares its political connotations as well as its etymological origins with "authority," it must be questioned for Fowles fully to engage and challenge the repressions at the heart of its plot: Will Charles choose "fallen" Sarah over ladylike Ernestina? Can Charles transcend the values of his culture? Can any of us?

What makes *The French Lieutenant's Woman* so characteristic a postmodernist novel is its concern with *rewriting*; it self-consciously remakes the Victorian novel. The critical recycling of preexisting cultural forms is one hallmark of postmodernist fiction: John Gardner rewrote the Old English classic *Beowulf* from the monster's perspective in *Grendel* (1971); in *Foe* (1986) J. M. Coetzee rewrote *Robinson Crusoe* from the perspective of a fictional woman who has shared Crusoe's captivity and subsequently been silenced by patriarchal history; and in *Wide Sargasso Sea* (1966) the Dominica-born Jean Rhys rewrote Charlotte Brontë's *Jane Eyre* from the perspective of the first Mrs. Rochester, the West Indian heiress whom the hero marries for her money and incarcerates in Thornfield Hall. You can see from those examples that the act of rewriting is implicitly political, reexamining materials from historically unacknowledged or marginalized perspectives; and although it admittedly sounds like a parody of political correctness to speak of the *Beowulf* monster in those terms, the moral and political force behind books like *Wide Sargasso Sea* and *Foe* certainly comes from their foregrounding the stories that Brontë and Defoe couldn't or wouldn't want to tell. You can see here the impact on the novel of the social justice movements of the 1960s – the women's movement and Civil Rights, for instance – when you consider how concerned postwar fiction is with stories that have previously gone untold.

If one strand of postmodernist rewriting was a political "speaking back" to the canon – *Beowulf, Robinson Crusoe, Jane Eyre*, and so on – another was recuperating what had never made it into the canon in the first place. What pop art was doing with advertising images in the 1960s, much contemporary fiction was doing with what the culture traditionally thinks of as lesser, ephemeral forms of writing: folklore, fairytale, children's books, and so on, critically revising the hierarchy that separates high from low art. Some early postwar rewritings are sobering, as when William Golding turned the boys' adventure story into a parable of human savagery in *Lord of the Flies* (1954), while later ones tend to be more emancipating in spirit, as in Angela Carter's short story collection *The Bloody Chamber* (1979), which rewrites well-known fairytales to bring out their subtexts of violence and eroticism: Carter's Little Red Riding Hood falls asleep between the wolf's tender paws, while a rewriting of "Beauty and the Beast" ends with the heroine shrugging water from her lovely new fur, as if for beauty to turn beast is sexier and more liberating than for the beast to become a man.

Postmodernism, politics, history

It is indicative that anonymous texts like myths and fairytales should supply material for postmodernist rewriting. These are texts without an original, and which belong to no one; again "authorship" is symbolically being renounced. Like *The Arabian Nights*, another important source of inspiration for postmodernist writers, these narratives have been transcribed, translated, and compiled, but not necessarily *authored*. This both appeals and contributes to a particular strand of the modern literary imagination, which privileges the provisional, plural, and impermanent over what purports to be universal, singular truth. For the postmodernist, reality itself is culturally constructed – and thus rewritable – rather than somehow universal or to be taken for granted. In his famous shorthand definition of postmodernism the cultural theorist Jean-François Lyotard wrote of an "incredulity toward metanarratives": among those "metanarratives," or overarching explanatory stories, is history itself, the authority and objectivity of which is now thrown into doubt.[21]

You see that skepticism in the frequency with which postmodernist fiction addresses the borderline between the fictional and the real by, for example, including in their fictional stories historical figures, people who really lived and yet whom we can access only through their media representations, their textual selves. For sure, the novel has, at other historical moments, included real-life figures – Queen Caroline is a character in Scott's *The Heart of Midlothian*, Mary, Queen of Scots a character in *The Princess of Clèves* – but these incorporations typically work to underwrite the authenticity and actuality of fictional stories by anchoring them to the real world. Postmodernist fiction, in contrast, uses these "celebrity" characters to cast doubt on the nature of historical knowledge itself, as when the Indian Prime Minister Indira Gandhi becomes a fantastical Cruella de Vil in Salman Rushdie's *Midnight's Children* (1981); when the historical Richard Nixon is raped by the mythical Uncle Sam in Robert Coover's *The Public Burning* (1977); when Harry Houdini shows up as a character in E. L. Doctorow's *Ragtime* (1975); when John F. Kennedy's presumed assassin becomes the protagonist of Don DeLillo's *Libra* (1988); when Marilyn Monroe is the heroine of Joyce Carol Oates's *Blonde: A Novel* (2000). These are the concerns of a postmodern culture of media-consciousness, a society of the spectacle, a culture of simulacra, being contemporaneously theorized by intellectuals such as Guy Debord (*Society of the Spectacle* [1967]) and Jean Baudrillard (*Simulacra and Simulation* [1985]). In the late twentieth century many novelists and theorists alike claimed that image precedes *and* determines reality "Is she fact or is she fiction?" asks the advertising slogan of the winged high-wire artist, Fevvers, in Angela Carter's *Nights at the Circus* (1984). In a late capitalist, hyper-mediated culture of the celebrity and the commodity (and Fevvers is both) Carter knows that it probably makes no difference.[22]

That even history is available to us only as text is the provocation for and central argument of many of these novels. The point is emphatically not that past events never *happened*, but that we can know them only in mediated forms, filtered by their representations, and that histories, the shaping and explanatory narrative records of these events, are contingent and humanly constructed.

"History isn't what happened. History is just what historians tell us," writes Julian Barnes in his novel *A History of the World in 10½ Chapters* (1989): "We make up a story to cover the facts we don't know or can't accept: we keep a few true facts and spin a new story round them. Our panic and our pain are only eased by soothing fabulation; we call it history."[23] Barnes's playful novel is one example of a very familiar late twentieth-century form that Linda Hutcheon has influentially termed "**historiographic metafiction**."[24] Historiography stands in the same relationship to history as metafiction does to fiction: if history is what happens, historiography reflects on how we write what happens; if fiction is storytelling, metafiction reflects on how we tell stories. If history has been written, it can be rewritten.

Not all instances of historiographic metafiction are as lighthearted as the beginning of Barnes's alternative history of the world, which opens with the story of Noah's Ark as seen from the point of view of a stowaway woodworm; see, for example, D. M. Thomas's controversial *The White Hotel* (1981), about a fictional patient of Freud's who dies in the Babi Yar massacre of Ukrainian Jews in 1941; Michael Ondaatje's *The English Patient* (1992) about the end of the Second World War as seen from the colonial perspectives that would subsequently get written out of a glorious Anglo-American story of good triumphing over evil; and Ian McEwan's *Black Dogs* (1992), set around the fall of the Berlin Wall, about a man trying to reconstruct a forty-year-old encounter with evil in the immediate aftermath of the Nazi occupation of France.

This is obviously a far cry from experiment for experiment's sake. While the departure from realist norms in postmodernist fiction served straightforwardly artistic ends for many of its most celebrated practitioners, weaning readers away from asking *what* happens and asking them to focus on the language that "happens," novelists would also give these newly self-referential narrative strategies a sharply political twist when they applied them to the problem of how *historical* narrative is constructed and understood. The relationship between narrative experimentation and historical representation is the subject of the coming interchapter on Thomas Pynchon's postmodernist classic, *The Crying of Lot 49*.

Thomas Pynchon, *The Crying of Lot 49* (1966)

Early in Pynchon's reworking of the detective novel, the suburban housewife Oedipa Maas learns that she has been assigned the task of executing the will of a former lover, the real estate mogul Pierce Inverarity. This daunting task will soon be dwarfed by a greater source of bafflement: Oedipa may have stumbled upon an ancient postal conspiracy stretching across two continents, from dynastic medieval Europe through a seemingly historyless modern California. But does the Tristero postal system really exist? Or is Oedipa losing her mind? Or is this a massive hoax orchestrated by the dying trickster, Pierce? Oedipa never finds out – nor do we.

The southern Californian setting of Pynchon's novel evokes the famous Los Angeles novels of Raymond Chandler, whose private eye can be counted on to get to the bottom of even global conspiracies. Pynchon's rewriting of a populist form, the detective novel, is an exemplarily postmodernist strategy, bridging the divide between high and low art. Such rewritings can produce pure kitsch, Pynchon announces at the outset, when Oedipa recognizes the muzak in the supermarket as "the Vivaldi Kazoo Concerto," high art (Vivaldi) bathetically rendered in a vulgar medium (the kazoo, of all absurdities), but *The Crying of Lot 49* will show that rewriting can also be more productively transformative, turning the familiar challengingly unfamiliar.[1] That detective fiction is Pynchon's source is particularly significant because this is the genre most concerned with the exposure of secrets by solitary human ingenuity. The novel details the failure of that paradigmatic belief that "all you needed was grit, resourcefulness, exemption from hidebound cops' rules, to solve any great mystery" (100).

Obsessed by the 1960s television investigator Perry Mason, Oedipa's lawyer is incapable of understanding that Perry Mason is a fictional character; he is one of many characters in the novel for whom the fictional and the real are interchangeable. Likewise, Oedipa's co-executor Metzger, a former actor who cannot differentiate between war and those war movies in which he acted. "I know this part," he tells her as they watch one of his old films, "For fifty yards out the sea was red with blood. They don't show that" (24). The suspicion that the fictional and the real may be interchangeable explains the novel's concern with "world making." "I'm the projector at the planetarium," a theater director tells Oedipa, "all the closed little universe visible in the circle of that stage is coming out of my mouth" (62); and Oedipa recalls a painting she once saw depicting girls imprisoned in a tower embroidering a tapestry "which spilled out the slit windows and into a void, seeking hopelessly to fill the void ... and the tapestry was the world" (11). To "project a world" as Oedipa keeps supposing she must (64, 69), is an image of solipsism because it places the perceiving individual in the role of sovereign creator; but the tapestry is also a gesture of expansiveness, to want to break out of your own solitude to imagine something greater than your perceiving, projecting self. The joke that Oedipa's destination is San Narciso is self-explanatory, but for all that Oedipa suspects that reality is intractably subjective, she is still motivated to unravel the Tristero conspiracy. The self-reflexive dimension is clear: if metafiction is, as in the title of Linda Hutcheon's book, "narcissistic narrative" because it cannot help looking at itself, Pynchon clearly wants the novel to be able to look outward even as he knows that such looking is always going to be distorted, privatized by the idiosyncrasies of the perceiving agent.

So what does Pynchon see? Well, even otherwise hostile critics have conceded that the best postmodernist fiction "constitutes an intellectual attack upon the atomized, passive and indifferent mass culture which, through the saturation of electronic technology, has reached its zenith in Post-War America" and that its sense of representational crisis comments sharply "on the historical crisis which brought it about."[2] *The Crying of Lot 49* supports those claims: haunted by his time as a used car salesman, Oedipa's husband, Mucho, "could never accept the way each owner, each shadow, filed in only to exchange a dented, malfunctioning version of himself for another, just as futureless, automotive projection of somebody else's life" (5). American commodity culture means attempting to satisfy metaphysical need with material acquisition: the dealership for which Mucho works is a member of the (too good to be true, but it is) National Automobile Dealer's Association, NADA, and so above the parking lot a sign waves "nada, nada, against the blue sky" (118). Or think of the "nothing" that is Pynchon's atomized San Narciso: "less an identifiable city than a grouping of concepts – census tracts, special purpose bond-issue districts, shopping nuclei, all overlaid with access roads to its own freeway" (13). Oedipa looks at this city and wants it to mean something, but ultimately wonders if the hints of meaningfulness she encounters are "only some kind of compensation" for the loss of transcendent meaning, compensation for her "having lost the direct, epileptic Word, the cry that might abolish the night" (95).

This is one of the novel's many references to Pentecost, celebrated on the fiftieth day after Easter Sunday, commemorating the moment when the apostles were given the gift of communicating in foreign tongues. Although tongues are literally ripped out in the fake Jacobean revenge tragedy through which Oedipa encounters Tristero, the Pentecostal image of linguistic plurality is deeply appropriate to a novel of global consciousness, a novel in which globalization is both the inevitable outcome of postmodern American capitalism and the challenge to its otherwise deleterious effects of atomization and ahistoricism. Cashing in on the Beatles' success, the novel's fake British band ("Blimey" says one; "Lord love a duck" says another [25–6]) are the comic face of globalization, but there are others less funny. Consider Pierce's new housing development, boasting an artificial lake into which are sunk "restored galleons, imported from the Bahamas; Atlantean fragments of columns and friezes from the Canaries; real human skeletons from Italy; giant clamshells from Indonesia" (20).

Let's pause on those skeletons since Oedipa doesn't. Here, they're just one component of a list of imported commodities for American dwellers of luxury homes, American solipsism having reached such a pitch that "real human skeletons from Italy" are no more remarkable than "giant clamshells from Indonesia." Surely this is what it means to be "sensually fatigued," the phrase Pynchon uses of Jacobean England's ominously gory tragedies, when decorative atrocity lies at the bottom of the luxury lagoon (49). The imported bones turn out to be the bodies of Second World War soldiers, while others become charcoal to make the filters for the cigarettes that Oedipa sees advertised on television: there is nothing that cannot be made grist to the corporate mill, Pynchon implies, and, just as bodies are turned into ash and ink in the violent Jacobean play Oedipa sees, they're turned into ash and decorative objects in Pynchon's postmodern America. The historical – and geopolitical – implications become clear when we learn that Oedipa's therapist, the deeply unfunny Dr. Hilarius, prescriber of tranquilizers to California housewives, has done his internship at Buchenwald, as if, knowing no moral boundaries, high capitalism is as corruptible as Nazi corpse-making was corrupt. At one point in the novel Oedipa learns in an army surplus store of a massive domestic demand for Nazi uniforms and swastika armbands: "This is America," she rebukes herself: "you live in it, you let it happen" (123).

A revelation of a kind, then, but the book refuses to give Oedipa the consolation of a conclusive ending: even in the novel's final sentence Oedipa still awaits the potentially revelatory "crying of lot 49" at the auction. But this isn't how postmodernist fiction works: if the novel is to culminate in a revelation we have to write it ourselves. The Tristero organization may or may not connect the Old World and the New; that the potential for reducing human beings to things certainly does is the never-to-be-spoken revelation that I take from *The Crying of Lot 49*. My purpose in giving historical motivations to the novel's formal withholdings is to suggest that characterizing metafiction as fiction about fiction is emphatically not to say that fiction is the *only* thing it is about.

Chapter 10

Novel, nation, community

> She had dedicated herself … to making sense of what Inverarity had left
> behind, never suspecting that the legacy was America.
>
> Thomas Pynchon, *The Crying of Lot 49* (1966)[1]

What seemed a private quest on the part of Pynchon's Oedipa Maas has suddenly turned public. The dead Pierce Inverarity has left behind not a private game for a former girlfriend, but a shared legacy: even in this atomized and narcissistic postmodern culture Oedipa sees that she remains part of a community, one among many of the collective inheritors of "America." Perhaps this comes as an unexpected revelation in a novel so preoccupied by what divides rather than unites people, but it is also a deeply significant one because it speaks to the novel's resources as a form. That is, because novels are typically both subjective and intersubjective, about social existence but also about individual experiences of social existence, among all the major literary genres this is the one most strongly associated with the imagining and perpetuation of communities. If there's one reason why the novel is the dominant literary form in the world today, this may be it.

Representing the part and the whole

A novel makes a part of something stand for the whole thing. Rhetoricians call this trope "synecdoche," the figure of speech by which a poem's sheep are "fleeces" and its ships "masts." Not even the most compendious of novels can include everything, so some fragment is made to *represent*, to stand in place of something larger than itself: in *The Crying of Lot 49* the freeway represents San Narciso; San Narciso, the American city; the American city, America.

Instructively, *representation* is also the characteristic form of democratic governance: elected leaders *represent* constituencies; they *stand in for* larger groups of people. Representation, then, is the common ground between politics and the novel: the fragment stands for something that cannot be presented in a 1:1 relation. If the novel really could include the world and if a parliament or senate could accommodate all of us we probably wouldn't need either of them.

A novel may be quite explicit about its "representative" qualities. The initially puzzling subtitle of the early American writer Charles Brockden Brown's gothic novel *Wieland* (1798) is "An American Tale": a common late eighteenth-century designation, the "national tale" formula alerts us to the representative nature of the story. The title character of *Wieland* kills his wife at the behest of a mysterious voice, and we never find out whether he was driven by a religious delusion or by an evil trick carried out by the sinister, dangerously fine-spoken ventriloquist Carwin. Why "an American tale"? What is it about the United States that this freakishly odd story stands in for? Perhaps it's the young country's ominously fanatical sense of its own mission? Or perhaps the possibility that your voice may be "thrown" articulates the anxieties of a new democracy? After all, the novel is set on the eve of American independence and written in the early days of representative government: and, in the context of democracy, what happens if what *sounds* like your "voice" is nothing more than a treacherously convincing illusion?

Perhaps needless to say, such explicit concern with representation, voice, and the fragment that stands for the whole is not unique to novels interested in politics in the traditional sense of governance. "Sixty million and more" reads the famous dedication to Toni Morrison's *Beloved* (1987), the story of the former slave Sethe who has murdered her infant daughter rather than see her enslaved. Sethe's story is the part that stands for the whole to which the dedication directs us, sixty million being an estimate of slavery's victims. And as the centrally canonical stature of *Beloved* attests, scholars in recent decades have been particularly attracted to novels that articulate perspectives traditionally kept from view. This is a form of narrative redress, the inclusion of the voices of those who have historically been subordinate, voiceless, and disempowered (what theorists sometimes refer to as "subaltern" perspectives). And although the relationship between fiction and the representation of communities may seem primarily a matter of content – a matter of who and what a novel represents – it has massive implications for narrative form.

Take, for example, the Nigerian novelist Chinua Achebe's very widely studied *Things Fall Apart* (1958), which tells the story of European imperialism from the perspective of those colonized during the so-called "scramble for Africa" at the end of the nineteenth century. Achebe's novel constitutes a riposte to

Joseph Conrad's *Heart of Darkness*, a corrective to its dehumanizing treatment of the Africans subjected to colonial rule: Conrad was "a bloody racist," Achebe famously announced in a talk on *Heart of Darkness*: "a thoroughgoing racist," he later amended.[2] First published under the British imprint Heinemann Educational, Achebe's novel has an "educational" dimension evidenced from the outset where we see how a Western readership is assumed: "Having spoken plainly so far, Okoye said the next half a dozen sentences in proverbs. Among the Ibo the art of conversation is regarded very highly, and proverbs are the palm oil with which words are eaten."[3]

Who is speaking? Someone who knows the Igbo/Ibo people well enough to generalize in an almost anthropological way about their habits ("Among the Ibo … "), but someone who is also speaking from *inside* that group, as you see when he confirms the Ibo taste for proverbs by deploying one himself ("proverbs are the palm oil with which words are eaten"). But to whom is he speaking? A reader who was also a member of this society wouldn't need to be told about the high regard in which "the art of conversation" is held. The narrative *enacts* rather than simply describes a community, and it does this by marking the difference between the insider (the narrator) and the outsider (the implied reader).

The reader's presumed ignorance substantially shapes Achebe's style because it makes for a heavily adjectival manner ("Okonkwo had just blown out the *palm-oil* lamp and stretched himself on his *bamboo* bed" [my emphasis]), and it means that the progress of the story is frequently interrupted by extensive explanation ("A snake was never called by its name at night, because it would hear. It was called a string").[4] The awkwardness of that almost pedantically explanatory narrative mode acts as a strategy of alienation, a means by which the Western reader is made to confront the limits of his or her knowledge of the world in which the story takes place. The narrative voice reads like a generic voice from the community the novel describes, but the reader is constantly being prompted to recognize his or her own exclusion from that community – a salutary prompt, perhaps, given how seemingly unproblematically Western novels (not to say Western works of criticism) can assume a white, Western reader.

A more recent and thus much more self-conscious example is the Dominican-American Junot Díaz's highly successful *The Brief Wondrous Life of Oscar Wao* (2007). With its extensive use of un-translated Spanish words and phrases there are whole passages of the novel where the Anglophone reader feels about as foreign in the world of the novel as its immigrant Dominican characters must feel on their arrival in New Jersey. In contrast with the somewhat teacherly tact of Achebe's novel, Oscar Wao has lengthy footnotes explaining with various degrees of impatience the relevant historical material: "For those of you who missed your mandatory two seconds of Dominican history ..." begins the first of these footnotes.[5] Who is this "you"? A Dominican reader will have had more than "two seconds"; this British reader is fairly certain she never even had that. The "you" appears to be an American "you" ("American" in the restricted sense of a US national, that is, and of non-Dominican descent) who is supposed to know *something* about the Caribbean but, the presence of the footnotes tells you, almost certainly doesn't. It's always worth asking what kinds of knowledge a narrative voice takes or refuses to take for granted because being able to answer this question allows us to see the specific communities a novel postulates – and all narratives assume (create) at least one.

E pluribus unum: the nation-making novel

Although the ignorance with which Achebe and Díaz are primarily concerned is that of the reader, there is a longstanding tradition of fiction that uses a displaced, disoriented protagonist in order to make the problem of cultural ignorance one of the novel's main cultural and political themes. Of course "ignorance surmounted" constitutes a classic novelistic story more generally – think of *Emma* or *Great Expectations* – but the variant in which the novel dramatizes the process of a character coming to know another *culture* has a special bearing on the relationship between the novel and the very particular kind of community we think of as the nation.

The Irish novelist Sydney Owenson, Lady Morgan held that the novel "forms the best history of nations," and in her unashamedly partisan, culturally nationalist *The Wild Irish Girl: A National Tale* (1806) a misbehaving English youth is sent unwillingly to a remote Connacht estate to mend his bad city-bred ways. But he must be weaned not only from his dissolute English habits but also from his ugly national prejudice against "semi-barbarous" Ireland and the "turbulent, faithless, intemperate, and cruel" Irish, soon seduced by hospitable and picturesque natives and the sublime Irish landscape.[6] Likewise, in the Scottish Tobias Smollett's *The Expedition of Humphry Clinker* (1771), Anglo-Welsh characters travel to Scotland as part of their tour of mainland Britain, where they come to realize that "the people at the other end of this island know as little of Scotland as of Japan," and are forced to admit that "the contempt for Scotland, which prevails too much on this side the Tweed, is founded on prejudice and error."[7] Perhaps needless to say, the speedy reeducation of these novels' protagonists should be that of the reader as well: "For the information of the *ignorant* English reader, a few notes have been subjoined," wrote the Irish novelist Maria Edgeworth in the preface to her self-professed "Hibernian tale" *Castle Rackrent* (1800): "Indeed, the domestic habits of no nation of Europe were less known to the English than those of their sister country, till within these few years."[8]

As these examples suggest, the novelists most concerned with the nation have typically been those from what would have been considered the "backward" or "barbaric" peripheries rather than from the nation's imagined center, English and metropolitan, of "civilization." In the context of the British Isles, it's no accident that Irish and Scottish novelists such as Edgeworth, Smollett, and Owenson should have been so concerned with the relationship between novel and nation: Scotland had become a stateless nation through the 1707 Act of Union, and long-since-occupied Ireland was incorporated into the United Kingdom in 1800. Indeed, just as Brockden Brown's "American Tale" appeared soon after American independence, the era of Scottish and Irish national stories also coincided with moments when boundaries of state and nation were in flux. From this we might infer that a number of writers have understood the novel as a valuable way of negotiating the borders of the community, whether they see new political conditions as potentially endangering (as in *Wieland*) or as an occasion for promoting and translating the national culture to their new compatriots (Owenson, Edgeworth, Smollett).

However, at the same time as Smollett gives his *English* readers a much-needed education in the virtues and accomplishments of the Scots, he gives his *British* community of readers an imaginative tour of the land they share; this is "arguably the first fully *British* novel," Robert Crawford writes.[9] The Scottish/British novel was being written when Great Britain was still comparatively new, and shows most explicitly of all how the act of describing a nation back to itself makes that nation more real. When the theorist of postcolonial literature and identity Homi Bhabha writes of "the performativity of language in the narratives of the nation" he is suggesting that to represent a national community is to *make* one.[10] "Performativity" in this context refers to the special linguistic formulae known as "performative speech acts," verbal formulations that have autonomous efficacy, that *do* something rather than describe it: just as the mere act of saying "I promise" constitutes promising, and to say "I apologize" is to apologize, the accounts we give of a nation help to *realize* (literally, "make real") the nation they describe. Self-representation need not necessarily be directed at implied outsiders as it is in a postcolonial novel like *Things Fall Apart* and novels of immigrant experience like *Oscar Wao*.

While the relationship between the novel and the nation is most immediately visible in those ethnographic novels like Smollett's that take their reader on a tour of their country, it potentially has a bearing on all fiction, for reasons explained by the theorist of nationalism Benedict Anderson in his much-cited book *Imagined Communities*. The nation is a *community* because it is "always conceived as deep, horizontal comradeship"; the nation is *imagined* because we will only ever know at most a few hundred of our fellow citizens but nevertheless have no difficulty conceptualizing them all leading their everyday existences alongside our own as we all travel through time "together."[11] Anderson points out that the nation-state arose at the same time as the novel, and that we can understand them both better if we see how they deal with collective experience, or, as he puts it, "community in anonymity."[12] This is the novel's characteristically "meanwhile" mode: while Stephen Dedalus is squabbling with Buck Mulligan in *Ulysses*, Leopold Bloom is making his breakfast; and, as the clock strikes noon in *Mrs. Dalloway*, Clarissa is laying out her dress for a party that evening while Septimus Smith walks to his psychiatrist's office. Bloom and Stephen will meet up that night, but Clarissa and Septimus will never meet (though Clarissa will hear at her party of the other's death). We imagine our countrymen and countrywomen with the sense of simultaneity that novels encourage; we need not know them to imagine that they are living their autonomous lives at the same time as we live our own.

Driving much of the thinking about novel and nation is the analogy between their forms. The novel is "the symbolic form of the nation-state," Franco Moretti argues, "and it's a form that (unlike an anthem, or a monument) not only does not conceal the nation's internal divisions, but *manages to turn them into a story*."[13] Timothy Brennan, likewise, argues that "It was the *novel* that historically accompanied the rise of nations by objectifying the 'one, yet many' of national life, and by mimicking the structure of the nation, a clearly bordered jumble of languages and styles."[14] So the novel resembles the nation in being a "bordered" singularity that emerges from plurality, and resembles the modern (democratic) nation in its ability to accommodate multiple styles of living, many worldviews. The nation and the novel-state are both composite formations: *e pluribus unum* – out of many, one – as in the old motto of the young American republic. Think of a novel like *Bleak House*, with its absolutely enormous cast of characters across all social strata: these characters have nothing in common but the nation and novel that hold them all together.

Multiculturalism and the languages of fiction

In the context of novel and nation no one matters more than Sir Walter Scott. Having established his reputation with novels that drew heavily on the communal life of his native Scotland – folkloric novels such as *Rob Roy* (1817) and *The Bride of Lammermoor* (1819) – Scott turned his attention to *English* national identity in order to erode comforting views of Englishness as "given," as something to be taken unquestioningly for granted. "I cannot but think it strange that no attempt has been made to excite an interest for the traditions and manners of Old England," Scott wrote in his preface to *Ivanhoe* (1820), a novel driven by the animosity between the Norman aristocracy and the Saxons they conquered in 1066.[15] That there is no historical support for such enmity is very telling because it shows how invested Scott was in the composition of nationhood out of cultural differences (remember Moretti's argument that novels *turn the nation's internal divisions into a story*). *Ivanhoe*'s main groups are the aristocratic Normans, the plebeian Saxons, and the ostracized Jews. Although Scott replays some hoary anti-Semitic stereotypes with the avaricious Isaac of York, the novel was otherwise so intelligently tolerant that even its first readers back in 1820 were disappointed that the hero ends up with the bland but ethnically appropriate Rowena rather than with the magnificent Jewish Rebecca, who resists assimilation even as the novel otherwise enacts a "melting pot" view of nationality in order to remind the English of their mongrel ancestry; to remind them that there *is* no essential Englishness.

Because Scott did more than any other writer to give the novel its substantiality as a means of cultural representation, you can see why I have emphasized his multiculturalism if you consider how the most dangerous forms of nationalism – the least tolerant, the most racist – are typically powered by fantasies of national homogeneity or "purity," as if there were a true national identity from which all other forms (ethnic, say, or religious) are inferior deviations, not quite the real thing. "My name is Karim Amir, and I am an Englishman born and bred, almost," begins Hanif Kureishi's *The Buddha of Suburbia* (1990), acknowledging both the factuality of the hero's Englishness (Karim was indeed born and raised in England) and the reality of a racism that refuses to see as English someone with a name like Karim Amir ("we were supposed to be English, but to the English we were always wogs and nigs and Pakis and the rest of it").[16]

There's an enduringly memorable showdown between the paranoid-purist and the cheerfully pluralist view of nationality in James Joyce's national novel, *Ulysses*, when the Jewish-Irish Bloom runs into the nationalist windbag The Citizen in Barney Kiernan's pub. The monstrous, monocular Citizen attacks Bloom because being Jewish he cannot also (the bigoted Citizen thinks) be properly Irish, but ideas of the "properly Irish" are exactly what this encounter mocks. This is from Joyce's long description of the kilted Citizen:

> From his girdle hung a row of seastones … and on these were graven with rude yet striking art the tribal images of many Irish heroes and heroines of antiquity, Cuchulin, Conn of hundred battles, Niall of

nine hostages, Brian of Kincora, the Ardri Malachi, Art MacMurragh, Shane O'Neill, Father John Murphy ... Dante Alighieri, Christopher Columbus, S. Fursa, S. Brendan, Marshall MacMahon, Charlemagne, Theobald Wolfe Tone, the Mother of the Maccabees, the Last of the Mohicans ... Herodotus, Jack the Giant Killer, Gautama Buddha, Lady Godiva ...[17]

Irish heroines and heroes of antiquity? Cúchulainn, surely, but what's so Irish about Herodotus, Dante, and Buddha? That Irish culture – any culture – shares some of its material with other cultures is Joyce's cosmopolitan and pluralistic point.

And intimately connected to that pluralism is the linguistic polyphony of this episode. Timothy Brennan, you'll recall, argued that the novel is a harnessed multiplicity ("a clearly bordered jumble of languages and styles"), a claim obviously indebted to Bakhtin's definition of the novel as a polyphonic or "many-voiced" form. The encounter between the pluralistic Bloom and the bigoted Citizen begins in the style of the portentously translated classical epic ("the loud strong hale reverberations of his formidable heart thundered rumblingly causing the ground, the summit of the lofty tower and the still loftier walls of the cave to vibrate and tremble"), turns into the styles of pub anecdote in demotic Hibernian-English ("So anyhow Terry brought the three pints Joe was standing and begob the sight nearly left my eyes when I saw him land out a quid"), of chivalry ("Who comes through Michan's land, bedight in sable armour?"), of mysticism ("he was now on the path to prālāyā"), of the newspaper report, of the minutes of meetings, of the Old Testament, and so on.[18] The sheer heterogeneity of the available forms of English is surely a riposte to the Citizen's unseeing, narrow-minded, potentially violent purisms. "After all," Bakhtin said, "one's own language is never a single language."[19]

It is because there are all sorts of ways in which English (or any other living language) can be spoken that it is necessary to be attentive to the politics of novelistic voice: to the different languages deployed in a novel, and, crucially, to the implied relationships among them. Consider how often a novel incorporates styles of speech marked by region and nation, ethnicity and class within the dialogue and yet deploys so-called Standard English for the voice of the narrator. Dickens's representations of England and the English are amazing archives of vocal multiplicity, and even in the most restrained of his novels you "hear" multiple styles of English. *Hard Times*, for example, includes the slurring of the circus ringmaster Sleary ("people mutht be amuthed"); the dignified demotic of the noble factory hand Stephen Blackpool ("I ha' seen more clear, and ha' made it my dyin' prayer that aw th' world may on'y coom toogether more, an get a better unnerstan'in o' one another'"); the bogus blustering of the "self-made man" Bounderby ("I passed the day in a ditch, and the night in a pigsty. That was the way I spent my tenth birthday. Not that a ditch was new to me, for I was born in a ditch"); the bombast of the Trade Union demagogue Slackbridge ("the hour is come, when we must rally round one another as One united power, and crumble into dust the oppressors that too long have battened upon the plunder of our families").[20] The narrator, however, masquerades as the voice from nowhere, a total contrast to the characters' sharply delineated styles of English. Implicitly, this is the language of the reader, too. Even if "educated middle-class Victorian Christian" sounds like a style to twenty-first-century readers it wasn't meant to sound like one.

In his very useful discussion of the uses of dialect in fiction, Cairns Craig quotes the contemporary novelist James Kelman on "a wee game going on between writer and reader and the wee game is 'Reader and writer are the same' and they speak in the same voice as the narrative and they're unlike these fucking natives who do the dialogue in phonetics."[21] Underlying Kelman's claim is the critique of the "classic realist text" discussed in Chapter 3, where there is a hierarchy of voices that presents the heterodiegetic narrator's perspective as reliable, the voice of characters (dialogue) as inherently subordinate, inferior. *Hard Times* exemplifies this hierarchy, and helps us to see the political grounds on which Kelman wants to erode the distinction between the written and the spoken, the taken-for-granted perspective of the middle class and the necessarily different voices of the "fucking natives." A new attention to the politics of novelistic languages has produced many of the most powerful experiments in modern fiction.

Almost any passage from Kelman's fiction could be used to make the point about discursive hierarchies – if his use of a phrase like "fucking natives" in the context of a literary-critical discussion doesn't already make it. However, I want to end instead with one of the writers who made his experiments possible. My example is from Lewis Grassic Gibbon's *Sunset Song* (1932), one of the finest working-class novels of the century, and one which, in a very unusual narrative strategy, deploys the second person ("you") used so often in ordinary speech and so seldom in written narrative, as if the narrator were one member of this community addressing another. The novel begins with a history of the aristocratic estate of which the novel's main characters are tenants:

> More than half the estate had gone in this driblet and that while the cripple sat and read his coarse French books; but nobody guessed that till he died and then his widow, poor woman, found herself own no more than the land that lay between the coarse hills, the Grampians, and the farms that stood out by the Bridge End above the Denburn, straddling the outward road. Maybe there were some twenty to thirty

holdings in all, the crofters dour folk of the old Pict stock, they had no history, common folk, and ill-reared their biggings [buildings] clustered and chaved [labored] amid the long, sloping fields. The leases were one-year, two-year, you worked from the blink of the day you were breeked to the flicker of the night they shrouded you, and the dirt of gentry sat and ate up your rents but you were just as good as they were.[22]

Here we are asked to look at the decline of the estate as if from "below": money is squandered ("in this driblet and that"); the heir fiddles while Rome burns (reading his "coarse French books"). Then we begin to hear about the ordinary people who live on the estate, the real subject of the novel: the ironic – but of course also true – "they had no history, common folk" reminds us of the relationship between social status and the ability to have your story recorded, to have your story considered *worth* writing.

Gibbon's narrative voice is meant to resemble the spoken voice. Closing the gap between speaking and writing that has left the experiences of working-class people unvoiced ("they had no history, common folk"), by breaking with the traditional hierarchy that separates narrative voice from dialogue, so-called Standard English from dialect, the narrator speaks much the same language as the people about and, implicitly, to whom he writes. I argued in Chapter 3 that attentive reading of narrative form requires us to ask "who speaks?" but that question about narrative technique may be asked in a different – and more culturally and politically relevant – way: Who *gets* to speak? How do they speak? And to whom?

Salman Rushdie, *Midnight's Children* (1981)

"I was born in the city of Bombay ... once upon a time," begins Saleem Sinai, the narrator of Sir Salman Rushdie's postcolonial classic *Midnight's Children*. But in keeping with what soon becomes recognizable as his Tristram Shandyish habit, Saleem immediately corrects his opening sentence: "once upon a time," won't do, not when Saleem was born at midnight on the very day India gained independence from Great Britain, August 15, 1947, and is thus "mysteriously handcuffed to history, my destinies indissolubly chained to those of my country."[1] Saleem Sinai, also known as "Snotface, Stainface, Baldy, Sniffer, Buddha, and even Piece-of-the-Moon," will go on to tell his life story, a narrative of identity formation where the identity being formed is not only his but his nation's (4).

The trouble with personal and national identities is that they must be both unitary and multiple. "I am the sum total of everything that went before me, of all I have been seen done, of everything done-to-me," Saleem announces: "I am everyone everything whose being-in-the-world affected was affected by mine. I am anything that happens after I've gone which would not have happened if I had not come. Not am I particularly exceptional in this matter; each 'I,' every one of the now-six-hundred-million-plus of us, contains a similar multitude" (441). But that a self or a nation that is *too* divided threatens to crumble out of existence gives its urgency to Saleem's narration: he feels that he is breaking apart, disintegrating into "(approximately) six hundred and thirty million particles of anonymous, and necessarily oblivious dust" – or the population of India (36). Democratic abundance and multiplicity are the keynotes of *Midnight's Children* and its vision of India, but abundance is overshadowed by the risk it brings of fragmentation and disintegration. The ineffectual democrat Saleem is one product and vision of the new India ("a lost federation of equals, all points of view given free expression" [252]), but the cacophonous model of the nation that the children of India's first midnight represent is constantly threatened by its own internal divisions. How do you keep the self, the nation, or the novel together?

That *Midnight's Children* may exceed the bounds of the novel form is suggested through Saleem's struggles with his down-to-earth interlocutor Padma, who plays Sancho Panza to his Don Quixote. "At this rate ... you'll be two hundred years old before you manage to tell about your birth," she complains when in the third chapter we're still hearing about Saleem's newly married grandparents; it's going to take another hundred pages to get Saleem's story as far as his own birth, reminding us again of Tristram Shandy, of the long struggle into existence of Tristram and the novel that tells his life story. In Saleem's account of his gestation, too, teller and text are one and the same: "What had been (at the beginning) no bigger than a full stop had expanded into a comma, a word, a sentence, a paragraph, a chapter; now it was bursting into more complex developments, becoming, one might say, a book – perhaps an encyclopedia – even a whole language ..." (111). Saleem is haunted by the possibility that neither novels nor nations are adequate to their contents, liable to be split apart by the multiplicities they are being asked to "contain."

On the other hand, Saleem believes that even a form-endangering multiplicity is preferable to its opposite. When his family crosses the newly instituted partition dividing India from Pakistan as Rushdie's own family had done, Saleem contends that a nation that is too united, too homogeneous, becomes culturally sterile: he finds himself resisting "the somehow barren certitudes of the land of the pure" (362) – the Urdu name "Pakistan" means "Land of [the] Pure" – and mourning India's "infinity of alternative realities" (373). Against cultural purity stands literary heterogeneity, and Saleem likens himself to Scheherazade spinning her thousand-and-one stories, "the number of night, of magic, or alternative realities – a number beloved of poets and detested by politicians, for whom all alternative versions of the world are threats" (248). Like Saleem, *Midnight's Children* has "a marked preference for the impure" (355), and you can see that preference in the novel's celebration of the mixed, the hybrid, the plural, and the heterogeneous. But that, too, brings risk: like one of the novels *Midnight's Children* most resembles, Günter Grass's national epic *The Tin Drum*, *Midnight's Children* opens on contested ground: in Grass, it's the German–Polish border and in Rushdie's novel it's Kashmir. Is Kashmir part of India or Pakistan? And is Oskar's city Danzig or Gdansk? In one sense, national borders are completely arbitrary; in another, they're dangerously real.

That *culture* knows no borders is the source of this novel's comic "fertility." This is a novel very self-consciously situated where such classic European fictions as *Don Quixote*, *Tristram Shandy*, and *The Tin Drum* meet oral classics of the East – the Hindu myths loved by the Muslim hero, for instance, and, above all, *The One Thousand and One Nights*. Indeed, reading *Midnight's Children* reminds you that some of its sources were *always* between two cultures: *Don Quixote* pretends to be based on the manuscript of a learned Arabic historian Cid Hamete Benengeli (much of Spain, remember, was part of the Islamic world through the Middle Ages); and the stories of *The One Thousand and*

One Nights have been part of Western culture (as "The Arabian Nights") since their translation into French and English early in the eighteenth century, as much a component of our mental furniture as Grimm's fairy tales. In culture, at least, there need be no "barren" purity of the single worldview, and some of the novel's best jokes are about the transformation of one culture in the minds of another. A resident of India's film capital, Mumbai ("Bombay"), home of Bollywood cinema, Rashid the rickshaw boy models himself on the hero of the wonderfully named "eastern Western" (50) in which the heroic cowboys are not herders of cattle – cows being sacred to India's Hindu population – but their vigilante protectors. Cultures are transformed in their encounter with one another, their very languages transformed: "The rapscallions have perpetrated an outrage!" announces the Muslim Mustapha Kemal, describing in British-era argot a Mafia-style protection racket named after a Hindu demon: "a dastardly crew, Madam; a band of incendiary rogues ... unscrupulous cut-throats and bounders to a man!" (76–8).

Cultural crossbreeding, the imaginative counterpart to hybrid vigor, is the novelistic corollary of the novel's liberal, pluralistic desire to give the lie to fantasies of national purity, understandings of the nation that rely on or impose ethnic homogeneity. After all, Saleem Sinai, child of India, may be half-English by "blood." In contrast to his father Ahmed Sinai's nativist fiction of Mughal ancestry – the authentic, pseudo-aristocratic "Indianness" he invents to impress the departing Briton William Methwold – Saleem's adopted ancestries are irreducibly plural. Just as his British-national/Indian-born/Pakistani-raised/US-resident author is subject to many influences, the character of Saleem has even more "presumptive fathers" than Grass's Oskar Matzareth: not just Ahmed Sinai (official father) and William Methwold (birth father – perhaps), but also Wee Willie Winkie (street entertainer), Hanif Aziz (Bollywood director), Schaapsteker/Sharpsticker (snake expert), and Picture Singh (snake charmer). Saleem has unusually blue eyes and, in what simultaneously suggests the Hindu elephant god Ganesh and one of Sterne's grubby jokes, he has an enormous nose: but did he inherit those characteristics from his Kashmiri grandfather, Aadam Aziz, or from the blue-blooded French grandmother of the last Englishman? Problems of reproduction and metaphors of fecundity run through this novel, but the "genetic" is never allowed to be taken as a foundational fact. After all, what is *believed* to be the case matters more than what objectively *is*. In a "collective failure of imagination" the Ahmeds' belated discovery that Saleem is not their biological son makes no difference: "we simply could not think our way out of our pasts" (131).

"Reality is a question of perspective," Saleem announces: "the illusion itself *is* reality" (189). The social, national, and geopolitical corollary of this sense that subjective perception may count for more than "objective" knowledge comes when power is transferred from British to Indian hands. As sunset falls on the Methwold Estate on the final day of British power, the bogus Samson William Methwold removes the wig no one knew he wore. The illusion of British imperial "virility" has been demystified, but as the clock counts down to Indian independence, new illusions will be required – a new "myth", "dream," "mass fantasy," or "collective fiction" to be known and experienced as India:

> A nation which had never previously existed was about to win its freedom, catapulting us into a world which, although it had five thousand years of history, although it had invented the game of chess and traded with Middle Kingdom Egypt, was nevertheless quite imaginary; into a mythical land, a country which would never exist except by the efforts of a phenomenal collective will – except in a dream we all agreed to dream; it was a mass fantasy shared in varying degrees by Bengali and Punjabi, Madrasi and Jat, and would periodically need the sanctification and renewal which can only be provided by rituals of blood. India, the new myth – a collective fiction in which anything was possible, a fable rivalled only by the two other mighty fantasies: money and God. (124–5)

Nations are not natural but fabricated, not discovered but continually remade. Nations *are* novels, and they're no less real for that. "Sometimes legends make reality," Saleem explains, "and become more useful than the facts" (47).

Concluding

Chapter XLIX: The conclusion, in which nothing is concluded

Samuel Johnson, Rasselas (1759)[1]

The anxiety, which in this state of their attachment must be the portion of Henry and Catherine, and of all who loved either, as to its final event, can hardly extend, I fear, to the bosom of my readers, who will see in the tell-tale compression of the pages before them, that we are hastening together to perfect felicity.

Jane Austen, Northanger Abbey (1817)[2]

The endings of novels are always bad, argued E. M. Forster, because everything needs to be satisfactorily wrapped up: "no wonder that nothing is heard but hammering and screwing." It would be much more rewarding if novelists could simply persevere until they got too bored or confused to keep going.[3] But whether we write six-page papers or six-hundred-page novels, all of us who write know how much an ending matters: this is where we are expected to provide clarity and revelation, to make readers feel that they have spent their time well in reading everything that has gone before. And it is because novelists know how much pressure we put on endings that so many of them joke about the high expectations we bring to their closing chapters. In Johnson's concluding chapter of *Rasselas* "nothing is concluded," while Austen puts an end to the suspenseful delay of *Northanger Abbey* (will the lovers Henry and Catherine overcome parental opposition?) with a wry acknowledgment that the reader, book in hand, literally feels the ending coming in "the tell-tale compression of the pages." My final chapter describes how novels end – and how they don't.

Apocalyptic thinking

Many critics have speculated that there is an intimate connection between how we imagine fictional endings and how we think about human life in time. That we make the inherently meaningless flux of time *meaningful* by imposing endings upon it is the influential argument of Frank Kermode's *The Sense of an Ending*, a study of what he takes to be a virtually universal Western tendency to think in apocalyptic terms. Conversationally we use the word "apocalypse" to mean any large-scale ending, but it tells you a great deal about our ideas of ending that the word literally means an unveiling, a revelation; indeed, some of the most famous novel endings explicitly recall that original meaning, as when, for instance, D. H. Lawrence's *The Rainbow* (1915) ends with the heroine Ursula Brangwen seeing in a rainbow "the earth's new architecture, the old, brittle corruption of houses and factories swept away, the world built up in a living fabric of Truth, fitting to the over-arching heaven."[4] This is an apocalyptic vision in the conversational sense of an obliteration – everything has been "swept away" – and in the literal sense of a revelation ("Truth" with a capital T). To end, then, is to reveal.

Although not all novels end as overtly "apocalyptically" as *The Rainbow*, we still *read* them apocalyptically. That is, we look forward to an end that will reveal to us the meaning of what we have read, which is why we do not feel that we have "read" a novel until we have *finished* reading it. For Kermode the implications of our investment in apocalypse go far beyond the literary, speaking to the absolute centrality of narrative itself: the meaning-making force of "the ending" is so engrained in our way of looking at the world, he argues, that we organize even the most banally repetitive of occurrences into stories with beginnings, middles, and ends. So, for example, we have come to hear the ticking of a clock as "tick tock" rather than "tick tick" or "tock tock" in order to make it a *story* with a beginning ("tick"), a middle (the silent pause), and an end ("tock"): "The clock's *tick-tock* I take to be a model of what we call a plot, an organization that humanizes time by giving it form; and the interval between *tock* and *tick* represents purely successive, disorganized time of the sort we need to humanize."[5] We give time meaning when we impose endings upon it, endings that retroactively transform into significance everything that precedes them.

Whereas Kermode takes a descriptive rather than evaluative approach to our need for endings, Michael André Bernstein argues that the fiction of the revelatory ending – fictional in both senses of novelistic and false – devalues human life in all its shapelessness, contingency, and ordinariness because it treats everything as a precursor to what then becomes a predestined, inevitable outcome. In short, that we *do* think "apocalyptically" doesn't mean we have to – or should. Bernstein's historical test case is the Holocaust, and his target those historical and fictional representations that present it as if it were the *outcome* of the whole history of European Jews, reading their history backwards from the Holocaust and inadvertently trivializing those lives lost by implying that they could *only ever* have been lost. Reading back from the "ending" we ourselves have constructed means that the present ceases to matter other than as it foreshadows (what we present as) the end: it "implies a closed universe in which all choices have already been made, in which human free will can exist only in the paradoxical sense of choosing to accept or willfully – and vainly – rebelling against what is inevitable." [6]

Bernstein's point is that what has happened has happened but *need* not have happened, and its implications for novelistic form become clear when he speculates that because our densely plotted major novels, novels that wrap everything up in their final pages, are "like monuments of inevitability, effortlessly enfolding each turn of events … into the larger structure of the whole" we respond with pleasure to those playful experimental texts that favor chance and contradiction, freeing us "from the too strictly plotted, the too seamlessly coherent story" and the totalizing determinisms of the tidy wrap-up.[7] Bernstein's exemplary novel is Robert Musil's *The Man Without Qualities* (1930–43): set on the eve of the First World War, the novel refuses to write the war, to use the war as an ending that would falsify (by purporting to sum up) everything that goes before. The novel remained unfinished on Musil's death.

Open endings

The end of a novel is traditionally where the desires of readers are gratified, its wish-fulfilling function sometimes as obvious as in those happy endings Henry James summed up as "a distribution at the last of prizes, pensions, husbands, wives, babies, millions, appended paragraphs, and cheerful remarks."[8] That James was writing of the Victorian ending will be obvious to all readers of modern fiction, which tends to turn the ending into a problem for the reader instead of a source of gratification. Think of the choice of endings John Fowles offers the reader – twice over – in *The French Lieutenant's Woman*, where, instead of linear progress toward a predetermined end, we have forking paths. Engaged to the heiress Ernestina, Charles is tempted by Sarah, the deserted mistress of a French sailor. The first "choice" of endings comes when Charles is on his way back to Ernestina from a trip to London, and must pass through the town where Sarah lives. Will he proceed on his homeward journey, or will he see Sarah? He does both: first, Fowles writes the Victorian-style ending, where Charles returns to Ernestina, and the novel "concludes" with what happened to everyone afterward. But of course we know that there remains a lot of novel yet to be read (no "tell-tale compression of the pages"), and another ending follows, in which Charles stops and has rapturous sex with Sarah. But that's not the ending either. Charles returns to Ernestina, breaks off his engagement, and then pursues Sarah. And now we get another choice: in the conventionally happy first ending, they are eventually reunited, and Charles meets the infant he never knew he fathered; in the ambiguous other, Sarah drives him away because she no longer needs him. Which is the correct ending to the book? In one sense, there *is* no correct ending; in another, whichever we read last is the one we're liable to think of as the "real" ending. The materiality of the novel, an inherently *linear* form because we read it from "end to end," necessarily compromises the illusion of choice.

Or, to give a more recent example of a novel with "multiple" endings, think of the trick ending of Ian McEwan's *Atonement* (2001). In the final pages, the reader discovers that the book she has been reading is an altogether different novel from the one she took it to be: what looked like the third-person narration of an expiated crime is really the first-person narration of a crime that can never be expiated because its victims did not (as the seemingly third-person narration described) survive. "How could that constitute an ending?" asks the "author" Briony in defense of her decision to rewrite what happened: "What sense or hope or satisfaction could a reader draw from such an account?"

> I know there's always a certain kind of reader who will be compelled to ask, But what *really* happened? The answer is simple: the lovers survive and flourish. As long as there is a single copy, a solitary typescript of my final draft, then my spontaneous, fortuitous sister and her medical prince survive to love.[9]

As in Fowles's novel and contrary to Briony's claims for the force of her rewriting of history, the less redemptive, less comforting second ending overwrites the happier first. Happy endings are not to be trusted, it seems; they tell us comforting lies.

Multiple endings may seem a radically postmodernist gesture, and when I used "Victorian" to summarize a particular type of ending in which rewards and punishments are distributed, and all the characters accounted for, I made it sound as if the question of ending were essentially a historical one – nineteenth-century novels end one way, modern novels another. In reality, some of the least conclusive endings come much earlier than we might expect. Always good for the historical counterexample, Sterne begins *A Sentimental Journey* (1768) as if in the middle of a conversation with " – They order, said I, this matter better in France – " and ends with an unfinished sentence: "So that when I stretch'd out my hand, I caught hold of the Fille de Chambre's – "[10] The chambermaid's hand? Or what? And what did the chambermaid do? We'll never know because the book has ended as it began, in the middle.

But in view of Sterne's characteristic eccentricity, it's even more telling that even a number of major *Victorian* novelists resisted the pressure to end in the resolutely optimistic, conclusively redemptive ways expected of them. Perhaps the best-known example is the suppressed first ending Dickens wrote for *Great Expectations*, in which Pip and Estella meet at the end and move on again; in the second version, the "final" version, Pip and Estella, chastened, are reunited, and Pip, famously, sees no shadow of another parting from her – a happy ending compared to the last, but when you read it knowing the earlier draft, there's something newly melancholy about Pip and Estella standing at twilight in the burned-out shell of Miss Havisham's Satis House.

More dramatic still is the ambiguous ending of Charlotte Brontë's final novel *Villette* (1853). Now working in the little Belgian school established for her by her beloved Paul Emmanuel, the narrator Lucy Snowe awaits the ship that brings him home from the Caribbean. But a terrible storm has arisen at sea, wrecking every ship in its path:

> Here pause: pause at once. There is enough said. Trouble no quiet, kind heart; leave sunny imaginations hope. Let it be theirs to conceive the delight of joy born again out of great terror, the rapture of rescue from peril, the wondrous reprieve from dread, the fruition of return. Let them picture union and a happy succeeding life.
>
> Madame Beck prospered all the days of her life; so did Père Silas; Madame Walravens fulfilled her ninetieth year before she died. Farewell.[11]

Have Lucy and Paul been reunited or not? In that superb final paragraph we learn only that the conspirators who drove Paul to the West Indies went on to live long prosperous lives they never "deserved," a reversal of fiction's habits of concluding justice. We suspect that Paul was drowned at sea, and the happier possibility becomes hopelessly unbelievable when Lucy implies that only the very innocent could expect it ("Trouble no quiet, kind heart," she urges herself, "leave sunny imaginations hope"). In a striking anticipation of the postmodernist insistence on the sheer wishful thinking that motivates the disavowed happy ending, Lucy's "farewell" gives the novel its conclusion; what it refuses to give the novel is the traditional form of **closure**.

Closure and anti-closure

Of course, novels always *end* in the sense that they stop; that there always comes a point after which there are no more pages left to read. But if one meaning of "ends" is "conclusions," the other is "objectives," which means that an ending is also a form of fulfillment. This is what we mean by "closure": something more than a simple finish, the satisfaction that comes when conflicts have been resolved and questions answered. We want to reach an ending that will confer meaning on the rest of the narrative, and we want to be taken there by an unexpected (but not arbitrary) route. "Closure occurs when the concluding portion … announces and justifies the absence of further development," writes Barbara Herrnstein Smith in her book on how poems end: "it reinforces the feeling of finality, completion, and composure which we value in all works of art; and it gives ultimate unity and coherence to the reader's experience of the poem by providing a point from which all the preceding elements may be viewed comprehensively and their relations grasped as part of a significant design."[12]

But if many texts allow you to enjoy that feeling of "wholeness" in an artistic work – and although the ending of *Villette* is a shocking one, it is also retrospectively totally true to the rest of the novel and especially to the withholding Lucy Snowe – others refuse to remain self-contained, and end less concerned with evoking their own artistic integrity ("the feeling of finality, completion and composure which we value in all works of art") than with opening the world of the text out on to the world of the reader. For example, by the time we reach the end of Conrad's novel about terrorism, *The Secret Agent* (1907), the domestic plot has left no loose ends: all the main characters are dead now that Verloc has killed Stevie and Winnie has killed Verloc and then herself. What could be more conclusive than that? But the novel's final sentences are devoted to what seemed a minor character, the terrorist known as the Professor, who stalks the streets of London with a bomb in his pocket: "Nobody looked at him," reads the ending: "He passed on unsuspected and deadly, like a pest in the street full of men."[13] Something similar happens when you get to the final page of Forster's *A Passage to India* (1924): the plot crisis has been resolved and all the main characters accounted for (death, marriage – the usual). A meeting in the closing pages between the estranged Indian doctor Aziz and the sympathetic Englishman Fielding raises the possibility of reconciliation only to defer it to some future date outside the novel ("No, not yet … No, not there").[14] For Forster to present a reconciliation of Aziz and Fielding, colonized India and colonizing Britain, would be as falsifying as for Conrad to end *The Secret Agent* as if terrorism were a thing of the past, as if it had died with the novel's main characters.

Although the critic Russell Reising is discussing American literature specifically, I think this is the kind of ending he has in mind when he raises "the possibility that no novel, no social text, can resolve in its imaginative work the crises, tensions, and vexations that characterize the social and cultural world of its genesis, that any appearance of having done so is tantamount to political, moral, and rhetorical bad faith."[15] And when Rachel Blau DuPlessis describes modern women authors "writing beyond the ending" in her book of that title, she argues that the cultural script for women is structured by one particular ending, the marriage that traditionally concludes the nineteenth-century novel; and *this* is the ending beyond which all modern women write (and of course the ending beyond which *Villette* writes, too, if you think about the difference between this novel and *Jane Eyre*). Critics, then, have been interested in *anti-closure* because they imagine closure as a form of containment whereby the radical energies of a novel – all the social and cultural problems it addresses, all the unruly passions and ambitions it raises – are finally boxed up and made politically harmless. "In essence, closure is an act of 'make believe,'" D. A. Miller argues in his brilliant book on closure in the seemingly "traditional" nineteenth-century novel: "a postulation that closure is possible."[16]

Ongoingness

Endings are never really endings, Dostoevsky argued in the closing paragraphs of *Crime and Punishment* (1865–6). The impenitent murderer Raskolnikov has been exiled to hard labor in Siberia, and the sequence of "crime" followed by "punishment" opens on to a third term and a new story: "redemption."

> But at this point a new story begins, the story of a man's gradual renewal, his gradual rebirth, his gradual transition from one world to another, of his growing acquaintance with a new, hitherto completely unknown reality. This might constitute the theme of a new narrative – our present narrative is, however, at an end.[17]

Beyond the limits of the crime and punishment narrative are other stories to be told, Dostoevsky proposes: beyond this novel are novels yet to be written. When one story ends, another begins.

This raises another sense in which novels are potentially endless, the opportunities they give other novelists as a prompt or starting point for their own work. Many of the classic novels discussed in this book have served in this capacity. Chief among them, perhaps, is *Don Quixote*, its narrative of holy madness a sort of blueprint for Dostoevsky's own *The Idiot* (1869), and a novel also rewritten by authors as radically different as Tobias Smollett (*The Life and Adventures of Sir Launcelot Greaves* [1760–1]), Charlotte Lennox (*The Female Quixote* [1752]), Richard Graves (*The Spiritual Quixote* [1773]), Jorge Luis Borges ("Pierre Menard, Author of the *Quixote*" [1939]), Graham Greene (*Monsignor Quixote* [1982]), and Kathy Acker (*Don Quixote: Which Was a Dream* [1986]). The list comprises everything from female conduct-and-courtship novel (Lennox) to cyberpunk (Acker), anti-Methodist satire (Graves) to political commentary (Greene) and postmodernist play (Borges). Writing a novel can be an act of interpretation, and all these writers reinterpreted Cervantes in the light of their own private interests as writers and in the new light of their culture's needs and concerns.

Which brings me to my inconclusive conclusion: that novels and novelists are potentially *endless* because they are constantly being rediscovered and rethought, rewritten by some critics and novelists and written out by others. Reputations rise, fall, and often rise again. Looking over what I have written in pursuit of an ending both adequate and true – or not inadequate and not untrue, to borrow a formula from a favorite poet – I realize that there are potentially as many introductions to the novel as there have been readers of the novel.[18] Since it took writing this book to make me see how much I think Sir Walter Scott matters to the history of the novel, it will at least be true to the book to use him as my final example. Scott sold more novels than all his contemporaries put together; sets of the Waverley Novels were given as wedding gifts through the nineteenth century (every home should have one!); Scott was the giant of the novel Victorian novelists sought to surpass.[19] And yet by the beginning of the twentieth century his standing was so low that he could be used as the very emblem of literary obsolescence in Virginia Woolf's *To the Lighthouse* (1927), while in a book on the novel published in the same year Forster used Scott only as a negative example, an instance of storytelling at its most primitive. At the end of the twentieth century, Scott would come back into view as one of the most formally interesting, culturally revealing, and, above all, historically significant of novelists. Throughout this book I have taken for granted Scott's importance in a way that would have been mystifying to some earlier generations and for others too self-evidently correct to be worth remarking. Many of the novels and novelists discussed in this book have been and will be subject to these fluctuations – lost to one generation of critics, found by another, lost and found again. It is because important novels continue to be written and important novelists *rewritten* that any introduction to the novel is a work in progress.

Notes

1 Why the novel matters

1 Charles Dickens, *Hard Times* (London: Penguin, 2003), 12.
2 Dickens, *Hard Times*, 9.
3 Clara Reeve, *The Progress of Romance*, vol. II (New York: The Facsimile Text Society, 1930), 78–9.
4 Milan Kundera, *The Curtain: An Essay in Seven Parts*, trans. Linda Asher (New York: HarperCollins, 2007), 8.
5 Samuel Johnson, "The New Realistic Novel," in *The Major Works*, ed. Donald Greene (Oxford: Oxford University Press, 2000), 175.
6 Johnson, "New Realistic Novel," 176.
7 Samuel Johnson, *Rasselas* (London: Penguin, 1985), 105.
8 Henry Fielding, *Joseph Andrews and Shamela* (London: Penguin, 1999), 61.
9 Daniel Defoe, *Moll Flanders* (Oxford: Oxford University Press, 2009), 2.
10 Fanny Burney, *Evelina* (Oxford: Oxford University Press, 2002), 9.
11 Burney, *Evelina*, 9–10.
12 Jane Austen, *Northanger Abbey* (London: Penguin, 2003), 36–7.
13 Richard Brinsley Sheridan, *The Rivals, The School for Scandal and Other Plays* (Oxford: Oxford University Press, 1998), 20.
14 Henry Fielding, *Tom Jones* (Oxford: Oxford University Press, 1998), 423.
15 Tobias Smollett, *The Expedition of Humphry Clinker* (London: Penguin, 1985), 160.
16 Nancy Armstrong, *Desire and Domestic Fiction: A Political History of the Novel* (Oxford: Oxford University Press, 1987), 26.
17 Samuel Richardson, *Clarissa* (London: Penguin, 2004), 1178.
18 Quoted in William B. Warner, *Licensing Entertainment: The Elevation of Novel Reading in Britain, 1684–1750* (Berkeley: University of California Press, 1998), 224.
19 Fielding, *Joseph Andrews and Shamela*, 29.
20 Samuel Richardson, *Selected Letters of Samuel Richardson*, ed. John Carroll (Oxford: Clarendon, 1964), 322.
21 John Bunyan, *The Pilgrim's Progress* (Oxford: Oxford University Press, 2003), 155.
22 D. H. Lawrence, "The Novel," in *Selected Critical Writings* (Oxford: Oxford University Press, 1998), 180.
23 D. H. Lawrence, "Morality and the Novel," in *Selected Critical Writings*, 174.

24 Selden L. Whitcomb, *The Study of a Novel* (Boston: D. C. Heath, 1905), 11.

25 Henry James, "The Art of Fiction," in *The Future of the Novel: Essays on the Art of Fiction*, ed. Leon Edel (New York: Vintage, 1956), 4.

26 James, "The Art of Fiction," 24–5.

27 Joseph Conrad, preface to *The Nigger of the "Narcissus," Conrad's Prefaces to his Works*, ed. Edward Garnett (London: Dent, 1937), 51.

28 Mark McGurl, *The Novel Art: Elevations of American Fiction after Henry James* (Princeton: Princeton University Press, 2001), 2.

29 Virginia Woolf, *To the Lighthouse* (Orlando: Harcourt, 2005), 211.

30 George Saintsbury, *The English Novel* (London: Dent, 1913), 270.

31 Lawrence, "The Novel," 178.

32 D. H. Lawrence, "Why the Novel Matters," in *Selected Critical Writings*, 206.

33 Leavis, *Fiction and the Reading Public* (London: Chatto & Windus, 1932), 73–4.

34 Leavis, *Fiction and the Reading Public*, 48.

35 Leo Tolstoy, *Anna Karenina* (Harmondsworth: Penguin, 1978), 160.

36 George Eliot, "The Natural History of German Life," in *Selected Essays, Poems, and Other Writings*, ed. Nicholas Warren (London: Penguin, 1991), 110.

37 F. R. Leavis, *The Great Tradition: George Eliot, Henry James, Joseph Conrad* (London: Penguin, 1983), 9, 28.

38 Leavis, *Fiction and the Reading Public*, 256.

39 Leavis, *The Great Tradition*, 37, 30, 10.

40 Georg Lukács, *The Theory of the Novel: A Historico-Philosophical Essay on the Forms of Great Epic Literature*, trans. Anna Bostock (Cambridge: The MIT Press, 1971), 41.

41 M. M. Bakhtin, "Epic and Novel," *The Dialogic Imagination*, ed. Michael Holquist, trans. Caryl Emerson and Michael Holquist (Austin: University of Texas Press, 1981), 20.

42 Quoted in Ann Douglas, "Introduction," Harriet Beecher Stowe, *Uncle Tom's Cabin* (London: Penguin, 1986), 19.

43 Stowe, *Uncle Tom's Cabin*, 624.

Interchapter: *Don Quixote*

1 Milan Kundera, "The Depreciated Legacy of Cervantes," *The Art of the Novel*, trans. Linda Asher (New York: Grove, 1988), 6.

2 William Congreve, *Incognita* (New York: Houghton Mifflin, 1922), 5–6.

3 Miguel de Cervantes, *Don Quixote de la Mancha*, trans. Charles Jarvis (Oxford: Oxford University Press, 1998), 21. Hereafter cited parenthetically.

2 Origins of the novel

1 Margaret Anne Doody, *The True Story of the Novel* (New Brunswick: Rutgers University Press, 1996), 1.

2 Doody, *True Story of the Novel*, 16.

3 J. Paul Hunter, *Before Novels: The Cultural Contexts of Eighteenth-Century English Fiction* (New York: Norton, 1990), 23–5.

4 The long prose fictions of the pre-modern East have yet to be integrated into the Western consensus on the rise of the novel. For clarifying summaries of early Japanese and Chinese accomplishments in prose fiction see Andrew H. Plaks, "The Novel in Premodern China," Adriana Boscaro's "Monogatari," and Judith T. Zeitlin, "Xiaoshuo," in *The Novel, vol. I: History, Geography, and Culture*, ed. Franco Moretti (Princeton: Princeton University Press, 2006), 181–213, 241–8, 249–61.

5 Ian Watt, *The Rise of the Novel: Studies in Defoe, Richardson, and Fielding* (Berkeley: University of California Press, 1957), 32.

6 Michael McKeon, *The Origins of the English Novel, 1600–1740* (Baltimore: Johns Hopkins University Press, 2002).

7 McKeon, *Origins of the English Novel*, 28, 293.

8 Watt, *Rise of the Novel*, 15.

9 Geoffrey Day, *From Fiction to the Novel* (London: Routledge, 1987), 7.

10 Walter Raleigh, *The English Novel, Being A Short Sketch of its History from the Earliest Times to the Appearance of* Waverley (New York: Scribner, 1895), 109.

11 William B. Warner, *Licensing Entertainment: The Elevation of Novel Reading in Britain, 1684–1750* (Berkeley: University of California Press, 1998), 25–6.

12 Warner, *Licensing Entertainment*, 29.

13 Doody, *True Story of the Novel*, 18.

14 Doody, *True Story of the Novel*, xix.

15 Jane Austen, *Emma* (Harmondsworth: Penguin, 1985), 53, 87.

16 Austen, *Emma*, 462, 463.

17 Emily Brontë, *Wuthering Heights* (Harmondsworth: Penguin, 1985), 76.

18 Brontë, *Wuthering Heights*, 77.

19 Terry Eagleton, *Heathcliff and the Great Hunger: Studies in Irish Culture* (London: Verso, 1995), 3; Eric Solomon, "The Incest Theme in *Wuthering Heights*," *Nineteenth-Century Fiction*, 14. 1 (June 1959): 80–3.

20 Brontë, *Wuthering Heights*, 98.

21 Brontë, *Wuthering Heights*, 222.

22 Charles Dickens, *Oliver Twist* (Oxford: Oxford University Press, 2008), 34.

23 Charles Dickens, *Great Expectations* (Harmondsworth: Penguin, 1985), 339.

24 Dickens, *Great Expectations*, 493.

25 George Eliot, *Daniel Deronda* (Harmondsworth: Penguin, 1995), 5.

26 Henry Fielding, *Tom Jones* (Oxford: Oxford University Press, 1998), 68; Samuel Richardson, *Selected Letters of Samuel Richardson*, ed. John Carroll (Oxford: Clarendon, 1964), 41.

27 William Baldwin, *Beware the Cat* (San Marino, Calif.: Huntingdon Library, 1995), xiv.

28 Homer Obed Brown, *Institutions of the English Novel: From Defoe to Scott* (Philadelphia: University of Pennsylvania Press, 1997), 177.

Interchapter: *Tristram Shandy*

1 J. D. Salinger, *The Catcher in the Rye* (Boston: Back Bay, 2001), 3.
2 Viktor Shklovsky, *Theory of Prose*, trans. Benjamin Sher (Normal: Dalkey Archive Press, 1991), 170.
3 Laurence Sterne, *The Life and Opinions of Tristram Shandy, Gentleman* (London: Penguin, 2003), 64. Hereafter cited parenthetically.

3 Narrating the novel

1 Percy Lubbock, *The Craft of Fiction* (New York: Viking, 1957), 20.
2 Henry James, *The Ambassadors* (London: Penguin, 2008), 6.
3 Jane Austen, *Persuasion* (Harmondsworth: Penguin, 1985), 36.
4 Jane Austen, *Pride and Prejudice* (London: Penguin, 2003), 5.
5 This formulation of the "classic realist text" is taken from Colin McCabe's *James Joyce and the Revolution of the Word*, 2nd edn (Basingstoke: Palgrave Macmillan, 2003); see especially 13–38. For an important critique of McCabe's position see David Lodge, "*Middlemarch* and the Idea of the Classic Realist Text," in *The Nineteenth-Century Novel: Critical Essays and Documents*, ed. Arnold Kettle (London: Heinemann, 1981), 218–38.
6 George Eliot, *Felix Holt, the Radical* (Harmondsworth: Penguin, 1995), 18.
7 Eliot, *Felix Holt*, 25–6.
8 Angus Wilson, *Anglo-Saxon Attitudes* (New York: NYRB Classics, 2005), 16, 17.
9 Jane Austen, *Emma* (Harmondsworth: Penguin, 1985), 37.
10 Austen, *Emma*, 54.
11 George Eliot, *Middlemarch* (London: Penguin, 2003), 10.
12 Eliot, *Middlemarch*, 211.
13 Eliot, *Middlemarch*, 278.
14 James Joyce, *A Portrait of the Artist as a Young Man* (London: Penguin, 2003), 3.
15 Virginia Woolf, *Mrs. Dalloway* (Orlando: Harcourt, 2005), 3.
16 Virginia Woolf, *To the Lighthouse* (Orlando: Harcourt, 2005), 41.
17 D. H. Lawrence, "The Thorn in the Flesh," in *The Prussian Officer and Other Stories* (Harmondsworth: Penguin, 1995), 34.
18 Quoted in Stephen Kern, *The Culture of Time and Space, 1880–1918* (Cambridge: Harvard University Press, 1983), 24.
19 James Joyce, *Ulysses* (New York: Vintage, 1990), 738.
20 William Faulkner, *As I Lay Dying* (New York: Vintage, 1991), 12.
21 Virginia Woolf, *The Waves* (Oxford: Oxford University Press, 1992), 8.
22 Albert Camus, *The Fall*, trans. Justin O'Brien (New York: Vintage, 1991), 73.
23 Christopher Isherwood, *Goodbye to Berlin*, *The Berlin Stories* (New York: New Directions, 1963), 1.
24 Aphra Behn, *Oroonoko* (New York: Norton, 1997), 8.

25 Daniel Defoe, *Robinson Crusoe* (London: Penguin, 2003), 47.
26 Nathaniel Hawthorne, *The Blithedale Romance* (Harmondsworth: Penguin, 1986), 245.
27 Emily Brontë, *Wuthering Heights* (Harmondsworth: Penguin, 2003), 3.
28 Bram Stoker, *Dracula* (London: Penguin, 2003), 240.

Interchapter: *Justified Sinner*

1 James Hogg, *The Private Memoirs and Confessions of a Justified Sinner* (Oxford: Oxford University Press, 1999), 92. Hereafter cited parenthetically.

4 Character and the novel

1 David Lodge, *Nice Work* (Harmondsworth: Penguin, 1989), 39.
2 David Lodge, *The Art of Fiction* (London: Penguin, 1992), 67.
3 Jane Austen, *Pride and Prejudice* (London: Penguin, 2003), 6–7.
4 Austen, *Pride and Prejudice*, 7.
5 Virginia Woolf, "Modern Fiction," in *The Virginia Woolf Reader*, ed. Mitchell A. Leaska (San Diego: Harcourt, 1984), 290.
6 Virginia Woolf, "Mr. Bennett and Mrs. Brown," in *The Virginia Woolf Reader*, 207–8.
7 Robert Liddell, *A Treatise on the Novel* (London: Jonathan Cape, 1947), 93.
8 Virginia Woolf, *Jacob's Room* (Oxford: Oxford University Press, 1999), 37; Virginia Woolf, *Mrs. Dalloway* (Orlando: Harcourt, 2005), 8.
9 Henry James, *The Portrait of a Lady* (Harmondsworth: Penguin, 1986), 253.
10 E. M. Forster, *Aspects of the Novel* (Orlando: Harcourt, 1955), 67.
11 James Wood, *How Fiction Works* (New York: Farrar, Straus, & Giroux, 2008), 129.
12 Deidre Shauna Lynch, *The Economy of Character: Novels, Market Culture, and the Business of Inner Meaning* (Chicago: University of Chicago Press, 1998), 9.
13 Henry James, *The Wings of the Dove* (London: Penguin, 2008), 285, 89.
14 George Eliot, *The Mill on the Floss* (Oxford: Oxford University Press, 1998), 247.
15 Charles Dickens, *A Tale of Two Cities* (London: Penguin, 2003), 16.
16 Charles Dickens, *Great Expectations* (Harmondsworth: Penguin, 1985), 5.
17 Joel Weinsheimer, "Theory of Character: *Emma*," *Poetics Today*, 1 (1979): 187
18 Alex Woloch, *The One vs. the Many: Minor Characters and the Space of the Protagonist in the Novel* (Princeton: Princeton University Press, 2003), 15.
19 John Mullan, *How Novels Work* (Oxford: Oxford University Press, 2006), 79.
20 W. J. Harvey, *Character and the Novel* (London: Chatto & Windus, 1965), 23.
21 Northrop Frye, *Anatomy of Criticism: Four Essays* (Princeton: Princeton University Press, 1990), 304–5.
22 Tobias Smollett, *Ferdinand Count Fathom* (Oxford: Oxford University Press, 1971), 2–3.

23 Sir Walter Scott, *Waverley* (Harmondsworth: Penguin, 1985), 33.
24 Lodge, *Nice Work*, 40.

Interchapter: *The Scarlet Letter*

1 Nathaniel Hawthorne, *The Scarlet Letter* (Harmondsworth: Penguin, 1986), 31. Hereafter cited parenthetically.

5 Plotting the novel

1 Madame de Lafayette, *The Princesse de Clèves*, trans. Robin Buss (London: Penguin, 2004), 46.
2 Graham Greene, *Brighton Rock* (London: Penguin, 2004), 3.
3 Italo Calvino, *If on a winter's night a traveler*, trans. William Weaver (Orlando: Harcourt, 1981), 3, 4.
4 Calvino, *If on a winter's night*, 210.
5 George Saintsbury, *The English Novel* (London: Dent, 1913), 268
6 Henry James, *The Wings of the Dove* (London: Penguin, 2008), 10.
7 James Joyce, *Ulysses* (New York: Vintage, 1990), 783.
8 T. S. Eliot, "'Ulysses', Order, and Myth," in *Selected Prose of T. S. Eliot*, ed. Frank Kermode (San Diego: Harcourt, 1975), 177.
9 Daniel Defoe, *Robinson Crusoe* (London: Penguin, 2001), 63.
10 Oscar Wilde, *The Importance of Being Earnest and Other Plays* (Oxford: Oxford University Press, 2008), 273.
11 Muriel Spark, *The Prime of Miss Jean Brodie* (New York: HarperCollins, 1999), 129.
12 E. M. Forster, *Aspects of the Novel* (San Diego: Harcourt, 1965), 86.
13 George Eliot, *Middlemarch* (London: Penguin, 2003), 621.
14 Gillian Beer, *Darwin's Plots: Evolutionary Narrative in Darwin, George Eliot, and Nineteenth-Century Fiction* (London: Routledge, 1983), 8, 47.
15 Eliot, *Middlemarch*, 95.
16 Charles Dickens, *Bleak House* (London: Penguin, 2003), 256.
17 Benjamin Disraeli, *Sybil* (Oxford: Oxford University Press, 2009), 65–6.
18 Ian Duncan, *Modern Romance and Transformations of the Novel: The Gothic, Scott, Dickens* (Cambridge: Cambridge University Press, 1992), 2.
19 Charles Dickens, *Our Mutual Friend* (London: Penguin, 1997), 131.
20 George Eliot, *The Mill on the Floss* (Oxford: Oxford University Press, 1998), 402.
21 Peter Brooks, *Reading for the Plot* (Cambridge: Harvard University Press, 1992), 4.
22 Walter Benjamin, "The Storyteller," in *Illuminations*, ed. Hannah Arendt, trans. Harry Zorn (London: Pimlico, 1999), 100.
23 Don DeLillo, *White Noise* (Harmondsworth: Penguin, 1986), 26.
24 Calvino, *If on a winter's night*, 259.

Interchapter: *Madame Bovary*

1 Gustave Flaubert, *Madame Bovary* (London: Penguin, 2003), 32–3. Hereafter cited parenthetically.
2 Richard Brinsley Sheridan, *The Rivals, The School for Scandal and Other Plays* (Oxford: Oxford University Press, 1998), 72.
3 Charlotte Lennox, *The Female Quixote* (Oxford: Oxford University Press, 1998), 327.

6 Setting the novel

1 Franco Moretti, *Atlas of the European Novel, 1800–1900* (London: Verso, 1998), 70.
2 Charles Dickens, quoted in John Forster, *The Life of Charles Dickens*, vol. II (New York: Scribner, 1907), 349.
3 Nathaniel Hawthorne, *The House of the Seven Gables* (London: Penguin, 1986), 1.
4 Hawthorne, *House of the Seven Gables*, 3.
5 M. M. Bakhtin, "Forms of Time and Chronotope in the Novel," in *The Dialogic Imagination*, ed. Michael Holquist, trans. Caryl Emerson and Michael Holquist (Austin: University of Texas Press, 1981), 100.
6 Bakhtin, "Forms of Time and Chronotope," 98.
7 Stendhal, *The Red and the Black*, trans. Roger Gard (London: Penguin, 2002), 85.
8 Patrick Parrinder, *Nation and Novel: The English Novel from its Origins to the Present Day* (Oxford: Oxford University Press, 2006), 29.
9 Jane Austen, *Northanger Abbey* (London: Penguin, 2003), 18.
10 Voltaire, *Candide*, trans. Roger Pearson (Oxford: Oxford University Press, 2006), 46.
11 Samuel Johnson, *Rasselas* (London: Penguin, 1985), 45.
12 J. Paul Hunter, *Before Novels: The Cultural Contexts of Eighteenth-Century English Fiction* (New York: Norton, 1990), 110; Tobias Smollett, *The Expedition of Humphry Clinker* (London: Penguin, 1985), 67.
13 Smollett, *Humphry Clinker*, 150.
14 Jane Austen, *Mansfield Park* (London: Penguin, 2003), 360–1.
15 Austen, *Mansfield Park*, 355, 363.
16 Jane Austen, *Pride and Prejudice* (London: Penguin, 2003), 353.
17 Austen, *Pride and Prejudice*, 235.
18 Austen, *Pride and Prejudice*, 239.
19 Raymond Williams, *The Country and the City* (Oxford: Oxford University Press, 1973), 50.
20 Williams, *Country and the City*, 50.
21 Edward W. Said, *Culture and Imperialism* (New York: Knopf, 1993), 80–97.
22 Jane Austen, *Northanger Abbey* (London: Penguin, 2003), 188.
23 Mary Shelley, *Frankenstein* (London: Penguin, 2003), 31, 164.
24 Bram Stoker, *Dracula* (London: Penguin, 2003), 7.

25 Henry James, *Hawthorne* (New York: Harper, 1901), 42–3.

26 Herman Melville, *Moby-Dick* (London: Penguin, 2003), 117.

27 Thomas Hardy, *The Mayor of Casterbridge* (London: Penguin, 2003), 29.

28 Hardy, *Mayor of Casterbridge*, 85.

29 D. H. Lawrence, *The Rainbow* (London: Penguin, 2007), 10–11.

30 Charlotte Brontë, *Shirley* (London: Penguin, 2006), 5.

31 Elizabeth Gaskell, *North and South* (London: Penguin, 2003), 14.

32 Charles Dickens, *Hard Times* (London: Penguin, 2003), 27.

33 Honoré de Balzac, *Père Goriot*, trans. A. J. Krailsheimer (Oxford: Oxford University Press, 1999), 6.

34 Émile Zola, *Thérèse Raquin*, trans. Andrew Rothwell (Oxford: Oxford University Press, 1998), 2.

35 Zola, *Thérèse Raquin*, 7.

36 Mieke Bal, "Over-writing as Un-writing: Descriptions, World-Making, and Novelistic Time," in *The Novel*, vol. II: *Forms and Themes*, ed. Franco Moretti (Princeton: Princeton University Press, 2006), 571.

37 Joseph Conrad, *The Secret Agent* (London: Penguin, 2007), 250.

38 Sam Selvon, *The Lonely Londoners* (New York: Longman, 2007), 72.

39 Peter Kalliney, *Cities of Affluence and Anger: A Literary Geography of Modern Englishness* (Charlottesville: University of Virginia Press, 1996), 110.

40 Don DeLillo, *Underworld* (New York: Scribner, 1997), 807, 810.

41 Samuel Beckett, *Company, Three Novels* (New York: Grove, 1996), 3.

42 Jonathan Swift, *Gulliver's Travels* (Oxford: Oxford University Press, 1998), 121.

43 Kurt Vonnegut, *Breakfast of Champions* (New York: Delta, 1999), 10.

44 Viktor Shklovsky, *Theory of Prose*, trans. Benjamin Sher (Normal: Dalkey Archive Press, 1991), 5.

45 Shklovsky, *Theory of Prose*, 6.

46 Shklovsky, *Theory of Prose*, 12.

Interchapter: *Bleak House*

1 Charles Dickens, *Bleak House* (London: Penguin, 2003), 257. Hereafter cited parenthetically.

7 Time and history

1 Ian Watt, *The Rise of the Novel: Studies in Defoe, Richardson, and Fielding* (Berkeley: University of California Press, 1957), 23.

2 Quoted in Geoffrey Day, *From Fiction to the Novel* (London: Routledge, 1987), 50.

3 Dominick LaCapra, *History, Politics, and the Novel* (Ithaca: Cornell University Press, 1987), 8.

4 Thomas Hardy, *Tess of the D'Urbervilles* (London: Penguin, 2003), 23.

5 Joseph Roth, *The Radetsky March*, trans. Michael Hofmann (London: Granta, 2003), 98.

6 Roth, *Radetsky March*, 120.

7 Joseph Conrad, *The Secret Agent* (London: Penguin, 2007), 28.

8 Stephen Kern, *The Culture of Time and Space, 1880–1918* (Cambridge: Harvard University Press, 1983), 11.

9 Charlotte Brontë, *Jane Eyre* (Harmondsworth: Penguin, 1985), 60, 92, 115.

10 William Faulkner, *The Sound and the Fury* (New York: Vintage, 1990), 85.

11 Ford Madox Ford, *Joseph Conrad: A Personal Remembrance*, *The Ford Madox Ford Reader*, ed. Sondra J. Stang (London: Paladin, 1987), 216–17.

12 Ford, *Joseph Conrad*, 217.

13 Ford Madox Ford, *The Good Soldier* (London: Penguin, 2002), 147.

14 Martin Amis, *Time's Arrow* (New York: Vintage, 1992), 120; Claude Lanzmann, "Hier ist kein Warum," in *Au sujet de Shoah* (Paris: Belin, 1990), 279.

15 Kurt Vonnegut, *Slaughterhouse-Five* (New York: Dell, 1991), 22, 2, 19.

16 W. G. Sebald, *Austerlitz*, trans. Anthea Bell (New York: Modern Library, 2001), 100–1.

17 Sebald, *Austerlitz*, 153.

18 W. G. Sebald, *The Emigrants*, trans. Michael Hulse (New York: New Directions, 1997), 23.

Interchapter: *To the Lighthouse*

1 T. S. Eliot, *Four Quartets* (Orlando: Harcourt, 1971), 40.

2 Virginia Woolf, *To the Lighthouse* (Orlando: Harcourt, 2005), 132, 136, 137. Hereafter cited parenthetically. Note that this is the American edition of the novel; the deaths of Mrs. Ramsay and Prue appear slightly differently (though also in parenthesis) in the British version.

8 Genre and subgenre

1 John Sutherland, *Bestsellers: A Very Short Introduction* (Oxford: Oxford University Press, 2007), 1.

2 Gustave Flaubert, *Madame Bovary* (London: Penguin, 2003), 78.

3 Northrop Frye, *Anatomy of Criticism: Four Essays* (Princeton: Princeton University Press, 1990), 247–8.

4 Virginia Woolf, *A Room of One's Own* (San Diego: Harcourt, 1981), 73–4.

5 Sutherland, *Bestsellers*, 3.

6 Brian McHale, *Postmodernist Fiction* (London: Routledge, 2001), 9–10.

7 Michael Denning, *Cover Stories: Narrative and Ideology in the British Spy Thriller* (London: Routledge, 1987), 29.

8 Hans Robert Jauss, *Toward an Aesthetic of Reception*, trans. Timothy Bahti (Minneapolis: University of Minnesota Press, 1982), 23.

9 Alastair Fowler, *Kinds of Literature: An Introduction to the Theory of Genre and Modes* (Cambridge: Harvard University Press, 1982), 20.

10 Jauss, *Toward an Aesthetic of Reception*, 23.

Interchapter: *The Ministry of fear*

1 Graham Greene, *The Ministry of Fear: An Entertainment* (London: Penguin, 2005), 54. Hereafter cited parenthetically.

2 Elizabeth Bowen, *The Heat of the Day* (New York: Anchor, 2002), 212.

9 Novel and anti-novel

1 Bernard Bergonzi, *The Situation of the Novel* (London: Macmillan, 1970), 34.

2 Günter Grass, *The Tin Drum*, trans. Ralph Manheim (New York: Vintage, 1990), 17.

3 Quoted in John Tinnon Taylor, *Early Opposition to the English Novel: The Popular Reaction from 1760–1830* (New York: King's Crown Press, 1943), 13.

4 Bergonzi, *Situation of the Novel*, 19.

5 Henry Green, *Surviving: The Uncollected Writings of Henry Green*, ed. Matthew Yorke (New York: Viking, 1993), 247.

6 Salman Rushdie, "In Defense of the Novel, Yet Again," in *Step Across This Line: Collected Nonfiction, 1992–2002* (New York: Random House, 2002), 51.

7 Muriel Spark, *The Comforters* (New York: New Directions, 1994), 57.

8 Robert Hosmer, "An Interview with Dame Muriel Spark," *Salmagundi* (Spring 2005), 147.

9 Roland Barthes, "To Write: An Intransitive Verb?," in *The Rustle of Language*, trans. Richard Howard (Berkeley: University of California Press, 1989), 15.

10 Patricia Waugh, *Metafiction: The Theory and Practice of Self-Conscious Fiction* (London: Routledge, 1996), 2.

11 Denis Diderot, *Jacques the Fatalist*, trans. David Coward (Oxford: Oxford University Press, 1999), 3.

12 Diderot, *Jacques the Fatalist*, 238.

13 Linda Hutcheon, *Narcissistic Narrative: The Metafictional Paradox* (Waterloo, Ontario: Wilfred Laurier University Press, 1980), 37, 43.

14 Henry James, "The Art of Fiction," in *The Future of the Novel: Essays on the Art of Fiction*, ed. Leon Edel (New York: Vintage, 1956), 3.

15 Alain Robbe-Grillet, *For a New Novel*, trans. Richard Howard (Evanston: Northwestern University Press, 1996), 12.

16 Robbe-Grillet, *For a New Novel*, 12, 10.

17 Robbe-Grillet, *For a New Novel*, 9.
18 John Barth, "Foreword," *The Floating Opera and The End of the Road* (New York: Anchor, 1988), v.
19 John Fowles, *The French Lieutenant's Woman* (Boston: Back Bay, 1998), 94.
20 Fowles, *French Lieutenant's Woman*, 95.
21 Jean-François Lyotard, *The Postmodern Condition: A Report on Knowledge*, trans. Geoff Bennington and Brian Massumi (Minneapolis: University of Minnesota Press, 1984), xxiv.
22 Angela Carter, *Nights at the Circus* (London: Vintage, 1994), 8.
23 Julian Barnes, *A History of the World in 10½ Chapters* (London: Picador, 1990), 242.
24 Linda Hutcheon, *A Poetics of Postmodernism: History, Theory, Fiction* (London: Routledge, 1988), 105–23.

Interchapter: *The Crying of Lot 49*

1 Thomas Pynchon, *The Crying of Lot 49* (New York: Perennial, 1999), 2. Hereafter cited parenthetically.
2 Charles Newman, *The Post-Modern Aura: The Act of Fiction in an Age of Inflation* (Evanston: Northwestern University Press, 1985), 5; Gerald Graff, *Literature Against Itself: Literary Ideas in Modern Society* (Chicago: University of Chicago Press, 1979), 57.

10 Novel, nation, community

1 Thomas Pynchon, *The Crying of Lot 49* (New York: Perennial, 1999), 147.
2 Chinua Achebe, "An Image of Africa," reprinted in *The Critical Tradition: Classic Texts and Contemporary Trends*, 3rd edn., ed. David H. Richter (Boston: Bedford/St. Martins, 2007), 1787.
3 Chinua Achebe, *Things Fall Apart* (New York: Anchor, 1994), 7.
4 Achebe, *Things Fall Apart*, 9.
5 Junot Díaz, *The Brief Wondrous Life of Oscar Wao* (London: Penguin, 2007), 2.
6 Sydney Owenson, Lady Morgan, *The Wild Irish Girl* (Oxford: Oxford University Press, 2008), 10, 13.
7 Tobias Smollett, *The Expedition of Humphry Clinker* (London: Penguin, 1985), 250, 318.
8 Maria Edgeworth, *Castle Rackrent* and *Ennui* (London: Penguin, 1992), 63, 121.
9 Robert Crawford, *Devolving English Literature*, 2nd edn. (Edinburgh: Edinburgh University Press, 2000), 55.
10 Homi K. Bhabha, ed., *Nation and Narration* (London: Routledge, 1990), 3.
11 Benedict Anderson, *Imagined Communities: Reflections on the Origins and Spread of Nationalism*, rev. edn. (London: Verso, 2006), 7, 6.

12 Anderson, *Imagined Communities*, 36.
13 Franco Moretti, *Atlas of the European Novel, 1800-1900* (London: Verso, 1998), 20.
14 Timothy Brennan, "The National Longing for Form," in *Nation and Narration*, ed. Homi K. Bhabha (London: Routledge, 1990), 49.
15 Sir Walter Scott, *Ivanhoe* (Oxford: Oxford University Press, 1998), 14.
16 Hanif Kureishi, *The Buddha of Suburbia* (London: Penguin, 1991), 3, 53.
17 James Joyce, *Ulysses* (New York: Vintage, 1990), 296–7.
18 Joyce, *Ulysses*, 296, 297, 297, 301.
19 M. M. Bakhtin, "From the Prehistory of Novelistic Discourse," in *The Dialogic Imagination*, ed. Michael Holquist, trans. Caryl Emerson and Michael Holquist (Austin: University of Texas Press, 1981), 66.
20 Charles Dickens, *Hard Times* (London: Penguin, 2003), 282, 264, 21, 136–7.
21 Cairns Craig, *The Modern Scottish Novel: Narrative and the National Imagination* (Edinburgh: Edinburgh University Press, 1999), 77–8.
22 Lewis Grassic Gibbon, *Sunset Song* (London: Penguin, 2007), 12.

Interchapter: *Midnight's Children*

1 Salman Rushdie, *Midnight's Children* (London: Penguin, 1991), 3. Hereafter cited parenthetically.

11 Concluding

1 Samuel Johnson, *Rasselas* (London: Penguin, 1985), 149.
2 Jane Austen, *Northanger Abbey* (London: Penguin, 2003), 233.
3 E. M. Forster, *Aspects of the Novel* (Orlando: Harcourt, 1955), 95–6.
4 D. H. Lawrence, *The Rainbow* (London: Penguin, 2007), 459.
5 Frank Kermode, *The Sense of an Ending: Studies in the Theory of Fiction* (Oxford: Oxford University Press, 2000), 45.
6 Michael André Bernstein, *Foregone Conclusions: Against Apocalyptic History* (Berkeley: University of California Press, 1994), 2.
7 Bernstein, *Foregone Conclusions*, 4, 9.
8 Henry James, "The Art of Fiction," in *The Future of the Novel: Essays on the Art of Fiction*, ed. Leon Edel (New York: Vintage, 1956), 8.
9 Ian McEwan, *Atonement* (New York: Anchor, 2003), 350.
10 Laurence Sterne, *A Sentimental Journey* (London: Penguin, 2005), 5, 118.
11 Charlotte Bronte, *Villette* (London: Penguin, 2004), 546.
12 Barbara Herrnstein Smith, *Poetic Closure: A Study of How Poems End* (Chicago: University of Chicago Press, 1968), 36.
13 Joseph Conrad, *The Secret Agent* (London: Penguin, 2007), 246.
14 E. M. Forster, *A Passage to India* (London: Penguin, 2005), 306.

15 Russell Reising, *Loose Ends: Closure and Crisis in the American Social Text* (Durham: Duke University Press, 1996), 2–3.

16 D. A. Miller, *Narrative and its Discontents: Problems of Closure in the Traditional Novel* (Princeton: Princeton University Press, 1981), 267.

17 Fyodor Dostoevsky, *Crime and Punishment*, trans. David McDuff (London: Penguin, 1991), 630.

18 In Philip Larkin's poem "Talking in Bed" it is "difficult to find / Words at once true and kind / Or not untrue and not unkind."

19 William St Clair, *The Reading Nation in the Romantic Period* (Cambridge University Press, 2004), 224.

Glossary

allegorical novel: coded **representation** of either a real-life historical event (e.g. Orwell's rendering of the Russian Revolution in *Animal Farm*) or an abstract theme (e.g. Bunyan's treatment of Christian spiritual development as a literal journey in *Pilgrim's Progress*).

anachronism: an event, object, concept, or person appearing within a historical setting where it could not have existed. Departures from historical reality may be made deliberately (e.g. for comic effect) as well as inadvertently.

anecdote: a brief narrative of a surprising/amusing incident: the **episodic** quality of the eighteenth-century novel makes for extensive use of anecdote but anecdotes are also deployed in the modern novel (e.g. in Conrad's fiction), with the emphasis falling less on the anecdote than on how it is told.

anti-novel: typically associated with mid-twentieth-century experimentation (thanks to the experimental *nouveau roman* or "new novel" practiced by novelists such as Nathalie Sarraute, Alain Robbe-Grillet, and Christine Brooke-Rose), the anti-novel disrupts familiar **realist** conventions of **plot**, **character**, or **point of view**. However, the term need not imply a historical period, and much earlier works of **metafiction** (e.g. Diderot's *Jacques the Fatalist*) have also been described thus.

Bildungsroman: the "novel of formation" narrates the development of a (usually but not always male) **protagonist** from childhood to socialized maturity. Goethe's *William Meister's Apprenticeship* is often considered the first and most influential, but later examples include *David Copperfield* and *Jane Eyre*. See also *Künstlerroman*.

canon/canonical: a canon is a body of writing consisting of works accepted as authoritative/authentic (e.g. those books of the Bible that Christianity takes as scripture). "Canonical" novels are those accorded classic status, and frequently studied and written about. As a result of critical unease with the idea of "self-evident" greatness (which ignored the fact that the canon was constituted mainly of the work of dead white men), in recent decades the canon has expanded to include the fiction of, for example, women, people of color, and non-Western writers.

character: a narrative actor, usually but not always human. Characters may also be animals (e.g. Anna Sewell's *Black Beauty*), objects (e.g. Charles Johnstone's *Chrysal, or, The Adventures of a Guinea*), or automata (e.g. Philip K. Dick's *Do*

197

Androids Dream of Electric Sheep?), but even non-human characters usually have recognizably human characteristics and motivations.

chronotope: this term was coined by Mikhail Bakhtin to designate a narrative unit in which place ("topos") and time ("chronos") are inextricably connected.

closure: the condition of completion and resolution achieved at the ending, when mysteries have been explained and questions answered. It is often considered characteristic of the **realist** novel that the plot be satisfactorily wrapped up at the end, when, typically, we learn the fates of all significant characters. **Modernist** and **postmodernist** fiction, in contrast, tends to resist the conventional tactics for attaining closure (marriage, death), often favoring a more open-ended or even deliberately arbitrary approach to ending.

codex: a brick-shaped sheaf of papers collated and bound between covers, the codex is the handwritten prototype of the traditional (post-scroll) form of the Western book.

defamiliarization: Soviet critics of the 1920s argued that defamiliarization (*"ostranenie"*) was the essential quality of literary art. Working against the numbing effects of familiarity and habit, art makes us see familiar things in unfamiliar ways. Viktor Shklovsky offers the example of a Tolstoy story narrated from the estranging perspective of a horse, incapable of understanding such human "norms" as private ownership.

detective novel: a novel centered on the solving of a crime, usually a murder (or several), by the novel's **protagonist**, who may be either a professional or amateur detective (typically a maverick of some kind). The invention of the genre is usually attributed to nineteenth-century writers like Edgar Allan Poe ("The Murders in the Rue Morgue"), Wilkie Collins (*The Moonstone*), and Arthur Conan Doyle (creator of Sherlock Holmes), but its golden age is typically considered the 1920s and 1930s.

dialogic: that the novel is a "dialogic" form – permits the articulation of multiple perspectives and worldviews – was central to Bakhtin's view of the novel: although no novel could be truly "monologic" – authoritarian in promulgating a single worldview – some were more "dialogic" than others.

dialogue: conversation between two (or sometimes more) **characters**.

embedded narrative: usually narrated by a character within the novel, an embedded narrative is a story included within – distinct from but often thematically related to – the main story.

epic: a long narrative poem involving a heroic protagonist and events of mythic and/or supernatural proportions, of particular interest to novel theorists trying to identify the differences between the novel and older narrative forms. The best-known examples are from classical antiquity, e.g. Homer's *The Odyssey* and Virgil's *The Aeneid*.

epigraph: a passage of text, either a quotation from another author or invented, which, placed at the beginning of a novel or a chapter, sets the tone or announces the concerns of what follows.

episodic novel: consists substantially of separate, potentially stand-alone incidents or "episodes," a common structure in novels centered on a journey. See also **picaresque**.

epistolary novel: most common in the eighteenth century, the epistolary novel consists primarily or entirely of written correspondence between characters, the author (where not "invisible") purporting to be merely its editor.

espionage novel: a common form of twentieth-century **thriller** centered on state politics, intelligence gathering, and the dangerous exposure of conspiracy.

fabula and syuzhet: the *fabula* (sometimes translated as "story") consists of the sequence events would form if chronologically arranged (or rearranged); the *syuzhet* (sometimes translated as "plot") is the sequence of events as we encounter them in the reading of a novel. The distinction is especially useful for reading novels that deploy such techniques of temporal disruption as **flashback** and **flashforward**.

fiction: although the term simply indicates that the content of a text is imaginary, "fiction" as a genre label is used to refer only to the **novel**, **novella**, and **short story** (and not to poetic or dramatic works, which may be every bit as made-up).

first-person narration: named for the grammatical first person singular, "I," first-person narration describes the practice of recounting the **narrative** from the perspective of a **character** within the fictional world of the story. However, an otherwise detached **narrator** will occasionally refer to himself or herself in the first-person (e.g. in the novels of Fielding and Dickens); in these cases, the novel is still categorized as **third-person narration** because the narrator is not a realized character within the story.

flashback and flashforward: also known as "analepsis" and "prolepsis." The linear progress of the **narrative** is interrupted by the depiction of something that happened earlier (flashback/analepsis) or that will happen later (flashforward/prolepsis) in the story. These deviations from linear time need have no motivating "pretext," but common narrative motivations include a **character**'s dreams or memories.

flat and round character: terms invented by the novelist E. M. Forster to describe the differences between **characters** that, exemplifying a single quality or idea, can be summed up in a single sentence and do not change in the course of the novel ("flat characters"), and psychologically complex characters, usually **protagonists**, who develop over the course of the story ("round characters"). In the **realist** novel, the distinction generally corresponds to the distinction between major and minor characters.

focalization: see **point of view**.

frame narrative: a narrative that contains one or many distinct stories and explains the motivations behind its/their telling. Among the earliest and most famous examples of narrative "framing" is the story of Scheherazade and her tyrant husband in *The Arabian Nights*; if she doesn't keep telling him irresistibly absorbing stories he will have her beheaded in the morning.

free indirect discourse/free indirect style: when the **narration** remains in the **third-person** and past tense, but we recognize the words and thoughts as those of a character even though there is no "he said" or "she thought" to indicate explicitly that the narrative is being filtered through his or her perspective.

genre fiction: a "genre" is a "kind," and genre fiction a way of classifying as one all the novels that fall into a recognizable sub-category of fiction: **gothic, thriller,**

science fiction, and so on, each of which has easily recognizable conventions and formulae. Importantly, however, the pejorative connotations of "genre" and "generic" are historically and culturally specific; that we take "originality" to be an aesthetic virtue does not mean that it is or has been universally understood as one. Also importantly, "literary" or non-genre fiction often deploys conventions associated with particular genres.

gothic novel: established in the eighteenth century, the gothic novel tells a story of mystery, **suspense**, and horror, deploying or implying elements of supernatural terror. Often set in a distant time and/or remote place, the gothic novel typically represents a contest between vulnerable purity (an innocent, victimized heroine) and ruthless evil (often in the form of a cruelly calculating male aristocrat).

heterodiegetic and homodiegetic narration: when the narrator is outside the world of the story (e.g. in the novels of Fielding, Austen, and Eliot), the narration is heterodiegetic; when the narrator is a character within the story (like Lockwood and Nelly Dean in *Wuthering Heights*, for example), the narration is homodiegetic. Corresponds to the distinction between **third-person narration** and **first-person narration**.

heteroglossia: coined by Mikhail Bakhtin, the term means "many-languagedness." One's language, Bakhtin claimed, is never a single language, and "heteroglossia" refers to (what he took to be) the novel's defining characteristic of linguistic plurality: there are the narrator's voice and the voices of all the characters. Because these voices – same language, usually, but in different forms – may contradict each other, the novel is inherently subversive of monolithic or doctrinaire authority, even that of its own author.

historical novel: a fictitious narrative that uses real-life historical personages and events. Sometimes the novel's purpose is to reflect imaginatively on how and why events happened, but more often is concerned with investigating the relationship between the individual and the society or culture of which he or she is a part. Although the historical novel is concerned with reconstructing a prior period, it is typically more useful as an archive of information about the attitudes of its own time.

historiographic metafiction: coined by the **postmodernist** critic Linda Hutcheon, the term refers to a common late twentieth-century form of highly self-conscious fiction-about-fiction; historiographic metafiction not only reflects on what happened in history but also on how we think we know what happened.

ideology: the values underpinning the habits and customs of a particular social group, values so taken-for-granted that they seem self-evidently true and universally applicable, as if they were the natural order of things rather than constructed by and specific to particular cultures. The novel's traditional relationship to the **representation** of society makes it a particularly useful archive of unconsciously held beliefs about, e.g., gender, money, labor, love, empire, and class.

implied author and implied reader: the implied author is the idea or image of an authorial sensibility that we infer from a text; not to be confused with either the real-life biographical author or the novel's **narrator**. Likewise, the implied reader is generally not the person who reads the novel but the reader we infer as an intended recipient of the story, a recipient whose knowledge, values, and interests are suggested by what the implied author can assume.

interior monologue: when the thoughts, feelings, and impressions are reproduced as the subconscious or semi-conscious flow of the character's mind, and presented as if narratively unmediated (**first-person** rather than **third-person narration**, no quotation marks).

intertextuality: the status of all texts, for some **postmodernist** thinkers and writers, as composites or amalgams of other texts; intertextuality may be understood in intentionalist terms (e.g. generated by deliberate allusions) or, more usually, as an inevitable condition of writing (since language is shared, belongs to no one).

intrusive narrator: an **omniscient third-person narrator** who doesn't simply tell the story but routinely comments on what is happening and on its implications, often linking the fictional world to phenomena observable in the real, non-fictional world.

Künstlerroman: the "artist novel," often semi-autobiographical, examines the development of an artist from childhood promise to maturity (e.g. Joyce's *A Portrait of the Artist as a Young Man*). See also ***Bildungsroman.***

magic/magical realism: closely related to and contemporary with the **postmodernist novel**, magical realist fiction is characterized by the intrusion of fantastical, supernatural, or folkloric happenings or phenomena into an otherwise meticulously delineated, realistic world, where they are treated as unremarkable, requiring no comment or explanation. Magical realism is strongly associated with the (internationally influential) modern Latin American novel.

metafiction: fiction that explicitly and self-consciously reflects on the nature, status, and procedures of fiction. See also **anti-novel, historiographic metafiction**, and **postmodernism/postmodernist**.

mimesis/mimetic: mimesis means the "copying" or "imitating" of reality in art. See also **realism/realist**.

modernism/modernist: the product of the revolutionary sensibilities of the early twentieth century, intent on liberating fiction (and all the arts) from taken-for-granted **realist** conventions of **representation**. Although there is little consensus on when literary modernism begins and ends, one influential dating of the period is 1890–1930. Characteristic of modernist fiction are experiments with **point of view, unreliable narration, interior monologue, flashback and flashforward**.

narration/narrative: "narration" is the recounting or representation of a story; "narrative" may refer to either the story or its telling. A narrative may be fictional (e.g. a novel or part of a novel) or non-fictional (e.g. a newspaper story).

narratology: the systematic, theoretical study of narrative form and structure, usually with an emphasis on prose fiction and film. The "ology" suffix denotes "study of" or "science of"; thus, narratology is the science of **narrative**.

narrator: the "speaker" in the narration, the conduit of the narrative: sometimes a character within the novel and sometimes not (see **heterodiegetic and**

homodiegetic). A novel always has a narrator, and sometimes more than one. Not to be confused with either the real-life biographical author or the **implied author**.

naturalism: associated with late nineteenth-century Europe (especially France) and early twentieth-century America, Naturalism is a self-consciously hyper-realist mode of fictional representation aiming at quasi-scientific objectivity in its tracing of environmental and hereditary causes and their effects. Characteristics include a preoccupation with lower-class life, sexual, criminal, and/or economic degradation, and a highly deterministic view of human action.

non-fiction novel: real-life events are reconstructed through novelistic techniques (plotting, **dialogue**, characterization, scene-making, and so on).

nouveau roman: see **anti-novel**

novel sequence: sometimes known as the *"roman fleuve"* (literally, "river-novel"), the novel sequence is a series of novels by the same author and deploying the same characters, context, or setting, although each novel has an autonomous plot, allowing it to be read alone and the series to be read selectively and/or non-sequentially.

novella: fictional prose narratives between around fifty and a hundred pages are often referred to as novellas, reflecting their brevity relative to the typical novel. These frequently take the form of a "tale" or extended **anecdote**, sometimes **framed** (e.g. James's *The Turn of the Screw*) but not necessarily (e.g. Kafka's *The Metamorphosis*).

omniscient narration: "omniscient" means "all-knowing," so omniscient narration refers to a **third-person narration** in which the **narrator** can present not only the sorts of external detail and information that might be accessible to characters in the story but also the feelings and thoughts of characters (which might well be unknown even to the character being discussed). An omniscient **narrator** may refrain from explicit judgment (e.g. Flaubert's *Madame Bovary*) or may, alternatively, provide a running commentary on the events being recounted (e.g. Fielding's *Tom Jones*).

paratext: the textual material accompanying the main text – e.g. index, cover image, footnotes, back-cover blurbs – that is not usually considered an integral part of the text but which may inform our reading of it (sometimes without our being conscious of it).

parody: a comic imitation of a form that takes itself seriously; of particular interest to novel theorists because of the debunking, illusion-stripping irreverence some view as integral to the form (e.g. *Don Quixote*'s parody of chivalric **romance**, Fielding's parody of *Pamela* in *Joseph Andrews*, Austen's of the **gothic** in *Northanger Abbey*, etc).

picaresque: named for the Spanish *pícaro* (rogue, rascal), the picaresque is an **episodic** form of early novel that recounts in a down-to-earth and usually comic way the enterprises and adventures of a morally dubious but likeable protagonist.

plot: although English-speakers typically think of the plot as the story, or "what happens," **narratology** uses "plot" to speak of the *organization* of events in a narrative: that is to say, not *what* happens in a story but *how* we encounter it. See also *fabula* and *syuzhet*

point of view: the vantage point of the narration; or, the position from which we are able to "see" the action. See also **first-person narration** and **third-person narration.**

postcolonial fiction: novels produced by authors with roots in countries or regions (e.g. India, Nigeria, the Caribbean) formerly colonized by European nations, and often written in the language of the former colonizer (which may be the novelist's own and only language) rather than in languages "indigenous" to the region (e.g. Indian novels in English not Urdu; Algerian novels in French not Arabic).

postmodernism/postmodernist: like **modernist**, the adjective designates both a period (here the second half of the twentieth century) and a kind of fiction: **metafictional** and anti-**realist**, formally experimental, skeptical and relativistic, transgressing the boundaries between high and low art and between literary and non-literary media.

prose: written language akin to normal non-literary speech (we all speak in prose), usually conforming to the demands of grammar but not evidencing poetry's traditional forms of syntactical organization (line breaks, meter, rhythm). With only very rare (e.g. Pushkin's *Eugene Onegin*) and debatable (e.g. Byron's *Don Juan*) exceptions, novels are written in prose.

protagonist: used to describe the main character/agent in a narrative, the term "protagonist" is simpler than "hero"/"heroine" since it implies no value judgment (e.g. the amoral, opportunistic Becky Sharp in Thackeray's tellingly subtitled *Vanity Fair: A Novel Without A Hero*).

realism/realist: "realist" designates the kind of fiction that minimizes its status as a constructed artifact, asking us to treat its prose as transparent, a window on reality; "realism" is also used to refer to the aura of lifelikeness and plausibility generated by a novel's attention to the concrete details of everyday life. Historically, the realist novel has been character-driven (concerned with the development of the protagonist), materialist (attentive to, for example, the power of money and status), and socially engaged (dealing with a range of social groups, sometimes with an activist intent).

representation: the reenactment or rendering of something via a particular medium (Michelangelo's David "represents" in sculpture the Biblical king; Dickens's *Bleak House* "represents" in prose fiction the Court of Chancery). Although an indispensable term, "representation" should be used cautiously since it implies the prior existence of what is being represented (hence the "re" prefix), which isn't always the case with **fiction.**

romance: (I) Long (and sometimes very long) fictional works written in verse or prose and characterized by a sequence of implausible adventures, idealized lovers, exciting quests, and astounding triumphs. Predating the novel by many centuries, romance, like **epic**, is of particular relevance to critics interested in the possible origins of the novel. (II) Sometimes used in the eighteenth century for what we would come to call novels, this older term was later reclaimed by some nineteenth-century writers, most notably Hawthorne, as a way of signaling that their novels would engage (e.g.) extreme emotional states, the subjective inner landscape, and unusual moral situations rather than be constrained by the perceived "real-worldliness" of the novel.

satire: witty or ironic writing that deflates its target, which may be particular kinds of writing – see **parody** – or social institutions, moral failings, worldviews, or beliefs, mostly to amuse but sometimes with an implicitly or explicitly reformist agenda.

science fiction: a genre of fictional writing, often futuristic, centered on scientific (or pseudo-scientific) and technological concepts: e.g. time travel, alien encounters, evolution/degeneration. Although, in theory, science fiction might be traced back at least as far as Swift's *Gulliver's Travels* (see, for example, the **dystopian satire** of the novel's third section), late nineteenth-century writers such as Jules Verne and H. G. Wells are typically credited with its "invention" and popularization.

sensation novel: a popular mid-**Victorian** form, a prototypical **thriller**, supplying a gripping tale of shocking secrets within respectable circles – bigamy, adultery, madness, murder.

sentimental novel/novel of sensibility: an eighteenth-century form that solicits the reader's sympathy for the trials of a virtuous hero or heroine, and encourages moral feeling and right action. "Sentimentality," crucially, did not have pejorative connotations for eighteenth-century readers; rather, it spoke to the moral virtue of being able to imagine yourself in another's situation.

setting: where, in terms of place, time, and socio-cultural context(s), the action of a novel takes place.

short story: a short fictional prose narrative. What counts as "short" may vary: to take two **modernist** classics, Kafka's "Before the Law" is around 600 words; Joyce's "The Dead" is over 15,000. If a fictional prose **narrative** is too short to be published alone as a book (rather than in a magazine or anthology or collection of stories), it is likely a short story rather than a **novella**.

stream of consciousness: a term coined by William James (brother of Henry James) to describe how we experience consciousness as a fluid stream – associative, fluctuating, defying rational order. Can be used to describe the general effects of a number of different narrative techniques for presenting interiority, including **interior monologue** and (in the hands of **modernist** novelists) forms of **free indirect discourse**, but these other terms are more usefully precise.

suspense: the means by which a text defers the clarification of its mysteries, the solution to the questions it asks; the solicitation of desires for knowledge and revelation that stop us from putting the book down.

theme: the cultural, political, social, moral, spiritual, emotional, psychological (and so on) questions and problems that a novel addresses.

third-person narration: the story is told from a perspective external to the characters being described (external in the sense that characters are referred to as "he," "she," "they," or, uncommonly, "it"). Usually **omniscient** but sometimes limited to the perspective of a single **character**, whose **point of view** we follow through, e.g., **free indirect discourse**.

thriller: novels of high **suspense**, usually aimed at a popular readership, centered on a mystery or conspiracy; these work by generating and exploiting the readerly pleasures of (temporary!) uncertainty and anxiety.

unreliable narrator: a **narrator** of compromised credibility, subscribing to perceptions or attitudes different from those of the **implied author**, and either unwilling or unable to provide an accurate or trustworthy rendering of the events he or she recounts.

utopia and dystopia: utopian and dystopian settings refer to places that do not exist in reality: a utopia is an idealized place, too good to be true, and a dystopia is a horrendously bad place, its evil usually the product of an oppressive and/ or corrupt political order. Despite the "topos" part of the word, utopian and dystopian settings may refer to different times rather than different places (e.g. Orwell *1984* is recognizably set in London, but in the future time designated by the title).

verisimilitude: the credibility, plausibility, and "lifelikeness" of a narrative that we know to be fictional.

Victorian novel: the British novel in the era corresponding to Queen Victoria's reign (1837–1901). Typically but not invariably, Victorian novels are quite long (published first as serializations and/or in multiple volumes), complexly plotted, and **realist** in form. The product of an era of rapid industrialization, urbanization, and socio-political reform (women's rights, the expansion of the franchise), the Victorian novel is typically panoramic in its **representation** of society, concerned with public institutions such as law and governance as well as cultural questions like class, marriage, and vocation.

Further reading

Anthologies of criticism and theory

Hale, Dorothy J. *The Novel: An Anthology of Criticism and Theory, 1900–2000*. Oxford: Blackwell, 2006.

Hoffman, Michael J., and Patrick D. Murphy. *Essentials of the Theory of Fiction*, 3rd edn. Durham: Duke University Press, 2005.

McKeon, Michael. *Theory of the Novel: A Historical Approach*. Baltimore: Johns Hopkins University Press, 2000.

Moretti, Franco. *The Novel*, 2 vols. Princeton: Princeton University Press, 2006.

1 Why the novel matters

Armstrong, Nancy. *Desire and Domestic Fiction*. New York: Oxford University Press, 1987.

Auerbach, Erich. *Mimesis: The Representation of Reality in Western Literature*. Trans. Willard R. Trask. Princeton: Princeton University Press, 1953.

Bakhtin, M. M. *The Dialogic Imagination: Four Essays*. Ed. Michael Holquist, trans. Caryl Emerson and Michael Holquist. Austin: University of Texas Press, 1981.

Ballaster, Ros. *Seductive Forms: Women's Amatory Fiction from 1684–1740*. Oxford: Clarendon, 1992.

Gallagher, Catherine. *Nobody's Story: The Vanishing Acts of Women Writers in the Marketplace, 1670–1820*. Berkeley: University of California Press, 1994.

Lukács, Georg. *The Theory of the Novel: A Historico-Philosophical Essay on the Forms of Great Epic Literature*. Trans. Anna Bostock. Cambridge, Mass: M.I.T. Press, 1974.

McGurl, Mark. *The Novel Art: Elevations of American Fiction after Henry James*. Princeton: Princeton University Press, 2001.

Spencer, Jane. *The Rise of the Woman Novelist: From Aphra Behn to Jane Austen*. Oxford: Blackwell, 1986.

Taylor, John Tinnon. *Early Opposition to the English Novel: The Popular Reaction from 1760–1830*. New York: King's Crown Press, 1943.

Warner, William B. *Licensing Entertainment: The Elevation of Novel Reading in Britain, 1684–1750.* Berkeley: University of California Press, 1998.

2 Origins of the novel

Brown, Homer Obed. *Institutions of the English Novel from Defoe to Scott.* Philadelphia: University of Pennsylvania Press, 1997.

Davis, Lennard J. *Factual Fictions: The Origins of the English Novel.* New York: Columbia University Press, 1983.

Day, Geoffrey. *From Fiction to the Novel.* London: Routledge, 1987.

Doody, Margaret Ann, *The True Story of the Novel.* New Brunswick: Rutgers University Press, 1996.

Hunter, J. Paul. *Before Novels: The Cultural Contexts of Eighteenth-Century English Fiction.* New York: Norton, 1990.

McKeon, Michael. *The Origins of the English Novel, 1600–1740,* 2nd edn. Baltimore: Johns Hopkins University Press, 2002.

Richetti, John. *The English Novel in History, 1700–1780.* London: Routledge, 1999.

Spacks, Patricia Meyer. *Novel Beginnings: Experiments in Eighteenth-Century English Fiction.* New Haven: Yale University Press, 2006.

Watt, Ian. *The Rise of the Novel: Studies in Defoe, Richardson, and Fielding.* Berkeley: University of California Press, 1957.

Williams, Ioan. *The Idea of the Novel in Europe, 1600–1800.* New York: New York University Press, 1979.

3 Narrating the novel

Abbot, H. Porter. *The Cambridge Introduction to Narrative,* 2nd edn. Cambridge: Cambridge University Press, 2008.

Bal, Mieke. *Narratology: Introduction to the Theory of Narrative,* 2nd edn. Toronto: University of Toronto Press, 1997.

Booth, Wayne C. *The Rhetoric of Fiction,* 2nd edn. Chicago: University of Chicago Press, 1983.

Chatman, Seymour. *Story and Discourse: Narrative Structure in Fiction and Film.* Ithaca: Cornell University Press, 1978.

Genette, Gérard. *Narrative Discourse: An Essay in Method.* Trans. Jane E. Lewin. Ithaca: Cornell University Press, 1980.

Herman, David. *The Cambridge Companion to Narrative.* Cambridge: Cambridge University Press, 2007.

Keen, Suzanne. *Narrative Form.* Basingstoke: Palgrave Macmillan, 2003.

Lubbock, Percy. *The Craft of Fiction.* London: Jonathan Cape, 1921.

Rimmon-Kenan, Shlomith. *Narrative Fiction,* 2nd edn. London: Routledge, 2002.

4 Character and the novel

Bayley, John. *The Characters of Love*. London: Constable, 1960.
Cohn, Dorrit. *Transparent Minds: Narrative Modes for Presenting Consciousness in Fiction*. Princeton: Princeton University Press, 1978.
Docherty, Thomas. *Reading (Absent) Character*. Oxford: Clarendon, 1983.
Forster, E. M. *Aspects of the Novel*. London: Edward Arnold, 1927.
Harvey, W. J. *Character and the Novel*. London: Chatto & Windus, 1965.
Lynch, Deidre Shauna. *The Economy of Character: Novels, Market Culture, and the Business of Inner Meaning*. Chicago: University of Chicago Press, 1998.
Phelan, James. *Reading People, Reading Plots: Character, Progression, and the Interpretation of Narrative*. Chicago: University of Chicago Press, 1989.
Price, Martin. *Forms of Life: Character and Moral Imagination in the Novel*. New Haven: Yale University Press, 1983.
Woloch, Alex. *The One vs. the Many: Minor Characters and the Space of the Protagonist in the Novel*. Princeton: Princeton University Press, 2003.

5 Plotting the novel

Beer, Gillian. *Darwin's Plots: Evolutionary Narrative in Darwin, George Eliot, and Nineteenth Century Fiction*. London: Routledge, 1983.
Benjamin, Walter. "The Storyteller," in *Illuminations*. Trans. Hannah Arendt. New York: Schocken, 1969.
Brooks, Peter. *Reading for the Plot: Design and Intention in Narrative*. New York: Knopf, 1984.
Caserio, Robert L. *Plot, Story, and the Novel: From Dickens and Poe to the Modern Period*. Princeton: Princeton University Press, 1979.
Duncan, Ian. *Modern Romance and Transformations of the Novel: The Gothic, Scott, Dickens*. Cambridge: Cambridge University Press, 1992.
Sutherland, John. *Victorian Novelists and Publishers*. London: Athlone, 1976.

6 Setting the novel

Fisher, Philip. *Hard Facts: Setting and Form in the American Novel*. Oxford: Oxford University Press, 1985.
Lehan, Richard. *The City in Literature: An Intellectual and Cultural History*. Berkeley: University of California Press, 1998.
Lutwack, Leonard. *The Role of Place in Literature*. Syracuse: Syracuse University Press, 1984.
Moretti, Franco. *Atlas of the European Novel, 1800–1900*. London: Verso, 1998.
Said, Edward W. *Culture and Imperialism*. New York: Knopf, 1993.
Williams, Raymond. *The Country and the City*. Oxford: Oxford University Press, 1973.

7 Time and history

Fleishman, Avrom. *The English Historical Novel: Walter Scott to Virginia Woolf*.
   Baltimore: Johns Hopkins University Press, 1971.
Heise, Ursula. *Chronoschisms: Time, Narrative, and Postmodernism*. Cambridge:
   Cambridge University Press, 1997.
Kern, Stephen. *The Culture of Time and Space, 1880–1918*. Cambridge: Harvard
   University Press, 1983.
LaCapra, Dominick. *History, Politics, and the Novel*. Ithaca: Cornell University
   Press, 1987.
Lukács, György. *The Historical Novel*. Trans. Hannah and Stanley Mitchell.
   London: Merlin, 1962.
Maxwell, Richard. *The Historical Novel in Europe, 1650–1950*. Cambridge:
   Cambridge University Press, 2009.
Ricoeur, Paul. *Time and Narrative*, 3 vols. Trans. Kathleen McLaughlin and David
   Pellauer. Chicago: University of Chicago Press, 1984–8.
White, Hayden. *The Content of the Form: Narrative Discourse and Historical
   Representation*. Baltimore: Johns Hopkins University Press, 1987.

8 Genre and subgenre

Bloom, Clive. *Bestsellers: Popular Fiction since 1900*. Basingstoke: Palgrave
   Macmillan, 2002.
Fowler, Alastair. *Kinds of Literature: An Introduction to the Theory of Genres and
   Modes*. Cambridge: Harvard University Press, 1982.
Frye, Northrop. *Anatomy of Criticism*. Princeton: Princeton University Press,
   1957.
Gelder, Ken. *Popular Fiction: The Logics and Practices of a Literary Field*.
   London: Routledge, 2004.
Hepburn, Allan. *Intrigue: Espionage and Culture*. New Haven: Yale University
   Press, 2005.
Radway, Janice A. *Reading the Romance: Women, Patriarchy, and Popular
   Literature*. Chapel Hill: University of North Carolina Press, 1984.

9 Novel and anti-novel

Alter, Robert. *Partial Magic: The Novel as a Self-Conscious Genre*.
   Berkeley: University of California Press, 1975.
Hutcheon, Linda. *Narcissistic Narrative: The Metafictional Paradox*. Waterloo,
   Ontario: Wilfred Laurier University Press, 1980.
A Poetics of Postmodernism: History, Theory, Fiction. London: Routledge, 1988.
The Politics of Postmodernism. London: Routledge, 1989.
Josipovici, Gabriel. *The World and the Book: A Study of Modern Fiction*, 3rd edn.
   Basingstoke: Macmillan, 1994.

McHale, Brian. *Postmodernist Fiction*. London: Routledge, 1987.
Robbe-Grillet, Alain. *For a New Novel: Essays on Fiction*. Trans. Richard Howard. New York: Grove, 1965.
Scholes, Robert. *The Fabulators*. New York: Oxford University Press, 1967.
Waugh, Patricia. *Metafiction: The Theory and Practice of Self-Conscious Fiction*. London: Methuen, 1984.
Zamora, Lois Parker, and Wendy B. Faris, eds. *Magical Realism: History, Theory, Community*. Durham: Duke University Press, 1995.

10 Novel, nation, community

Bhabha, Homi, ed. *Nation and Narration*. London: Routledge, 1990.
Boehmer, Elleke. *Colonial and Postcolonial Literature*, 2nd edn. Oxford: Oxford University Press, 2005.
Craig, Cairns. *The Modern Scottish Novel: Narrative and the National Imagination*. Edinburgh: Edinburgh University Press, 1999.
Crawford, Robert. *Devolving English Literature*, 2nd edn. Edinburgh: Edinburgh University Press, 2000.
Eagleton, Terry. *Nationalism, Colonialism, and Literature*. Minneapolis: University of Minnesota Press, 1990.
Innes, C. L. *The Cambridge Introduction to Postcolonial Literatures in English*. Cambridge: Cambridge University Press, 2007.
Parrinder, Patrick. *Nation and Novel: The English Novel from its Origins to the Present Day*. Oxford: Oxford University Press, 2006.

11 Concluding

Bernstein, Michael André. *Foregone Conclusions: Against Apocalyptic History*. Berkeley: University of California Press, 1994.
Duplessis, Rachel Blau. *Writing Beyond the Ending: Narrative Strategies of Twentieth-Century Women Writers*. Bloomington: Indiana University Press, 1985.
Kermode, Frank. *The Sense of an Ending: Studies in the Theory of Fiction*. Oxford: Oxford University Press, 1967.
Miller, D. A. *Narrative and its Discontents: Problems of Closure in the Traditional Novel*. Princeton: Princeton University Press, 1981.
Reising, Russell. *Loose Ends: Closure and Crisis in the American Social Text*. Durham: Duke University Press, 1996.
Torgovnick, Marianna. *Closure in the Novel*. Princeton: Princeton University Press, 1981.

Index

Cambridge Introductions to …

AUTHORS

Margaret Atwood Heidi Macpherson

Jane Austen Janet Todd

Samuel Beckett Ronan McDonald

Walter Benjamin David Ferris

J. M. Coetzee Dominic Head

Joseph Conrad John Peters

Jacques Derrida Leslie Hill

Emily Dickinson Wendy Martin

George Eliot Nancy Henry

T. S. Eliot John Xiros Cooper

William Faulkner Theresa M. Towner

F. Scott Fitzgerald Kirk Curnutt

Michel Foucault Lisa Downing

Robert Frost Robert Faggen

Nathaniel Hawthorne Leland S. Person

Zora Neale Hurston Lovalerie King

James Joyce Eric Bulson

Herman Melville Kevin J. Hayes

Sylvia Plath Jo Gill

Edgar Allen Poe Benjamin F. Fisher

Ezra Pound Ira Nadel

Jean Rhys Elaine Savory

Edward Said Conor McCarthy

Shakespeare Emma Smith

Shakespeare's Comedies Penny Gay

Shakespeare's History Plays Warren
    Chernaik

Shakespeare's Tragedies Janette Dillon

Harriet Beecher Stowe Sarah Robbins

Mark Twain Peter Messent

Edith Wharton Pamela Knights

Walt Whitman M. Jimmie
    Killingsworth

Virginia Woolf Jane Goldman

William Wordsworth Emma Mason

W. B. Yeats David Holdeman

TOPICS

The American Short Story Martin
    Scofield

Comedy Eric Weitz

Creative Writing David Morley

Early English Theatre Janette Dillon

English Theatre, 1660–1900 Peter
    Thomson

Francophone Literature Patrick
    Corcoran

Modern British Theatre Simon Shepherd

Modern Irish Poetry Justin Quinn

Modernism Pericles Lewis

Narrative (second edition) H. Porter
    Abbott

The Nineteenth-Century American Novel
    Gregg Crane

The Novel Marina MacKay

Postcolonial Literatures C. L. Innes

Postmodern Fiction Bran Nicol

Russian Literature Caryl Emerson

Scenography Joslin McKinney and
    Philip Butterworth

The Short Story in English Adrian Hunter

Theatre Historiography Thomas
    Postlewait

Theatre Studies Christopher Balme

Tragedy Jennifer Wallace

Victorian Poetry Linda K. Hughes